ROMANS REALIZED

Other books by Don DeWelt:

SACRED HISTORY AND GEOGRAPHY

ACTS MADE ACTUAL

IF YOU WANT TO PREACH

THE CHURCH IN THE BIBLE

BIBLE STUDY TEXTBOOK

ROMANS REALIZED

A New
Commentary
Workbook
Teaching Manual

DON DeWELT

Professor of
New Testament and Homiletics
Ozark Bible College, Joplin, Missouri

Paraphrase by JAMES MacKNIGHT
Summary by MOSES E. LARD

College Press, Joplin, Missouri

DEDICATION

To
  Dan,
  Anne Louise,
  Chris

PREFACE

THIS BOOK, like all other *Bible Study Textbooks*, is written for participation. You might read some books just for information, but not this one. This book has no use apart from *your* knowledge of Paul's letter to the Romans. We plan a fine bibliography of commentaries to which you can refer (see pp. 269, 270); and we plan to include some commentary of our own. But the comment of others and ourselves is *not* your personal knowledge of the epistle of Paul to the Romans. *What does Paul say to you?* Indeed, what does he say to all men? — and we believe Paul says the same thing to all men. But until you discover *for yourself* — with whatever aids you need — *what Paul says to you*, the purpose of the Word of God has fallen to the ground and the purpose of this book has not been realized. When you have experienced that wonderful exhilaration of knowing that "when the apostle wrote, this is what he meant; and this is how it refers to my life," we then will be happy. For that is why we wrote this book —and all *Bible Study Textbooks*.

CONTENTS

INTRODUCTION

WE FEEL there are several important features that should commend this book to you. Here they are; consider them carefully before going further:

FIRST: The entire text of the book of Romans is from the American Standard Version of 1901.

SECOND: A paraphrase of the text by James MacKnight is given. He is one of the finest commentators on the epistles. This paraphrase becomes a short commentary and literal translation. We believe it will help you immeasurably in your understanding of this wonderful epistle.

THIRD: A summary of the text by Moses E. Lard. This summing up in concise words the thought of the section is a fine way to learn at a glance the thought of the apostle.

FOURTH: A comment and explanation on every verse by Don DeWelt. We have intentionally limited our comment. Our purpose in preparing this study is not to add another commentary on Romans to the hundreds that are already in print. This book is intended to be a mental and spiritual stimulator. We want to "stir up your sincere mind" and cause you to know *for yourself* and *of yourself* (as much as is humanly possible) what Paul has written.

FIFTH: More than 1,000 questions on the entire book. These can either be answered orally, or the answers written in a notebook. The latter form is the method we have used most often.

SIXTH: A "review in outline form" that runs through the book. This will call to your mind the structure of the book as you progress in study.

SEVENTH: Preliminary questions appear at the beginning of each section. These questions are called *Realizing Romans*. They are intended for you to answer *before* you study anything but the text. *After* you have studied the aids, perhaps you will wish to return and change your answers; but *do answer* all the questions in *Realizing Romans before* you proceed in the rest of the study.

EIGHTH: Note the chart of the whole epistle as found on page 15. We follow this outline in our comments.

NINTH: There are two special studies in the back pages of this book. These studies were written by Wilbur Fields and the author.

Yours in His Happy Service,
DON DEWELT

9

GENERAL INTRODUCTION TO THE EPISTLE
OF PAUL TO THE ROMANS

A. *Paul the Apostle, the Author.*

1. Since the first word of the epistle gives the name of the author, There is no need to give reasons for attributing this letter to "Paul, a servant of Jesus Christ, called to be an apostle . . . "

2. There has been no weighty controversy in any period of history concerning the authorship of the book.

3. Notice that Paul, the inspired author, dictated this epistle to his scribe, Tertius (Ro. 16:22).

B. *The Time and Place of Writing.*

1. Paul dictated this epistle during the three months' stay in Corinth on the third missionary journey in about 57 or 58 A.D.

2. *Reasons* for the Conclusions Concerning the Time and Place of Writing.

a. Paul was taking the contribution of the churches of Macedonia and Achaia to the saints at Jerusalem. Ro. 15:25-26: ". . . but now, I say, I go to Jerusalem, ministering unto the saints. For it has been the good pleasure of Macedonia and Achaia to make a certain contribution for the poor among the saints that are at Jerusalem."

b. Paul and certain other brethren were in Corinth on the third missionary journey at this time and were on their way to Jerusalem with the offering for the saints. Ac. 19:21; 20:3, 16, 23. (Macedonia, together with Achaia, made up the whole of Greece, Corinth being in Achaia.) Though the offering is not here mentioned, we know that they had it because of what Paul said in Acts 24:17-18. He said, "Now after some years I came to bring alms to my nation, and offerings: amidst which they found me purified in the temple. . ."

c. We know that it was written at Corinth because the names of two people associated with this city are mentioned as being present with Paul at the time of writing. Ro. 16:23: "Gaius my host, and of the whole church, saluteth you. Erastus the treasurer of the city saluteth you . . ."

(1) Gaius was one of the few baptized by Paul in the city of Corinth. I Co. 1:14.

(2) Erastus is identified with Corinth in Acts 19:22 and also in II Tim. 4:20.

C. *The Persons Addressed in This Epistle.*

For some information concerning the Roman Christians, we are quoting from D. D. Whedon, who sums up in a few words what other writers have taken pages to say.

"When the Roman general Pompey conquered the Jewish nation and captured Jerusalem, a large body of Jewish prisoners were sent to Rome and sold as slaves. Their rigid adherence to the peculiarities of their faith rendering them very impracticable servants, their masters were glad to emancipate them, and, perhaps respecting their conscientiousness, assigned them a quarter beyond the Tiber as a residence. . . As the residence of freedmen, exiled from aristocratic Rome, in a low ground, where the flat boats from the seaport at Ostia had their wharves, and low shops abounded, it was scarce a respectable section. It was a symbol of truth abased in the world. The worship of the true Jehovah dwelt in these humble abodes, overlooked by the haughty temple of the Capitoline Jove. How has history reversed the contrast! Yet even here the stately synagogue rose, the rabbi established his school, and a hierarchy ruled in power. Nor was monotheism without its influence on imperial Rome herself. So prevalent was the tendency of thoughtful persons toward Judaism as to become the subject of satire to more than one of the Roman poets. And so crowded were the synagogues on the Saturday-Sabbath with Roman ladies that one poet recommends the young men to go thither to get sight of the beauty and fashion of Rome!

"The 'strangers of Rome', (Ac. 2:10) returning from Pentecost to this humble Jewish quarter, were probably the first germ of Roman Christianity. They were purely Jewish. The only probable fact we have of history is that such excitements arose among the Jews (about A. D. 50) as to attract the notice of the city government, which received intelligence that the disturbances came from one Chrestus, obviously a modification of the name of Christ. (See . . . Acts 18:2) . . . the government ordered the Jews in a body to leave Rome. By this decree it seems that the elements of the first Roman church . . . were swept away.

"It is from this epistle to the Romans that we get our next glimpse of the church at Rome. In this respect the catalogue of names in chapter 16 has a singular interest. The banished Aquila and Priscilla have returned. There is a goodly number of Paul's friends there. And if we may judge of the whole from this catalogue we should say that the church was almost entirely Gentile, and far more Greek than Roman. Of the 28 names there but two are Jewish, and the Greek are twice as many as the Latin. The Church had existed there many years, (15:23); they had attained a reputation through the Christian world,

(1:8). Though not founded by Paul, the church recognizes his apostleship; nor has he any misgivings that it is an anti-Pauline Church, nor does he recognize the existence of any opponents or maligners.

"The next view we have is not so much of the Church as of the escort of friends who met Paul at Appii Forum to conduct him to Rome (Acts 28:15) ... The career of the Church of Rome since that period is one of the wonders of history. Its spiritual empire, rising like the shadow of Rome's past imperial power, has exercised a mightier sway over the civilized world. That Peter was once at Rome and suffered martyrdom there is probably true; but that he was founder or Bishop of its church is supported by no adequate authority. And the stupendous despotism of Popery based its existence not upon the sacred canon, or upon primitive history, but upon forged documents that powerfully imposed upon the ignorance of the dark ages, but cannot claim to stand the test of modern criticism."

D. *The Design of the Epistle as Related to its Place in the New Testament.* Although it is not the first letter by Paul (being rather, the sixth), its place after the book of Acts is logical, for it contains a discussion of the grounds on which a sinner is justified before God.

1. In Acts we are told what to do to be justified; in Romans we are told of the "how" and "why" of justification.

2. We could say that Acts is a discussion of justification externally, and Romans a discussion of justification internally.

E. *The Purpose as Related to the Ones to Whom it is Addressed.*

1. There is no doubt that one purpose for this epistle was to take the place of an intended but deferred visit (1:11-13).

2. Upon its being delivered by Phoebe (16:1-2) to the church in Rome, it would serve as a letter of personal introduction.

3. It would also serve to establish more firmly the already accepted fact of Paul's apostleship.

4. This epistle was written to teach and instruct all Christians.

a. Because it is not written as a defense of some particular fact or teaching, we conclude that there was no immediate problem of such proportion as to make this epistle apologetic.

b. It was written to teach and instruct Christians, some of whom were misled and ignorant, but willing to receive instruction and to follow it, concerning the great theme of "Justification by Faith for the Jew and the Gentile."

c. It was written to teach and instruct not only the Christians at Rome, but all the Christians of that day: hence, to teach and instruct us also and with the same divine authority.

QUESTIONS FOR SELF-EXAMINATION

1. Who was the divinely inspired author of the book of Romans?

2. In what place was this book written?

3. Why do you believe it to have been written at this place?

4. On what missionary journey was the book written?

5. Why do you believe that it was written on this journey?

6. About what year was this epistle written?

7. Did the inspired author write the epistle himself? If not, who did?

8. Were there Jews in Rome before there were Christians there?

9. If so, how did they happen to be there?

10. How did the first Christian teaching probably reach Rome?

11. Is there any evidence that Peter founded the church at Rome?

12. Were the Christians in Rome mostly Jewish or Gentile?

13. Is the epistle to the Romans Paul's first letter?

14. Show how "Romans" logically follows the book of Acts.

15. For what purposes was this epistle written?

A Chart Showing the General Outline of the Book of Romans

THE BOOK OF ROMANS

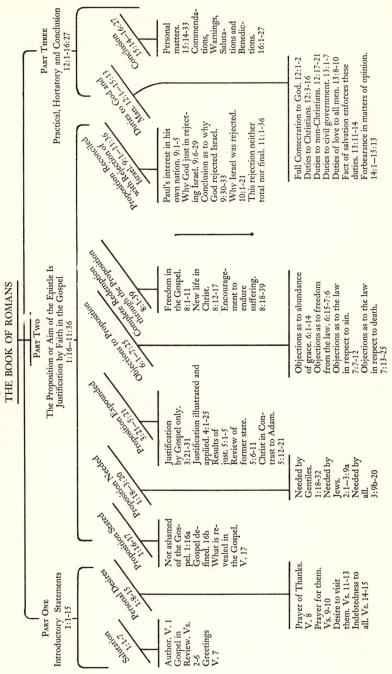

PART ONE
Introductory Statements
1:1-15

PART TWO
The Proposition or Aim of the Epistle Is
Justification by Faith in the Gospel
1:16—11:36

PART THREE
Practical, Hortatory and Conclusion
12:1-16:27

Salutation 1:1-7

Author. V. 1
Gospel in Review. Vs. 2-6
Greetings V. 7

Personal D'sires 1:8-15

Prayer of Thanks. V. 8
Prayer for them. Vs. 9-10
Desire to visit them. Vs. 11-13
Indebtedness to all. Vs. 14-15

Proposition Stated 1:16-17

Not ashamed of the Gospel. 1:16a
Gospel defined. 16b
What is revealed in the Gospel. V. 17

Proposition Needed 1:18-3:20

Needed by Gentiles. 1:18-32
Needed by Jews. 2:1-3:9a
Needed by all. 3:9b-20

Proposition Expounded 3:21-5:21

Justification by Gospel only. 3:21-31
Justification illustrated and applied. 4:1-25
Results of just. 5:1-5
Review of former state. 5:6-11
Christ in Contrast to Adam. 5:12-21

Objections to Proposition 6:1-7:25

Objections as to abundance of grace. 6:1-14
Objections as to freedom from the law. 6:15-7:6
Objections as to the law in respect to sin. 7:7-12
Objections as to the law in respect to death. 7:13-25

Complete Redemption through the Proposition 8:1-39

Freedom in the Gospel. 8:1-11
New life in Christ. 8:12-17
Encouragement to endure suffering. 8:18-39

Proposition Reconciled with Rejection of Israel. 9:1-11:36

Paul's interest in his own nation. 9:1-5
Why God just in rejecting Israel. 9:6-29
Conclusion as to why God rejected Israel. 9:30-33
Why Israel was rejected. 10:1-21
This rejection neither total nor final. 11:1-36

Duties to God and Man. 12:1-15:13

Full Consecration to God. 12:1-2
Duties to Christians. 12:3-16
Duties to non-Christians. 12:17-21
Duties to civil government. 13:1-7
Duties of love to all men. 13:8-10
Fact of salvation enforces these duties. 13:11-14
Forbearance in matters of opinion. 14:1-15:13

Conclusion 15:14-16:27

Personal matters. 15:14-33
Commendations, Warnings, Salutations and Benedictions. 16:1-27

15

A GENERAL CONSIDERATION OF THE ENTIRE EPISTLE

Preliminary Remarks

It will be our procedure to follow the outline as given on the preceding chart, and to enlarge upon the points of the chart by way of illumination and explanation.

To receive the most good from this section of the study, the book of Romans must be read carefully. Follow this study with your mind open, and the real meaning of our comments will be readily understood.

PART ONE

INTRODUCTORY STATEMENTS, 1:1-15
SALUTATION, 1:1-7

Text

1:1-7. Paul, a servant of Jesus Christ, called to be an apostle, separated unto the gospel of God, 2 which he promised afore through his prophets in the holy scriptures, 3 concerning his Son, who was born of the seed of David according to the flesh, 4 who was declared to be the Son of God with power, according to the spirit of holiness by the resurrection from the dead; even Jesus Christ our Lord, 5 through whom we received grace and apostleship, unto obedience of faith among all the nations, for his name's sake; 6 among whom are ye also, called to be Jesus Christ's: 7 to all that are in Rome, beloved of God, called to be saints: Grace to you and peace from God our Father and the Lord Jesus Christ.

REALIZING ROMANS, 1:1-7

Summaries, paraphrases, and commentaries are all fine; *but they are no substitute for your own knowledge of the inspired book.* What do *you* think of the salutation of this book? I refer to verses 1-7 of the first chapter. Here are a few questions that are framed to stir up your sincere mind; answer them before you read farther.

1. Why not refer to himself first as an apostle and then as a servant?
2. Are not a servant and an apostle the same?
3. When was Paul called to be an apostle?
4. Are you an "apostle" in any sense of the term? Look up the meaning of the term before you answer in the negative (cf. Acts 14:14).

5. Specify several features of the "good news that was promised afore by the prophets in the holy scriptures." (We could give you references to look up, but this would not develop *your* initiative.)

6. He was "born of the seed of David." Of what special significance is that?

7. What is the "spirit of holiness" here spoken of? Would it be accurate to say "Holy Spirit"?

8. In what sense did the resurrection proclaim Jesus as the Son of God? Are we not all sons of God?

9. Who is the "We" of verse five? Do not be too quick to answer, "Paul and the other apostles." Who was with Paul when he wrote?

10. What is there in "the faith" to obey? Can it be law? How then can it be faith? Is God's salvation dependent upon man's obedience?

11. "For His name's sake"—We often say, "for Jesus' sake." Is this the same? What is a name's sake? Do not look these answers up in a commentary (even if it is mine). Do your answering and writing and thinking BEFORE you read someone else's comment and conclusion. After all, they are only men — fallible like yourself, sincere, intelligent, but *not* infallible. Think for yourself: you are no parrot!

12. In what sense do we belong to Jesus? How much of us? Is this really true or just a fine phrase?

13. You *are* a saint. All the Christians in Rome were saints. What does this word mean? Or perhaps we should say, what *did* it mean?

14. If the saints in Rome received what Paul wished for them as in verse seven, what would it mean to them? Just what is the "grace" God and Christ were to give them?

Paraphrase

1:1-7. Paul a servant of Jesus Christ, and an apostle called expressly as the other apostles were, and separated by him to preach the good news from God,

2 Which he promised before, by his prophets in the holy scriptures, should be preached to the Gentiles,

3 Concerning the coming of his Son to save the world, who, as it was foretold, was born of a woman descended from David, the king of Israel, with respect to his flesh,

4 But was declared the Son of God, with great power of evidence, with respect to his holy spiritual nature, by his resurrection from the dead, after he had been crucified by the Jewish rulers for calling himself the Son of God, even Jesus Christ our Lord.

5 From whom, since his resurrection, I have received miraculous powers and apostleship, in order that through my preaching him as the Son of God, the obedience of faith may be given to him, among all the Gentiles, on account of his being the Son of God.

6 Among the number of which Gentiles are also ye the called disciples of Jesus Christ.

7 Being thus commissioned, I write this letter to all who are in Rome; and more especially to those who are the beloved of God, on account of their faith, to the called seed of Abraham, to the saints by profession. May grace be multiplied to you, and peace from God our Father, and from the Lord Jesus Christ.

Summary

Paul, a called apostle, is set apart to preach God's gospel, which he had before promised, through the prophets, in the holy Scriptures. The gospel respects his Son, who was born of the seed of David, as to his flesh, but determined, by power, to be God's Son, as to his spirit, by the resurrection of the dead. This Son is Jesus Christ our Lord. From him Paul received favor in becoming a Christian, and the office of an apostle, both these being received to induce men in all nations to believe and obey Christ. He writes this Letter to all the holy who are in Rome.

Comment

The apostle begins his epistle with a beautiful and solemn salutation in the form of one sentence containing 126 words (in the American Standard Version). Note this very helpful outline of the salutation. In this outline you can note the marvelous progression of connected thought.

1. Paul. vs 1a
   a. A servant (slave) of Jesus Christ.
   b. Called to be an apostle (one sent).
   c. Separated unto the gospel.
2. The Gospel. vs 1b-2a
   a. Of God.
   b. Promised afore through his prophets in the holy scriptures.
   c. Concerning his son.

3. His Son. vs 2b-5a
    a. Born of the seed of David according to the (his) flesh.
    b. Declared to be the Son of God with power according to the (his) (pure) holy spirit (or his inward man), by the resurrection from the dead.
    c. We (Paul and others) have received from him grace and apostleship.
4. Our grace and apostleship. vs 5b
   For the obedience of the faith among all nations for his name's sake.
5. All the nations. vs 5c-6
    a. Obedient to the faith.
    b. Romans among them.
    c. Belong to Jesus Christ.
6. Greetings to those in Rome. vs 7
    a. Beloved of God.
    b. Called saints.
    c. Grace and peace to you from God our Father and the Lord Jesus Christ.

Here are a few comments on these verses. Our purpose will be to place a devotional, evangelistic emphasis upon these truths:

Paul. How very many expressions the apostle could have used to describe himself. What a man thinks of himself in the revealing light of God's presence is a true indication of his spiritual stature. The first relationship Paul felt he sustained to Christ was not that of an apostle, but rather a servant or slave. The term "slave" is used sometimes in an official capacity of one who represents another in an official sense, This is *not* the use made of the word here. Paul places himself along with all other servants of Christ. He is just another common slave of Christ. Paul feels that he has been bought and paid for by Christ Jesus. To use his own words, he "is no longer his own; he has been bought with a price" (1 Cor. 6:19, 20).

How do we think of ourselves? What is my first answer to the question, "Who am I?" Do I think of myself first of all as a preacher, an elder, a deacon, a teacher? If I do, I am not thinking as I should. I am first of all, and most of all, a slave to King Jesus.

It might come as a shock to some to learn there are *seventeen* apostles in the New Testament! Yes, there are! Here they are; count them up: (1-12) The Twelve apostles; (13) Matthias; (14) Barnabas, Acts 14:14; (15) James, the Lord's brother, Gal. 1:19; (16) Christ, Heb. 3:1; (17) Paul.

This use of the term "apostle" is easily explained in the meaning of the word. "Apostle" means "one sent." In a very special sense, the Twelve were *sent* by Christ to "the lost sheep" of the house of Israel. Paul was *sent* "far hence to the Gentiles" (Ac. 26:18, 19). Barnabas was *sent* by the church at Antioch (Ac. 13:1-3). Evidently James was *sent* by the church in Jerusalem (Ac. 15:13). Christ was *sent* by God, our heavenly Father (Jn. 3:16). Matthias was apparently *sent* by the church in Jerusalem.

Paul never forgot the heavenly vision by which he was called and sent forth (Ac. 26:1ff). Have not many of us forgotten the heavenly vision of our conversion in which we were called and sent into the world to bear fruit unto God?

Saul of Tarsus was not only a slave of Jesus Christ, and one who was called to be sent, but he was also *sanctified*, or *separated*.

Paul was separated unto something. It was not a negative separation, but he was separated *unto* something. Paul's separation was for a purpose — that he might proclaim the "good news."

The Gospel. Somehow, we do so miss the impact of this word. Our message needs to be of the *good news*. The joy of the angel's announcement at Bethlehem needs ever to grip our hearts. Oh, for the exuberance of the youngster who bursts through the doorway to shout out in short exclamations the joy of some childish "good news." No, we need more, the unspeakable happiness of a released prisoner who has found pardon instead of condemnation. To Paul, the message he preached could vary according to the needs of his hearers or readers, But however varied, it was always a word that would finally produce happiness! Our message can only be *good news* to others when it is indeed this to us.

Has *God* spoken to your heart and mind? Paul knew his message was from God. Do you? Do I? We are not speaking of direct communication to us, as to the inspired spokesmen. But we do speak God's truth; we have God's message. (1:1-7)

Text

1:8-13. First, I thank my God through Jesus Christ for you all, that your faith is proclaimed throughout the whole world. 9 For God is my witness, whom I serve in my spirit in the gospel of his Son, how unceasingly I make mention of you, always in my prayers 10 making request, if by any means now at length I may be prospered by the will of God to come unto you. 11 For I long to see you, that I may impart unto you some spiritual gift, to the end ye may be established; 12 that is, that I with you may be comforted in you, each of us by the other's faith, both yours and mine. 13 And I would not have you ignorant, brethren, that oftentimes I purposed to come unto you (and was hindered hitherto), that I might have some fruit in you also, even as in the rest of the Gentiles.

REALIZING ROMANS, 1:8-13

15. Who proclaimed "the faith" of the Romans? Were other churches and Christians talking to Paul about the faith of the Roman church? In what other way could the faith of the church at Rome be made known?

16. What is meant by "the whole world" as used by Paul? Had he been in "the whole world"?

17. Why did Paul call God to witness the truth of his statement? Would not the Romans believe him?

18. Paul served God in, or with, "his spirit." What is meant? Jesus said "to worship in spirit and truth" (Jn. 4:24). Is this what Jesus had in mind?

19. Paul refers to his prayers for many Christians. If he prayed "unceasingly" for the Romans, (28 persons mentioned in chapters 15-16), for the Ephesians, Colossians, Philippians, Corinthians, and others, he must have spent a good deal of time just calling out the names in his prayers. Is this a fair evaluation of what he meant?

20. "If by any means . . . I may be prospered by the will of God to come unto you" (vs. 10). What does Paul mean by *"means"*? Can you think of some specific *means* through which the will of God was working out? Is the will of God working out in your life? Read carefully Jas. 4:13-15 in this connection.

21. What is the "spiritual gift" Paul wanted to impart to the saints in Rome? Let us have no hasty answers. Are you sure you do not know? There are some definite possibilities as to meaning. Name one. Perhaps there is only one.

22. Please note now that verse 12 explains or enlarges on verse 11. How could the faith of Paul "comfort" the saints? Vice versa? Is there a better word than "comforted" to use here? Use one, and then look up the original from one source or another.

23. Who "hindered" Paul—Satan or God? Consider this question in light of the one we asked on "any means" (Ques. No. 20).

24. What "fruit" did Paul expect? Was it the fruit of the Spirit in the saints or the fruit of salvation in sinners? It does seem to me that more weight is to be found on one side of this question than on the other. Which is it?

Paraphrase

1:8-13. And first, I thank my God through Jesus Christ, on account of all of you who have embraced the gospel, that your faith in Jesus Christ is so conspicuous, that it is spoken of throughout the whole Roman empire.

9 In saying I am thankful for your conversion, I speak the truth; for I call God to witness, whom, with the utmost earnestness, I serve in the ministry of the gospel of his Son, that constantly I make affectionate mention of you.

10 Always in my prayers, requesting that by some means, now at length, I may have a prosperous journey to Jerusalem, (ch. xv. 25) by the will of God, under whose direction I execute my ministry, and then to come to you.

11 For I greatly desire to see you, that I may impart to you some spiritual gift, in order that ye may be established against the heathens, who wish to bring you back to idolatry, and the Jews, who would subject you to the law.

12 And this is proposed, that I may be comforted together with you, through the mutual faith both of you, whose faith will be confirmed by these gifts, and of me, whose faith will be confirmed when I see unbelievers converted by these gifts.

13 Now, brethren, lest ye should be surprised that I, who am the apostle of the Gentiles, and who have expressed such a desire to see you, have never yet preached in Rome, I would not have you ignorant, that oftentimes I purposed to come to you, (though I have been hindered hitherto), in order that I might have some fruit of my ministry among you, the idolatrous inhabitants of Rome also, even as among the other Gentiles.

Summary

Paul is thankful that the belief of the disciples in Rome is spoken of everywhere. He always mentions them in his prayers, and desires at some time a prosperous journey to them. He longs to see them, and to impart to them some spiritual gift to strengthen them. From their mutual belief, he hopes to derive much comfort. Paul had often purposed to come to them, and had been hindered. He desired some fruit among them, such as he had in the other nations.

Comment

After this, he then expresses his personal desires for those in Rome in a prayer of thanksgiving, a prayer on their behalf, and a statement of his desire to visit them for the purpose of mutual helpfulness. In speaking of his desired but hindered visit, he mentions that the purpose of his visit would be to "have some fruit in you also, even as in the rest of the Gentiles." (1:8-13)

Text

1:14-15 I am debtor both to Greeks and to Barbarians, both to the wise and to the foolish. 15 So, as much as in me is, I am ready to preach the gospel to you also that are in Rome.

REALIZING ROMANS, 1:14-15

25. Why separate the Greeks from the Barbarians if he was debtor to all?
26. What particular debt would Paul owe to the Greeks? Would it be different from that to the Barbarians? Of course, we know he owed the gospel to both of them, but he felt an individual debt to each. What was it?
27. Suppose the foolish laughed at him, and the wise snubbed him—what then?
28. Did Paul have any doubts about what he had to offer? Then why did he say, "*as much* as in me is"?
29. What were the circumstances that made Paul "ready" to preach?

Paraphrase

1:14-15. Being the apostle of the Gentiles, I am bound to preach both to the Greeks, however intelligent, and to the Barbarians; both to the philosophers and to the common people.

15 Therefore, notwithstanding your great proficiency in the sciences, I am willing, according to my ability, to preach the gospel even to you unbelieving Gentiles, who are in Rome.

Summary

He is debtor to preach the gospel to all men, and therefore to those at Rome.

Comment

This thought led him to say that he was debtor to both Greek and Barbarians, both to the wise and to the foolish, and hence ready to preach or bring glad tidings (the gospel) to those at Rome also. (1:14-15)

1. Without referring to previous material, give the general outline of Part One.

PART TWO
Justification by Faith in the Gospel, 1:16—11:36
The Proposition Stated, 1:16-17

Text

1:16-17. For I am not ashamed of the gospel: for it is the power of God unto salvation to every one that believeth; to the Jew first, and also to the Greek. 17 For therein is revealed a righteousness of God from faith unto faith: as it is written, But the righteous shall live by faith.

Realizing Romans, 1:16-17

30. Is there any "natural" tendency to be ashamed of the good news? How can we call it "*good news*" and be ashamed?

31. The gospel is God's power. The power of God is manifested in other ways in this material world; but there is a real difference in the power of creation and the power unto salvation. What is it?

32. What is included in the word "believeth" as in vs. 16? There is more to believing than a mere mental assent. Just what is the nature of believing?

33. Was the gospel God's power to salvation for the *Jew first?* If so, in what sense was this true?

34. The good news reveals God's righteousness. Is this a revelation of the righteous character of God, or is this a revelation of some action by God in providing righteousness for man? Please do not forget the "good news", or gospel, is defined by Paul in I Cor. 15:1-4.

35. How is the word "faith" used as in verse 17? Note please that one faith leads to another. Explain how this is true. Do not just mentally "throw up your hands" with the thought you can't explain this. This is as much your job as anyone else's. What does it mean? To start with, you might remember that the word "faith" is used in several ways in the New Testament (Cf. Jude 3; Heb. 11:1, 2; Rom. 14:23; 10:17).

36. The last statement of verse 17 states that the righteous (who are they?) shall *live* by faith. What life is this discussing? Remember, please, you are under no obligation to accept *any* man's conclusion. But you *are* under obligation to God to attempt to understand His Word: otherwise He would never have "delivered it once and for all to the saints" (Jude 3). If scientists will spend years and years of life—to say nothing of millions of dollars— to discover the laws of God in the physical world, is the thought incredible that we should spend much time and energy in

thought and prayer that we might comprehend His higher moral and spiritual law as revealed in His Word?

Paraphrase

1:16-17. For although the learned among you think it foolishness, I am not ashamed of the gospel of Christ, because it is the power of God (I Cor. 1:24), the powerful means which God makes use of for working out salvation to every one who believeth; to the Jew first, and also to the Gentile.

17 First, the gospel is the power of God for salvation, to every one who believeth; because the righteousness of God's appointment by faith is revealed in it, in order to produce faith in them to whom it is preached. And to this righteousness the Jews cannot object, since it is written, But the just by faith shall live.

Summary

He is not ashamed of the gospel, for it is God's power for salvation to all who believe. In it is revealed God's justification by belief in order to induce belief.

Comment

In these two verses we have a proposition stated that takes nearly the whole book to develop. In verse 16a "the gospel" is spoken of as of great importance. In verse 16b we find that the gospel is of importance because "it is the power of God unto salvation". "In it" or "therein" (that is, in the gospel) is revealed "a righteousness of God" which is imputed (attributed) to man by his faith in the gospel. Simply stated, the gospel contains God's answer to Job's question, "Can a man be just before God?" The gospel contains God's method for making man just in His sight.

The apostle's proposition, stated accurately in fewer words, could very well read, "Justification by Faith in the Gospel." We repeat again this condensed proposition with explanation given in parentheses: Justification (being declared to be as if we had never sinned) by (through or by the means of) faith (which includes repentance, confession and baptism) in the gospel (which contains the facts of the death, burial and resurrection of Christ. These facts are the basis for God being both just and justifier.). (1:16-17)

2. Where do we find the proposition of the book of Romans?
3. Why was Paul not ashamed of the gospel?
4. Why is the gospel called "The power of God unto salvation"?
5. What is the brief statement of Paul's proposition to this book?
6. What is the meaning of justification? Of "by"? What does "faith" include?
7. What three facts are contained in the gospel? What basis do they form for God?

Rethinking in Outline Form

PART ONE

PART TWO

Text

1:18-25. For the wrath of God is revealed from heaven against all ungodliness and unrighteousness of men, who hinder the truth in unrighteousness; 19 because that which is known of God is manifest in them; for God manifested it unto them. 20 For the invisible things of him since the creation of the world are clearly seen, being perceived through the things that are made, even his everlasting power and divinity; that they may be without excuse: 21 because that, knowing God, they glorified him not as God, neither gave thanks; but became vain in their reasonings, and their senseless heart was darkened. 22 Professing themselves to be wise, they became fools, 23 and changed the glory of the incorruptible God for the likeness of an image of corruptible man, and of birds, and four-footed beasts, and creeping things. 24 Wherefore God gave them up in the lusts of their hearts unto uncleanness, that their bodies should be dishonored among themselves: 25 for that they exchanged the truth of God for a lie, and worshipped and served the creature rather than the Creator, who is blessed for ever. Amen.

Realizing Romans, 1:18-25

37. *Where* is God's wrath revealed? Not *from* where, but where? To say simply *"from heaven"* will not answer the whole question. If you wanted to show someone the revelation of God's wrath, where would you look?

38. Is there some difference between "ungodliness and unrighteousness," or was this said only for emphasis?

39. You will observe that Paul says certain men "hinder" the truth—a most interesting word. Look up (even in our text here) a fuller meaning of the word. What does the word "hinder" suggest as to man's responsibility to the truth?

40. Mark carefully the phraseology in verse 19. Knowledge of God is manifested in *two* places: *to* man, and *in* man. Does this mean that man is born with some innate knowledge of God, *or* that he is born with the faculty by which he can learn of God? Could it mean both? If so, how? Come on, friend. Do not bog down in your thinking processes. This is too important a matter to be treated lightly. This is most intriguing: think it out! Verse 20 will help you.

41. What two things about God can we learn from nature? What two things *can't* man learn from nature?

42. What should be the *natural* response of man upon viewing the "handiwork" of God? (Cf. Psa. 19:1-6)

43. If it is natural for man to understand some things about God through the creation, then it would be fitting to say that they were "senseless" who failed to acknowledge these things. How is it that the thought entered some persons' minds that they could attribute creation to some other source?

44. Will you note the use of the term "heart" in verse 21. Compare it with Psa. 14:1. Note that man does not say with his *mind* "there is no God." What causes a man to become "a fool"? Read verse 22.

45. In what way is God "incorruptible"? Is there some order in the idolatry described in verse 23?

46. I thought God never gave up, and taught us never to give up. Here it is stated that God *did* give up. (Cf.vs. 24) With today's emphasis upon the physical body, there is a real danger that men will fall into the same trap. How is the body dishonored?

Paraphrase

1:18-25. Next, the gospel alone is the power of God for salvation, because it alone grants pardon to sinners on repentance: wherein the law of nature, vs. 32 and in the law of Moses, the wrath of God is plainly revealed against all impiety and unrighteousness of men; who conceal the truth concerning God from the vulgar, by their unrighteous institutions.

19 Of this crime, all the Greek legislators, statesmen, and philosophers, have been guilty: Because that which may be known of God, is known among them; for God hath manifested it to them, by his works of creation.

20 For his invisible attributes, even his eternal power and Godhead, though not discernible by the eye of the body, ever since the creation of the world, are clearly seen by the eye of man's mind, being understood by the things which he hath made; so that they are inexcusable. (The apostle means that the Greek legislators and philosophers were inexcusable)

21 Because, though they knew God, they did not glorify him as God, by teaching the people what they knew concerning him; neither did they give him thanks, by making him the object of their worship; but became foolish by their own reasonings concerning the worship fit for the vulgar; and their imprudent heart was darkened, so as to relish idolatry equally with the vulgar.

22 Thus, the Grecian statesmen and philosophers, who assumed the pompous title of wise men, became fools in their public institutions of religion:

23 For they misrepresented the perfections of the incorruptible God, by an image made in the likeness of corruptible men, and of birds, and of beasts, and of reptiles, and thereby led the vulgar to believe that God was like the animals whose images they worshipped.

24. Therefore also, as the just punishment of their impiety in likening him to men and beasts, God, through the lusts of their own hearts impelling them, gave these pretended wise men up to every sort of uncleanness; whereby they dishonored their own bodies between themselves.

25 I speak of the legislators, philosophers, and priests, who changed the truth concerning God into falsehood, by likening him to men and beasts; and who, pretending to worship God under these symbols, worshipped and served the creature rather than the Creator, who is to be praised for ever. Amen.

Summary

The wrath of God is revealed from heaven against the impiety and injustice of all men who keep down the truth. The Gentiles had the truth, for God had made it known to them. But when they knew God, they did not glorify him as God. By their reasonings they be-

8. Paul has now presented the universal plan for salvation. What is his next logical step?

came foolish, and dull in heart, and exchanged the honor due to God for the worship of idols. For this, God gave them up to base passions, and as the result, they dishonored their bodies among themselves.

Comment

Since Paul has just laid down a universal plan for obtaining justification, it is only logical to read in the ensuing verses of the universal need for this plan, thus giving the reason for its inception. In verse 18 we find the general heading for the development of the thought of the universal need. "The wrath of God is revealed from heaven against all ungodliness and unrighteousness of men who hinder the truth in unrighteousness." We will find as we examine the lives of men universally that they deserve nought but the wrath of God; and that this heavenly vengeance is brought upon man by his disobedience to what he knows to be God's law.

The Gentiles (the heathen) were (and are) desperately in need of this justification found in the gospel, for they held the truth down or hindered it by their unrighteousness. Notice that they were not ignorant of the truth, but, having the truth, they did not choose to obey it, but rather to suppress it (vs. 18). Paul then tells us of the truth they possessed. He speaks of their knowledge of God's everlasting power and divinity which they attained from the material creation about them. Paul remarks that this truth about God has thus been accessible from the creation of the world.

In view of God's wrath which he must visit upon them, such persons have no excuse to offer, for even though they knew God to be the one of all power and the one truly divine being, they did not choose to accept him as such, and gave him neither glory nor thanks. They looked rather to their own accomplishments and wisdom, and thus became not humble before this great Creator, but vain, and with this false use of their senses their heart was darkened.

Though such action appeared as the mark of wisdom to the Gentiles, it was rather the mark of folly, for they thus exchanged the glory of the incorruptible God for the glory of corruptible man and

9. Why is God's wrath brought upon man as suggested in verse 18?
10. What truth regarding himself did God manifest to the Gentiles?
11. In what manner did God reveal this truth to the Gentiles? For how long?
12. Why were the Gentiles spoken of said to be without excuse?
13. What would you say was the primary cause of their sin? the secondary? the result?
14. With what attitude did these Gentiles regard themselves?
15. For what did they exchange the glory of the incorruptible God?
16. What was the awful act committed throughout this whole descent?
17. They are said to have exchanged the truth of God for a lie. What was the truth and what was the lie?

even of birds and four-footed beasts and creeping things. In this whole descent, there was the awful act of exchanging what they knew to be truth (that God was the creator and thus the natural object of worship) for what they knew to be a lie (that man, the creature was to be worshipped). Such action led them to participate fully in the lusts of their hearts, which brought about uncleanness and dishonoring of the body, and God had to give them up. (1:18-25)

Text

1:26-32. For this cause God gave them up unto vile passions: for their women changed the natural use into that which is against nature: 27 and likewise also the men, leaving the natural use of the woman, burned in their lust one toward another, men with men working unseemliness, and receiving in themselves that recompense of their error which was due. 28 And even as they refused to have God in their knowledge, God gave them up unto a reprobate mind, to do those things which are not fitting; 29 being filled with all un-righteousness, wickedness, covetousness, maliciousness; full of envy, murder, strife, deceit, malignity; whisperers, 30 backbiters, hateful to God, insolent, haughty, boastful, inventors of evil things, disobedient to parents, 31 without understanding, covenant-breakers, without natural affection, unmerciful: 32 who, knowing the ordinance of God, that they that practise such things are worthy of death, not only do the same, but also consent with them that practise them.

REALIZING ROMANS, 1:26-32

47. Are there some passions that are not vile? Is it true that "there is nothing good or bad; only thinking makes it so"?

48. Isn't a sexual pervert or deviate sick? Should we censure people who are ill? Paul attributes the responsibility of sexual perversion to whom? It would amaze you to know the statistics on sexual perversion in your own "Christian America." Is there any hope for these people? Do you truly believe your answer?

49. Oh, to constantly have God in our knowledge! This is the answer to this sordid picture. Read carefully verses 28-32, and see if you can divide and subdivide the words into some sort of ladder downward. Show how one leads to another—if they do.

50. Verse 32 reveals the worst quality of these people. What is it?

51. Why does Paul give us this description as in verses 18-32? Do you believe Paul met such people in his travels? Were there any in some of the churches who formerly "walked in these things"? Specify.

Paraphrase

1:26-32. I say, because they changed the truth concerning God into a lie, God left them to be led by the most shameful lusts. For even their women changed the use of their bodies into that which is contrary to nature, burning with lust towards one another.

27 In like manner also, the men, forsaking the natural use of the women, burned with their lust towards one another, men with men working habitually that which is shameful, whereby they received in their own minds and bodies that punishment for their error concerning God which was fit. The idolatry whereby they dishonored God, naturally led them to dishonor themselves, by lascivious practices, in imitation of their gods.

28 And as the Grecian legislators and philosophers did not approve of holding the knowledge of God with that worship which is due to him, God delivered them and their people over to a dead conscience, so that they practiced habitually those things which are not suitable to human nature:

29 Being not slightly tinctured, but filled with every kind of injustice, uncleanness, treachery, covetousness, malicious dealing; full of envy, murder, strife, cunning, habitual bad disposition, whispering evil of their neighbors.

30 Revilers, haters of God on account of his purity, insolent towards their inferiors, proud, boasters of qualities which they did not possess, inventors of unlawful pleasures, disobedient to parents;

31 Imprudent in the management of affairs, having no regard to the faith of covenants, without natural affection to their children and relations, implacable towards their enemies, unmerciful to the poor:

32 So utterly corrupt are they, that although they know the law of God, that they who practice such things shall be punished with death, they not only commit these crimes themselves, but even take delight in and encourage those who practice them; which is a demonstration that their wickedness is not to be cured by their own natural powers.

Summary

Being abandoned of God, both their men and women degraded themselves by their vile practices. They received in their own bodies the due reward of their error. They rejected God from their knowledge, and he rejected them. After this they became filled with every vice and crime. These they not only practiced themselves, but even

18. Why did God give them up? What was the recompense for their sin?
19. To what extent did these Gentiles indulge in sin?

had delight in others for practicing them. All this they did, knowing the decree of God, both against their sins and against themselves. They therefore sinned willfully and recklessly.

Comment

Why did God give them up? Because they refused to have him in their knowledge. How could they have him before their mind while they indulged in such vile passions as attributed to both men and women in verses 26-27a? In all this free reign of lust there was to be found the sure recompense of their error in their own bodies (27b). Because they abandoned their minds to sin and gave God no place in their knowledge God gave them up to do those things which are not fitting (28). The Gentiles were (and are) "filled" with the terrible catalog of sins described in verses 29-31.

The final toll of the bell of doom in all of this willful sin is that they who knew the law of God and realized that they who did such things under such conditions were worthy of the penalty of the wrath of God, actually encouraged others to do the same (32). (1:26-32)

Rethinking in Outline Form

II. Proposition Needed. 1:18—3-20

   1. Needed by the Gentiles. 1:18-32

   a. Needed by the Gentiles because they were under the wrath of God. vs. 18a

   (1) They were objects of God's wrath for the following reasons:

   (a) Although they had a knowledge of God's power and divinity through creation, they through their sin stifled this truth. 18b-20

   (b) Deliberately ignoring their knowledge of God they entered into vain speculation. This ended in the worst type of idolatry. 21-23

   (c) God had to give them up because of their absolute moral degradation. 24-32

   2. Needed by the Jews. 2:1—3:9a

Text

2:1-11. Wherefore thou art without excuse, O man, whosoever thou are that judgest: for wherein thou judgest another, thou condemnest thyself; for thou that judgest dost practice the same things. 2 And we know that the judgment of God is according to truth against them that practice such things. 3 And reckonest thou this, O man, who judgest them that practice such things, and doest the

20. What is the final word of condemnation given against the Gentiles?

same, that thou shall escape the judgment of God? 4 Or despisest thou the riches of his goodness and forbearance and longsuffering not knowing that the goodness of God leadest thee to repentance? 5 but after thy hardness and impenitent heart treasurest up for thyself wrath in the day of wrath and revelation of the righteous judgment of God; 6 who will render to every man according to his works: 7 to them that by patience in well-doing seek for glory and honor and incorruption, eternal life: 8 but unto them that are factious, and obey not the truth, but obey unrighteousness, shall be wrath and indignation, 9 tribulation and anguish, upon every soul of man that worketh evil, of the Jew first, and also of the Greek; 10 but glory and honor and peace to every man that worketh good, to the Jew first, and also to the Greek: 11 for there is no respect of persons with God.

Realizing Romans, 2:1-11

52. Why introduce the thought of judgment (on man's part) at this particular time? How does it relate to what has just been said?
53. Read carefully through these eleven verses and mark the three principles or standards of judgment God will use in judgment. They are in verses 2, 6, 11. Name them.
54. Who are the persons of whom the apostle speaks in verse two? (the 'them' of the verse.)
55. Do you belive that God will ever punish a man who does not know he is guilty?
56. The goodness of God does not lead all men to repentance. What is needed in our understanding before this is true?
57. What is repentance? Write out *your* definition.
58. What would be a synonym for the word "hardness" as in verse 5?
59. Will there be measures of punishment on the day of judgment?
60. In what way will we be judged "according to our works"? I thought we were saved by grace through faith.
61. Is Paul saying here that some Gentiles will be given eternal life even if they had no opportunity to hear of Christ, but continued to obey the law they knew? (Cf. 2:6, 7)
62. Why all the variety of words to describe punishment? i.e. "wrath, indignation, tribulation, anguish."
63. In what sense is God no respector of persons? How does the acceptance of Christ relate to this thought?
64. Will God give heaven to the Gentile who never heard of Christ, and never had opportunity, but lived up to the law of right and wrong that he did know? Be careful with this question; do not be too hasty on either side of the subject.

Paraphrase

2:1-11. Since all who practice these crimes are worthy of death, thou are inexcusable, O man, whosoever thou art, who thus judgest, and yet expected that thyself shall be saved: for whilst thou judgest the Gentiles worthy of death, thou condemnest thyself; because thou who thus judgest, committest the very same things.

2 Besides, we know that the sentence of God contained in the curse of the law of Moses is agreeable to truth, even when it is pronounced upon the Jews who commit such crimes, and condemns them to death.

3 This being the case, dost thou think, O Jewish man, who condemnest those heathens who commit such sins, and yet committest the same sins thyself, that thou shalt escape the sentence of God because thou are a son of Abraham, and a member of God's visible church?

4 Or dost thou misconstruct the greatness of his goodness, in bestowing on thee a revelation of his will, and forbearing to punish thee, and his being slow to anger with thee, by inferring from these things that God will not punish thee; not knowing that this goodness of God is designed to lead thee to repentance?

5 Whatever thou mayest think, in proportion to thy own obduratness and impenitency of heart, thou layest up in store for thyself punishment, to be inflicted on thee in the day of punishment, when there shall be an illustrious display of the righteous judgment of God made before the assembled universe;

6 Who will render to every man, not according to his external privileges, but according to the real nature of his works:

7 To them, verily, who by perseverance (I Thess 1:3) in faith and holiness, according to the light which they enjoy, seek glory, honor, and immortality, he will render eternal life:

8 But to them who, being of a proud skeptical disposition, dispute against, and obey not the truth concerning God and his will, made known to them, but obey unrighteousness from false principles and evil inclinations, anger and wrath shall be rendered.

9 I speak of all men without exception: for I say, the severest punishment will be inflicted on every man who practices evil; upon the Jew first, or heaviest, because his sins are aggravated by superior advantages, and also upon the Gentile, because, being taught his duty by the light of nature, he is justly punishable.

10 On the other hand, I affirm, that eternal life shall be to every one who practices good; first or chiefly to the Jew, who, through his superior advantages, hath made greater progress in virtue, and also

to the Greek, whose improvement hath been in proportion to his advantages.

11 For there is no respect of persons with God: A wicked Jew shall not escape at the judgment, because he is a son of Abraham; neither shall a wicked Gentile be spared, because he lived without revelation.

Summary

The Jew constantly condemned the Gentile for doing certain things, but in doing so he condemned himself, for he did the same things. God's just judgment is against all who do such things as the Jew did. Therefore he cannot escape condemnation. The goodness and patience of God are designed to lead men to repentance, but the Jew misconstrues these and does not repent. By this course he heaps up for himself wrath in the last day, when God will render to every one according to his deeds. To the good he will give eternal life; on the disobedient he will inflict wrath. There is no partiality with God.

Comment

While this passage (like the rest of the book) was written primarily for the edification of Christians, it seems to have an equally important secondary purpose—to convert the non-Christian Jew. This is seen in the fact that Paul is here addressing his remarks directly to the Jew, as a careful reading will substantiate.

With the above thought in mind we can realize that the eyes of the Jewish reader must have reflected the sense of self-righteousness he felt within his heart as he read Paul's conclusion of the state of the Gentiles. The apostle now turns to the other half of that world of "Gentiles" and "Jews." He is to finally demonstrate that they are in reality less excusable than the Gentiles, and thus laboring under a greater need for the gospel. Verse one indicates nothing of the persons addressed, and the argument continues in this concealed form until the 17th verse. Since this is true, the Jew would read and hear these words without the veil of prejudice over his mind and would imagine Paul to be continuing in his discussion of the sinful state of the heathen. This being so, he would readily assent to the principles laid down in these verses; and yet before he knew it, he would begin to behold his natural face in the mirror.

21. What is the primary and secondary purpose of Rom. 2:1—3:9a?
22. How does Paul begin his discussion of the need of the Jew?
23. Why does he do it in this way?
24. Why would it be ridiculous to excuse a man who practiced the same sins he condemned in another?
25. Explain the purpose of the personal note in Rom. 2:3.

It would seem ridiculous to excuse the man who judged or condemned another and at the same time practiced the very sins he condemned (vs. 1). This evident fact is based upon the eternal truth that
God will render judgment upon the basis of truth, not upon heredi-
ty or position. The judgment of God will be against all such hypo-
crites (vs. 2).

Making it still more personal (to the Jewish reader): this is a good
principle but personally speaking do *you*, O man, who are doing this
very thing, suppose that *you* will escape the judgment of God? Notice here the inspired author has anticipated the thoughts of the
Jewish mind which were probably as follows: "He seems to be applying this to me also, but I'll escape somehow; for although I am
guilty of the above stated charges, I see no immediate judgment of
God. He will overlook it. After all, I mean well and I am a son of
Abraham and bear the mark of circumcision." (vs. 3).

To correct this erroneous view, the inspired writer then points
out that all this goodness of God, both in forbearing his judgments,
and this suffering long with the offender, and in giving him a place
in the family of Abraham, along with the mark of circumcision, is but
directed to the end that he might repent. The fact that God has not
sent his judgment upon you is evidence that He is giving you a period
of time for repentance. And now if you fail to repent, you will despise all the riches of His goodness. But what are you doing? Why,
through your hard and impenitent heart you are storing up for yourself a great portion of wrath in the day of wrath and revelation of the
righteous judgment of God. vs. 3-5.

In this great day of judgment the Judge of the world will have
one rule which He will be sure to use, and it won't be whether you
are a son of Abraham and bear the mark of circumcision or not. The
rule of judgment will be "according to works." Then follow examples of the two classes of people who will appear before God to be
judged by this rule. There are those who through patient continuance (stedfastness) in well doing seek for glory and honor and incorruption; these shall be given eternal life. Notice: There is no indication here that sinless perfection is the requirement for receiving
eternal life, but rather a constant, unwavering and honest effort to attain "glory and honor and incorruption" by doing that which they

26. What was the purpose of God's long-suffering?
27. To whom was this long-suffering of God especially directed?
28. What did the Jew do instead of repenting?
29. What was the Jew doing for himself by not repenting?
30. On what basis will God judge these Jews and Gentiles?
31. What is meant by "patient continuance" of Rom. 2:7?
32. What will be given to those who so continue in well doing?

know to be right—right according to God's law. This may not seem to you to be true, but please conclude this part of the study before reaching a definite conclusion. Then there are those who through a proud, self-centered spirit, dispute against that which they know to be right and obey not the truth, but unrighteousness; to them shall be meted out the punishment due for such willful disobedience: wrath, indignation, tribulation, and anguish. This punishment will be rendered to every soul of man who works evil. Note that they are lost, but not because they simply fell short of perfection. They are lost not only because they did not even try, but rather because they stedfastly disobeyed and deliberately opposed God, clamoring against His law. (Cp. 1:18b, 25, 28a) Although the Jew and Greek will be judged by the same rule (according to works), the Jew, because of his superior knowledge and opportunity is under a greater responsibility; hence he will receive more severe judgment than the Gentile who was less privileged. (Cp. Lu. 12:47-48) Thus we see that in the judgment, the Jew and Greek will each receive a fair consideration. Behold and admire the impartiality of God's coming judgment. Truly God is no respector of persons. (2:1-11)

Text

2:12-16. For as many as have sinned without the law shall also perish without the law: and as many as have sinned under the law shall be judged by the law; 13 for not the hearers of the law are just before God, but the doers of the law shall be justified; 14 (for when Gentiles that have not the law do by nature the things of the law, these, not having the law, are the law unto themselves; 15 in that they show the work of the law written in their hearts, their conscience bearing witness therewith, and their thoughts one with another accusing or else excusing them); 16 in the day when God shall judge the secrets of men, according to my gospel, by Jesus Christ.

REALIZING ROMANS, 2:12-16

65. Having a law such as the Jews is no advantage in being justified; with or without law, men are lost. But *why* are they lost? Is it because they do not have Christ, or because they fail to keep their law?

66. What is "the law" of verse 12? Does this verse say that there is no possibility of being saved without Christ, or is it discussing the principle God will use in judgment?

67. Who are "the hearers of the law" in verse 13? Are there any comparable persons today? Who are they?

33. In reference to the judgment, what is meant by "the Jew first"?

68. I thought the law was unable to justify anyone. Here, it says the doers of the law shall be justified.
69. How could a person who had not the law "do by nature" the things of the law?
70. Note carefully what is written on their heart: *Not* the law, but "the work of the law." What is the work or purpose of law?

Paraphrase

2:12-16. As many, therefore, as have sinned without revelation, shall also perish without being judged by revelation; their punishment will be less on account of their want of revelation. And as many as have sinned under revelation shall be judged by revelation, their guilt being aggravated by the advantages which they enjoy. They shall be punished in proportion to their guilt.

13 For not those who have enjoyed revelation are esteemed just in the sight of God, but those only who do (vs. 10) the things enjoined in revelation shall be justified at the judgment.

14 When, therefore, the Gentiles who have not revelation, do, by the guidance of their reason and conscience, the things enjoined by revelation, these persons, though they have no external revelation to direct them, furnish a revelation to themselves, by obeying that by which they may be justified through Christ, equally with the Jews.

15 These show plainly, that the distinction between virtue and vice, inculcated in revelation, is written not on tables of stone, but on their hearts, their conscience bearing witness thereto, as also their debates with one another; in which they either accuse one another of evil actions, or else defend each other when so accused.

16 What I have said concerning God's rendering to every one according to his works, and concerning the judgment of those who have sinned, whether under law or without law, will happen in the day when God will judge the inward dispositions of men by Jesus Christ, according to the gospel which I preach.

Summary

The Gentiles who have sinned without a written law will be judged without one, while the Jews will be judged by the law under which they live. Nations who have no written law are law to themselves in so far as they know right from wrong. What they know in this respect is attested by their conscience, and shown by their mutual accusations and acquittals.

34. Explain the meaning of Rom. 2:12.

Comment

Taking up the case of the Jew and Greek from a closer viewpoint, Paul now states the basis of judgment (Notice: the basis of *judgment*, NOT the basis of *justification*) for those without the law as well as those with the law (the Mosaic law). As many as have sinned who have not the law of Moses, will be judged by the law they do have, the law of nature. Paul does not tell us exactly what this law is, but he undoubtedly gives us the basis of it in chapter one, verse twenty. And if justice demands it, they will perish. Their judgment will be totally apart from the law of Moses. It is well to notice here that the case of the Gentiles presented in the first chapter would seem to indicate that nearly all, if not all of the Gentile world would be lost, being judged upon the basis of the law of nature. But those who have sinned under the law of Moses, what about them? They will be judged upon the very law they have transgressed. The apostle points out in verse 13 that what he has said in verse 12 is true because of the previously stated facts that God's judgment will be "according to works" and "without respect of persons." (Cp. 2:6,11) In effect, he says: "Just because you hear the law read in your synagogues every sabbath, you need not rest easily; for this will mean nothing toward your acquittal on the day of eternal equity. I repeat again, it is the 'doing of the law' that counts before God." Paul has thus removed the Jew's last vestige of hope of being counted as a special object of favor, and has placed before him the mirror where he can see his need of the gospel. 2:12-13.

It would be quite probable that some learned Jew would offer this objection: "Now how could the Gentiles be judged by this rule (that the doers of the law shall be justified) since they have no law?" This objection is answered in the parenthetical statement of verses 14-15. The apostle says that even though the Gentiles have not "the" *law*, if they do by nature (naturally) the things of "the" law, they thus become "a" law unto themselves. This strange circumstance is explained in the fact that they have an accurate, though perhaps limited, knowledge of right and wrong which they received from the law of nature, and possibly through tradition. Thus the distinction between virtue and vice (which is the "work of the law") is

35. Upon what is the Gentile's law probably based?
36. What is the conclusion to be drawn from chapter one regarding the spiritual standing of the Gentiles in judgment?
37. In respect to the law, who is going to be justified in God's sight?
38. Why is the parenthetical statement of vs. 14-15 here inserted?
39. Explain in your own words verses 14-15.

written upon their hearts. That it is written upon their hearts is demonstrated by their actions. Inwardly their conscience assents to the fact that right is preferable to wrong. When the decision of the will is made and the deed is done, their thoughts or inward reasonings either accuse them if the deed was wrong, or excuse them if it was right. The Gentile will be judged according to his conscientiousness in keeping the law of nature and the Jew according to his conscientiousness in keeping the law of Moses. (Cp. 2:6, 7, 10) (We notice here a certain element of mercy extended to those who never heard the gospel.) The apostle has now clearly explained the way God will judge them "according to their works," 2:14-15.

It is here necessary to point out that the thought of verse 13 is broken by the parenthetical statement of verses 14-15, and is not completed until verse 16. Completely stated the thought is as follows: "For not the hearers of the law are just before God, but the doers of the law shall be justified; in the day when God shall judge the secrets of men, according to my gospel, by Jesus Christ." When God begins to mark the secrets of our hearts, "O Lord, who can stand?" But that will be absolutely fair judgment, will it not? Paul says that this is the message of the gospel he preaches, and that God will commit all decisions unto Jesus Christ, and act through him on that great day of judgment. 2:(13), 16. (2:12-16)

Rethinking in Outline Form
THE NEED OF THE GOSPEL AMONG THE JEWS, 2:1-16

The Jews Were Truly in Need of Justification, for:
If God's judgment was going to be:

1. According to truth. vs. 2
2. According to works. vs. 6
3. With no respect of persons. vs. 11
4. According to doing and not hearing. vs. 13

Then the Jews were tragically in need, for:

1. According to truth. vs. 2

a. The Jews condemned others and practiced what they condemned. vs. 1

b. The Jew felt he would be treated in a special manner. vs. 3

c. He misunderstood God's mercy as a license for sin and not an opportunity to repent. vs. 4

40. What thought is broken by this parenthetical statement?
41. How does this thought read when the parenthetical statement is left out?
42. To whom has God committed judgment? Cp. Jn. 5:22.

d. By his hard heart and unrepentant attitude he was only increasing his coming wrath. vs. 5

2. According to works. vs. 6

a. To the steadfast well-doer, eternal life. vs. 7

b. To the factious and disobedient, hell. vs. 8

c. This will be given to everyone, Jews and Greeks, vs. 9-10

3. With no respect to person. vs. 11

a. Even the Gentles will be judged by this standard. They do "by nature" their law and will be judged accordingly. vs. 14-15

In the day when God shall judge the secrets of the hearts of men it will be:

1. According to truth.

2. According to works.

3. With no respect for persons.

4. According to doing.

If this be so, and it is, then the Jew is truly, tragically, in need . . . for he is condemned ON ALL FOUR POINTS.

Text

2:17-24. But if thou bearest the name of a Jew, and restest upon the law, and gloriest in God, 18 and knowest his will, and approvest the things that are excellent, being instructed out of the law, 19 and art confident that thou thyself art a guide of the blind, a light of them that are in darkness, 20 a corrector of the foolish, a teacher of babes, having in the law the form of knowledge and of the truth; 21 thou therefore that teachest another, teachest thou not thyself? thou that preachest a man should not steal, does thou steal? 22 thou that sayest a man should not commit adultery, dost thou commit adultery? thou that abhorrest idols, dost thou rob temples? 23 thou who gloriest in the law, through thy transgression of the law dishonorest thou God? 24 For the name of God is blasphemed among the Gentiles because of you, even as it is written.

Realizing Romans, 2:17-24

71. Is there any real significance in the name "Jew" other than the fact that it distinguishes them from the Gentiles?

72. In what sense were the Jews "resting upon the law"? To what purpose or intent?

73. Make a list of the characteristics of the Jews here given by Paul. There are eleven of them; see if you can find them all.

74. Was there one of these qualities that was not true or desirable?

75. In what sense were the Jews glorying in God? Explain the expression.

76. What is the difference, if any, of "knowing His will" and "approving the things that are excellent"?
77. Tie up the expression "being instructed out of the law" with the two preceding phrases; i.e., show the relationship.
78. Did God ever intend for the Jewish nation to be a guide to the blind?
79. Show the tremendous significance of revelation as expressed in these words.
80. Is it true that all who are now without revelation are blind—in the dark, ignorant, and foolish?
81. Can you see any application to present-day church members?
82. In what sense had the Jew failed to teach himself?
83. What definition of teaching does this verse (21) give?
84. Do you believe these Jews were actually committing adultery and at the same time teaching others not to?
85. Why would a Jew rob a temple of idols? Would it be to worship them?
86. Note in verse 23 that transgression of the law is more serious than the transgression of a divine will. It has judgment implications.
87. Can God be dishonored?
88. What is the meaning of "blasphemed" as here used?

Paraphrase

2:17-24. What improvement have ye Jews made of revelation? Behold, thou hast the honorable appellation of a Jew, and restest in the law as a complete rule of duty and boastest in God as the object of thy worship;

18 And knowest what God requires, and approvest the things that are excellent, being instructed by the law, which is a revelation from God, and a much surer rule than philosophy;

19 And boastest that thou thyself art a guide in matters of religion to the Gentiles, who, notwithstanding their philosophy, are blind, and a light to all who are in the darkness of heathenism;

20 A reprover of the foolish, a teacher of persons as destitute of spiritual ideas as babes:—those titles thou assumest, because thou hast a just representation of religious knowledge and truth in the scriptures.

21 Is thy behaviour suitable to those high pretensions? Thou then who teaches the Gentiles, why teachest thou not thyself? Thou who preachest to them, Do not steal,—dost thou steal?

22 Thou enlightened Jewish doctor, who sayest to the Gentiles, Do not commit adultery,—dost thou commit adultery? Thou who

abhorrest idols, dost thou rob temples of the tithes destined for the support of the worship of God? as if impiety were criminal in heathens, but pardonable in thee.

23 Thou who boastest of revelation, dost thou, by breaking the precepts of revelation, dishonor God who bestowed it on thee? (See vs. 4)

24 I do not charge you Jews with these crimes rashly: For, as it was written to your fathers, so I write to you, the name of God is evil spoken of among the Gentiles through your wickedness, who call yourselves his people.

Summary

The Jew made great pretensions to superior knowledge; yet he acted as though he himself needed to be taught. He was inconsistent in his conduct. He preached not to do this, but did it. He taught not to do that, but did it. He boasted in the law, yet broke it. He abhorred idols; yet robbed temples of them to serve them. He affected great reverence for God; yet dishonored him by breaking his law. He even brought his name into disrepute among surrounding nations.

Comment

The Jewish readers of this letter have no doubt by this time come to see the personal application of what has been said, so the open statement of verse seventeen, directed as it is to the Jew, would be no great surprise. The 142 words of this remarkable sentence contain an undeniable exposé of Jewish sins which demonstrate the need in their lives for the gospel of Christ. Notice the apparently complimentary touch of these words along with the masked sarcasm which finally bursts forth into open denunciation of undeniable sins. Hear Paul speak to the heart of these Jews: (Ro 2:17-20)

First, he spoke of their high standing.

a. Bore the proud name of a Jew. (Proud because it meant "praise" Gen. 29:35.)
b. Rested upon the law.
c. Glorified in God.
d. Knew His will.

43. How does the universal need of the gospel help to answer question one?
44. How does the basis of judgment help to answer the question?
45. In what manner is the guilt of the Jew (chap. 2) and Gentile (chap. 1) made known?
46. Why wouldn't the Jew be surprised to hear his name mentioned as in verse 17?
47. What form does the 142-word sentence of the Jewish exposé take? Why?
48. Why was the name "Jew" a proud name?
49. Who was blind, in darkness, a babe, foolish?

e. Were able to discriminate in a very close way as to right and wrong because of their instruction in the law.
f. A confident guide to the blind Gentile.
g. A light to those in darkness.
h. An instructor of the foolish.
i. A teacher of those who were so destitute of spiritual knowledge as to be counted as "babes."
j. All these things were theirs because they had the law and in it the knowledge and truth which made such a standing possible (2:17-20).

He then condemned their hypocrisy. To the question now asked by Paul there could be but one answer. Here is the question, which contains the crux of the whole matter: "Thou therefore that teachest another, teachest thou not thyself?" (2:21a)

a. What about your teaching on stealing? How does it compare with your actions?
b. And your prohibitions against adultery—are you practicing the very thing you prohibit?
c. How you do abhor idols! But is it you who are entering temples of these idols to steal the very objects you abhor?
d. Summing up the matter, you present a strange paradox. You glory in the law of God and then by your transgressions of the law you dishonor Him who originated the law.
e. It is as in the days of your fathers—the name of Jehovah is sneered at among the Gentiles because of you (2:21b-24). (2:17-24)

Text

2:25-29. For circumcision indeed profiteth, if thou be a doer of the law; but if thou be a transgressor of the law, thy circumcision is become uncircumcision. 26 If therefore the uncircumcision keep the ordinances of the law, shall not his uncircumcision be reckoned for circumcision? 27 and shall not the uncircumcision which is by nature, if it fulfill the law, judge thee, who with the letter and circumcision are a transgressor of the law? 28 For he is not a Jew who is one outwardly; neither is that circumcision which is outward in the flesh: 29 but he is a Jew who is one inwardly; and circumcision is that of the heart, in the spirit not in the letter; whose praise is not of men, but of God.

REALIZING ROMANS, 2:25-29

89. In what sense would circumcision be of any profit? I thought we were answerable to the gospel.

50. What phrase contains the crux of the whole matter? Explain.

90. Either a man is circumcised or not. After being circumcised, how could he be "uncircumcised"?
91. Paul seems to understand circumcision in an entirely new light. Does this have any application to Christian baptism? cp. Col. 2:12-14. If so, what?
92. What is the meaning of the word "judge" in vs. 27?
93. What is "the letter" of vs. 27?
94. Do outward forms have any significance at all?
95. In this section a good synonym for "circumcision" would be___?
96. Could we as Christians keep the spirit of the Faith and not the letter, and yet still be acceptable with God? Explain.

Paraphrase

2:25-29. Whilst ye continue wicked, it is foolish to expect salvation because ye are circumcised; for cimcumcision, indeed, as the sign of God's covenant, will profit thee, if thou keepest the law of faith enjoined in the covenant; but if thou be a transgressor of that law, thou are in the condition of a wicked Gentile.

26 And if a heathen, instructed by right reason, and by the grace of God, perform the precepts of the law of faith, will not God treat him as a person circumcised, by bestowing on him justification, the blessing promised to Abraham's seed?

27 And will not every uncircumcised Gentile, who, under the direction of reason and conscience, without revelation, practises the faith and obedience enjoined in the covenant with Abraham, condemn thee as a transgressor of that covenant, though a Jew by the circumcision which is according to the letter of Moses's precept?

28 For he is not a son of Abraham, and an heir of the promises, who is one by natural descent only; neither is true circumcision that which is outward in the flesh:

29 But he is a Jew who is one in the temper of his mind; and circumcision is that of the heart, by cutting off evil desires, according to the spirit, not according to the letter of the law. Of such a real Jew, the praise will not be from the Jews, who will disown him if he is uncircumcised, but it will come from God, who, knowing his heart, will acknowledge him as one of Abraham's spiritual seed.

Summary

Circumcision is of no value unless the law is kept. The Gentile who keeps the law, though not circumcised, will be accepted. The Jew who breaks the law, though circumcised, will be condemned. The Judaism and circumcision which save men are in the heart and spirit, and not outward in literal fleshly marks.

51. What means of special approval did the Jew attempt to use?

Comment

Properly humbled, the Jew now searches for some way to bolster his deflated ego. He harkens back to the old prejudice of special favor supposedly found in circumcision. Paul speaks of the true meaning of circumcision after this fashion: Circumcision is indeed of profit if you are a doer of the law, but if you are not, of what value is your circumcision? You had just as well be uncircumcised. And speaking of the matter of uncircumcision, that person who does not bear this rite, if he keeps the ordinance of the law, will he not be considered as if he were circumcised? And would not such a person judge and shame you who have the law and circumcision, yet are a transgressor? As shocking as it may sound, being a Jew is not a matter of outward form, nor circumcision a mere physical rite, for God recognizes a man as a Jew from the condition of his heart. Likewise with circumcision, it also is of the heart and not of the letter. The circumstances are thus constituted so God may do the praising (since the name "Jew" means "praise") and not man. 2:25-29.

Text

3:1-9a. What advantage then hath the Jew? or what is the profit of circumcision? 2 Much every way: first of all, that they were intrusted with the oracles of God. 3 For what if some were without faith? shall their want of faith make of none effect of the faithfulness of God? 4 God forbid: yea, let God be found true, but every man a liar; as it is written,

That thou mightest be justified in thy words,

And mightest prevail when thou comest into judgment. 5 But if our unrighteousness commendeth the righteousness of God, what shall we say? Is God unrighteous who visiteth with wrath? (I speak after the manner of men.) 6 God forbid: for then how shall God judge the world? 7 But if the truth of God through my lie abounded unto his glory, why am I also still judged as a sinner? 8 and why not (as we are slanderously reported, and as some affirm that we say), Let us do evil, that good may come? whose condemnation is just. 9 What then? are we better than they?

Realizing Romans, 3:1-9a

97. Who is asking this question of vs. 1? i.e., for whom is Paul asking it?

98. Why imagine there would be an advantage and profit? cf. vs. 1.

99. The Jews had the oracles of God, but they did them no good. How did such oracles relate to Christ?

52. How could the circumcised become uncircumcised and vice versa?

53. How could Paul say that circumcision was of the heart when it plainly was in the flesh?

100. Paul says, "much in *every way*." Can you find more than one way mentioned?
101. Show how the thought, "10,000,000 Jews can't be wrong," was used as an argument by the Jews against Jesus as the Messiah.
102. Meaning of the words, "faithfulness of God," as in vs. 3?
103. The truth of God is totally apart from man. In what way?
104. Why should anyone think God would not be justified in His words?
105. In what sense could God come into judgment?
106. Does the end ever justify the means? In vs. 5 Paul is suggesting that some feel this is true. Read this verse over very carefully and try to show how.
107. On what basis or by what standard will God judge the world?
108. Paul "turns the tables" on the Jewish objectors. Read verses 7 and 8 to see if you can discover in what manner this is done.
109. How could good possibly result from doing evil? Do not say that some feel that it could. Explain *why* they felt it.
110. Who are the "we" and the "they" of vs. 9?
111. There is a wonderful lesson on the dangers of "having a form of godliness and denying the power thereof." See if you can find it.

Paraphrase

3:1-9a. If our privileges will procure us no favor at the judgment, and if the want of these privileges will be no disadvantage to the Gentiles, What is the pre-eminence of the Jew above the Gentile? and what is the advantage of circumcision?

2 It is great in every respect; but chiefly, indeed, because the Jews were intrusted with the oracles of God; especially that concerning the blessing of the nations in Abraham's seed.

3 But what benefit have we received from the oracles of God, if the greatest part of us have not believed on him whom ye call the seed, and are to be cast off? Will not their unbelief destroy the faithfulness of God, who promised to be a God to Abraham's seed in their generations?

4 By no means: the faithfulness of God will not be destroyed by the rejection of the Jews. But let God be acknowledged true to his covenant, although every Jew be a liar, in affirming that Jesus is not the promised seed, and be rejected on that account: for as it is written, in all cases God will be justified in his threatenings, and will appear just as often as he punishes.

5 But if our unrighteousness, in rejecting and crucifying Jesus, establisheth the faithfulness of God in casting us off from being his people, what shall we infer? Is not God unrighteous, who likewise

47

destroyeth us as a nation for that sin? (I write this in the character of an unbelieving Jew.)

6 By no means: for, if no sin can be righteously punished which is attended with good consequences, how shall God judge the world? How shall he render to every man according to his works?

7 Your account is not satisfactory; for if the truth of God, in casting off and punishing our nation, hath been manifested to his great honor through our lie, in affirming that Jesus is not the promised seed, why am I, an individual, farther punished also as a sinner? My being involved in the rejection and destruction of the nation, is punishment sufficient.

8 And to carry your objection farther, why not add, as we are slanderously reported by you Jews to practise, and as many affirm the apostles order, Certainly let us do evil, that glory may accrue to God from our pardon? Of those persons who teach and practise such things, the condemnation is both certain and just.

9a Well, then, since the pre-eminence of the Jews above the Gentiles consists in their superior advantages, do we acknowledge that we excel the Gentiles in piety?

Summary

The Jews, in being such, possessed many peculiar advantages, among the most important of which was being entrusted with the revelations of God. Still, though thus highly favored, many of them were very unfaithful. But this will have no effect upon God's faithfulness. He will remain true, though all men should prove false. Moreover, even when the Jew's injustice had the effect to display the justice of God, still God must punish the injustice, and he does right in doing so. We must not do evil that good may come, and we will certainly be punished if we do.

Comment

The argument of Paul would suggest three objections to the Jewish mind. These objections and their answers are the subjects of the first nine verses of the third chapter. The objections are:

a. If the moral Gentile is better off than the immoral Jew (as you seem to point out in your words concerning circumcision, etc.) what becomes of the Jew's advantages? 3:1

Answer: He still has many advantages. First of all, he has been and is the depository for the oracles of God, the advantage being that within these oracles are the promises of the coming Messiah; thus the

54. What was the first of the three objections the Jews had to justification by faith?
55. What particular advantage did having the oracles of God give the Jew?

Jew was privileged to be the one who could recognize and welcome the Christ when He came. Besides this paramount advantage the oracles also gave him the will of God for his life, and he could thus conduct himself accordingly and receive the approval of God and the benefits of right living in his own person. 3:2

Paul, although saying there were many advantages, here only mentions one and does not take up a discussion of any others until chapter nine, verse four.

b. The second objection is suggested by the answer of the first. Since the Jews have the oracles of God, which contain God's will, will not their unbelief and consequent disobedience cancel His promises? 3:3

Answer: God forbid. If every Jew on earth were a liar it would not affect the truthfulness of Jehovah. It is even as the Psalmist has said: God is just in every word spoken and in every case brought to trial he is only proved true. So your faithfulness or lack of it cannot alter the character of God; it can only magnify his eternal righteousness. 3:4

c. Again we find the objection growing out of the answer to the foregoing. Here it is: If our unrighteousness only results in the magnifying of God's righteousness, is he not unrighteous to visit us with wrath? (Paul speaks in the first person in giving this objection, thus indicating that he is speaking as an unbelieving Jew.) 3:5

Answer: How then shall God judge the world? If, as you say, God now excuses evil and counts it as good because it serves the purpose of establishing his faithfulness, what will be the standard for judgement? Wrong is wrong and sin is sin under whatever conditions it is enacted and regardless of what the final results might be. On what other basis could He judge all men according to their works and be no respector of persons? 3:6

The apostle then places before the mind of the Jew the illustration that completes in a unique way the answer to the third objection. He puts himself in the role of the Jew who has offered this objection and then says: "You believe what I have been telling you concerning the Messiahship of Jesus of Nazareth is a lie, do you not? Well, if the truth of God (which you claim to have) is made to abound, or to be more evident by my lie, why are you calling me

56. State in your own words the second objection.
57. What is the answer?
58. Give in your own words the third objection. How is it answered?
59. How would the third objection destroy the basis for judging the world?
60. Explain the illustration the apostle uses to complete the answer to the third objection.

a sinner? (My, what an application of their own principle!) "Indeed," says the apostle, "why not do the very thing some of you are accusing me of—do evil that good may come?" Why, the justice of condemning those who would so slander the apostle is self-evident. 3:7-8

In chapter two the need of the Jews was thoroughly dealt with; they were laid under the wrath of God and were thus shown to be without hope except it be in the gospel. In concluding his demonstration of the need of the Jew, Paul found it necessary to digress in order to answer the objections of chapter 3, verses 1-8. Now he returns to the subject and speaks of the pride of the Jews. 3:9a. Even though the Jews see themselves as lost along with the Gentiles, they somehow imagined that in spite of their sin and failure and because of the favors God has bestowed upon them (2:17-20) they still were a little bit better than the Gentiles. Paul places himself with them in voicing this egotistical question: "What then? are we better than they?" He then immediately rebels at the thought and denies it with the strong words, "No, in no wise." 3:9a

Rethinking in Outline Form

2. Needed by the Jews. 2:1—3:9a
   a. Reasons why the gospel means of justification was needed by the Jew:
      (1) He possessed the law but did not practice it. Since man is to be judged by the law under which he lives, the Jew, like the Gentile, is tragically in need. 1-16
      (2) The Jew boasts of his high standing given him by his possession of the law, but all the while his practice shows him to be no better than the Gentile. 17-24
      (3) His effort to seek special consideration because of circumcision avails nothing, for the true meaning and purpose of circumcision shows it to be of value only to the one who keeps the law. Even the uncircumcised can be counted as circumcised through obedience to his law. 25-29
      (4) The three objections of the Jew to this position are completely answered by Paul. 3:1-9a

Text

3:9b-20. No, in no wise: for we before laid to the charge both of Jews and Greeks, that they are all under sin; 10 as it is written, There is none righteous, no, not one;

61. How is it that the Jew could consider himself somewhat better than the Gentile?

11 There is none that understandeth, There is none that seeketh after God;

12 They have all turned aside, they are together become unprofitable; there is none that doeth good, no, not so much as one:

13 Their throat is an open sepulchre; With their tongues they have used deceit; The poison of asps is under their lips.

14 Whose mouth is full of cursing and bitterness:

15 Their feet are swift to shed blood;

16 Destruction and misery are in their ways;

17 And the way of peace have they not known:

18 There is no fear of God before their eyes.

19 Now we know that what things soever the law saith, it speaketh to them that are under the law; that every mouth may be stopped, and all the world may be brought under the judgment of God: 20 because by the works of the law shall no flesh be justified in his sight; for through the law cometh the knowledge of sin.

Realizing Romans, 3:9b-20

112. Where in the Roman epistle had Paul proven both Jews and Greeks guilty of sin?

113. In what sense is "there none righteous"?

114. The lack of understanding as in vs. 11a was limited to understanding on what subject?

115. There have been "seekers after God" in all ages and places. In what sense is vs. 11b true?

116. Note the responsibility of vs. 12a. What is it?

Paraphrase

3:9b-20. I acknowledge no such thing; for I have formerly proved both Jews and Gentiles to be all guilty of sin.

10 With respect to the Jewish common people, they have been wicked in all ages; as it is written, There is not a righteous man, no, not one.

11 In the same psalm, ver. 2, it is said, There is none that understandeth his duty; there is none that worshippeth God as he ought to do.

12 And in ver. 3 it is said, They are all gone out of the way of righteousness, they are employing themselves together in works which are utterly unprofitable to themselves and to society: there is none of them who does any good action; there is not so much as one.

13 Also it is said, Psal. v. 9. Their throat is an open sepulchre sending forth by their rotten speech an offensive stench; with their fair

speeches they deceive; their speech being deadly, the poison of asps is under their lips; Psal. cxl. 3.

14 On other occasions, giving way to their malicious dispositions, their mouth is full of cursing and bitter imprecations; Psal. x. 7.

15 Their works correspond to their words; for they make haste to commit murder, as Isaiah hath testified, chap. lix. 7.

16 They occasion destruction and misery to all who follow them.

17 But such practices as lead to the happiness of mankind, they neither have known nor desired to know.

18 All this wickedness they commit, because, as is said Psal. xxxvi. 1. There is no fear of God before their eyes; they fear not God's displeasure.

19 Now these things are said, not of the heathens, but of the Jews; for we know that whatever things the law saith, it saith to them who are under the law; that every Jew may remain silent, as condemned by the law; and that all the world, Jews as well as Gentiles, may be sensible [*aware*] that they are liable to punishment before God.

20 Wherefore, by works of law, whether natural or revealed, moral or ceremonial, there shall no man be justified meritoriously in God's sight, (Psal. cxliii. 2.); because law makes men sensible that they are sinners, without giving them any hope of pardon; consequently, instead of entitling them to life, it subjects them to punishment.

Summary

In point of guilt, then, are the Jews any better than the Gentiles? None at all. All are alike under the dominion of sin, and therefore are alike guilty. This is proved by the very scriptures which the Jews have. The law condemns all, and justifies none. Therefore, by law, no one may expect to be acquitted in the presence of God. Instead of being justified by law, men only learn from it that they are sinners.

Comment

Continuing the thought of verse nine, the apostle explains why the Jews were as needy as the Gentiles. He says, "We before laid to the charge both of Jews and Greeks that they are all under sin." At the time that he answers the question of the Jew, he lays down a proposition which sums up all he has previously said. The last portion of the ninth verse through the twentieth carries the conclusion of the whole matter. All that was needed in Paul's splendid argument was a substantiation from the Old Testament. This he gives, and shows in the use of the quotations from the Old Testament that they spoke

62. What is the purpose of verses 10-18?

not only of the sin and need of the Jew, but also spoke with equal force of the sin and need of the Gentile. 3:9b

a. We find a description of the sinful state of both Jew and Gentile. 10-12

b. Then the practice of sin is noted. 13-17

    (1) The practice of sin in their speech is pointed out. Vs. 13-14

    (2) Then sin through overt acts is discussed. Vs. 15-17

c. Finally the cause of such ungodliness is found: "There is no fear of God before their eyes." 18

In explanation of the above quotations Paul states that it is a well-known fact that whatever judgments are pronounced in a law are directed against those persons in possession of the law. In this case the Jews were such persons. When violations of the law are pointed out, and the offenders are truly guilty, there is nothing they can say to defend themselves. This was exactly the circumstance in respect to the Jew. But in addition to this effect, there was another: the whole world is brought under the judgment of God. How can this be true? How can the whole world be brought under God's wrath by pointing out violations of the law of Moses? We can understand this: first, by realizing that the sins described are counted as sin because *God so designated them in His law;* second, that those Gentiles who practiced the same sins would likewise be guilty because they knew or had the opportunity to know what was right (as we have already shown). The clear statement in the law brought to the surface the truth that all subconsciously felt: the whole world was under the judgment of God. 3:19

"Because" is the first word of the twentieth verse, indicating that a reason is now to be given for what has just been said. Paul had just said that the whole world was under the judgment of God as a result of the giving of the law. He now says this is true "because by the works of the law shall no flesh be justified in his sight." This is the grand conclusion toward which the apostle has been leading from chapter one, verse eighteen. He stated that in the gospel was to be found a means whereby man could be declared just before God. The Jew imagined he did not need the gospel, for he felt that there could be found justification through the law. Paul pointed out that the law indeed formed a basis for judgment, but as to obtaining justification through the law, this was proven to be an impossibility. To

63. How do these verses apply with particular force to the Jews?

64. How was the whole world brought under the wrath of God?

65. What was the grand conclusion toward which Paul had been leading from 1:18?

66. How could one be "just" under the law?

be just through the law, absolute obedience would have been essential, and this no Jew (or Gentile) accomplished. Indeed, it has been shown that, using the law under which they lived as a basis for judgment, they could not even be constituted conscientious, much less, "just." The inspired writer points out that sin is brought to light by the law; hence, (because of sin made known) no one can be justified by the law. The giving of the law made known the fact that all men had been and were transgressing God's standard of righteousness. These transgressions made justification through the law impossible. Looking into our own lives and then into the law we see that we are practicing the very sins spoken against. This being true, is it not absurd to think that we are just through the law? 3:20

Rethinking in Outline Form

3. Needed by All—Both Jews and Gentiles. 3:9b-20
   a. The need of both Jews and Greeks shown from the words of the Old Testament. 9b-18
      (1) Their sinful state. 10-12
      (2) The practice of sin. 13-17
         (a) The practice of sin through words. 13-14
         (b) The practice of sin through actions. 15-17
   b. All the world has sinned. Not even the Jew can claim exemption from the consequences of his sin, for when the law of Moses denounces those consequences, it speaks especially to the people to whom it was given. The law was so designed that the Jew, too, might have his mouth stopped from all excuse, and that all mankind might be held accountable to God. vs. 19
   c. This is the conclusion of the whole argument. By works of law (i.e., by an attempted fulfillment of law) no mortal may hope to be declared righteous in God's sight, for the only effect of law is to open men's eyes to their own sinfulness, not to enable them to do better. That method, the method of works, has failed. A new method must be found. vs. 20 (Sandy, p. 76)

Text

3:21-26. But now apart from the law a righteousness of God hath been manifested, being witnessed by the law and the prophets; 22 even the righteousness of God through faith in Jesus Christ unto all them that believe; for there is no distinction; 23 for all have sinned, and fall short of the glory of God; 24 being justified freely

67. What is the twofold task involved in establishing truth? How does this fit into justification by faith?
68. What twofold relationship does the "righteousness" have?

by his grace through the redemption that is in Christ Jesus: 25 whom God set forth to be a propitiation, through faith, in his blood, to show his righteousness because of the passing over of the sins done aforetime, in the forebearance of God; 26 for the showing, I say, of his righteousness at this present season: that he might himself be just, and the justifier of him that hath faith in Jesus.

REALIZING ROMANS, 3:21-26

117. Should we stumble over the word "believe" in vs. 22? Be careful—we can stumble over it through overemphasis as well as underemphasis. What is the safe course?
118. Show the two ways in which "there is no distinction."
119. What is "the glory of God" as in vs. 23?
120. We are justified "by" and "through" something. Explain.
121. Redemption is a wonderful word—it suggests a kidnaping. In what way is this true?
122. Use a Bible dictionary if necessary to look up the word "propitiation." This has an Old Testament background—what is it?
123. How does the death of Christ show the righteousness of God?
124. God's righteousness was shown on the cross because of "sins done afore time." In what way?
125. Show how the following qualities of God were manifested on Calvary: mercy, justice, love, wisdom.

Paraphrase

3:21-26. But now, under the gospel, a righteousness appointed by God as the means of the justification of sinners, without perfect obedience to law of any kind, is made known: And it is no new method of justification, being taught both by the law and the prophets;

22 Even the righteousness which God hath appointed to be through faith of Jesus Christ, (the faith which Jesus Christ hath enjoined), graciously counted unto all, and rewarded upon all who believe: for there is no distinction between Jew and Gentile in the method of justification;

23 Because all have sinned, and come short of praise from God: so that being all involved in guilt and misery, the same remedy must be applied to all:

24 Being justified by faith, not meritoriously, but of free gift, by a great exercise of God's grace, through the redemption which is procured for them by Christ Jesus:

25 Whom God hath set forth a propitiatory, from which he will dispense pardon to sinners, through faith in his blood, for a proof

of his own righteousness in not instantly punishing the sins which were before the coming of Christ committed through God's forbearing to punish Adam with immediate death, in the view of the obedience of Christ.

26 For a proof also of his righteousness in not punishing sins committed in the present time, and henceforward, in order that, at the judgment, he may appear just, when acquitting him who is a performer of the faith enjoined by Jesus: and that whether he be a Jew or a Gentile.

Summary

But although justification by law is impossible, still God has revealed another way of justifying men, a way, too, that is attested both by the law and the prophets. He has revealed a plan of justifying people by means of their belief in Jesus Christ, revealed it to all, both Jews and Gentiles. This justification takes its rise in God's favor; it is procured by a ransom which has been accomplished by Christ. Christ effected this ransom by his blood, and we attain the benefit of it by believing in him and obeying him. This ransom enables God to be just while forgiving the sinner, provided he is a believer in his Son.

Comment

"But now apart from the law a righteousness of God hath been manifested . . ." This righteousness of God is twofold: relating to the fact that God is righteous, and that man is to be made righteous, or just. The procedure of declaring man just is "apart from the law," and yet the law and prophets both spoke of it through type and prophecy. 21. This righteousness is that which comes through faith in Jesus Christ. It is given unto all that exercise this belief, "for there is no distinction." There is no distinction as to who can thus receive this righteousness; neither is there a distinction as to who needs this righteousness, "for *all* have sinned," and thus fall short of the glory of God. 22-23. This justification "takes rise in the favor of God." It is bestowed freely on all because of the redemption price paid by Jesus Christ. 24. Jesus Christ was set forth by God to be a covering for our sins, through faith in his blood. This covering for sins is the answer to the problem of those in the Old Testament who had no provision for the washing away of sins. The sins done aforetime in the days of the old covenant were passed over with the thought that one day the provision for their covering would be

69. In what two respects is there "no distinction"?
70. What is the meaning of the word "propitiation"?
71. What do "the sins done aforetime" have to do with the death of Christ?

found in the blood of Christ. 25. Behold now the wonderful righteousness of God at this present season. Through the substitutionary death of His Son, the justice of God in respect to punishment for sin and the mercy of God in respect to forgiving sin find a wondrous agreement and satisfaction. The wisdom of God searched the love of God for a way to reconcile the justice of God with the mercy of God and the result was the sending of his own son to die in the stead of man. 26.

Text

3:27-31. Where then is the glorifying? It is excluded. By what manner of law? of works? Nay: but by a law of faith. 28 We reckon therefore that a man is justified by faith apart from the works of the law. 29 Or is God the God of Jews only? is he not the God of Gentiles also? Yea, of Gentiles also: 30 if so be that God is one, and he shall justify the circumcision by faith, and the uncircumcision through faith.

31 Do we then make the law of none effect through faith? God forbid: nay, we establish the law.

REALIZING ROMANS, 3:27-31

126. Who would be tempted to glory? Why?

127. How does faith exclude pride?

128. In what sense can we refer to faith, or the exercise of it, as "a law of faith"?

129. If a man did not try to keep the law—whatever it might be— could he be justified by faith? If not, how could he be justified "apart from the works of the law"?

130. Why ask the question of 29a?

131. Every Jew would admit God was God to Gentiles as well as Jews. Why?

132. Is there any difference in "by faith" and "through faith" of vs. 30?

133. In what sense is the law established through faith?

Paraphrase

3:27-31. Since all are justified by the free gift of God, Where is boasting? It is excluded. By what law? Of works? Do the laws which require perfect obedience exclude it? No. But it is excluded by the law which makes faith the means of our justification.

72. What two qualities in the nature of God are reconciled in the death of Christ?

28 We conclude then, that by faith Jew and Gentile is justified without works of law; without perfect obedience to any law, as the meritorious cause of their justification.

29 To show that God will justify the Gentiles by faith, equally with the Jews, let me ask, Is he the maker and judge of the Jews only? and not of the Gentiles also? Most assuredly of the Gentiles also.

30 Seeing there is one God of Jews and Gentiles, and they are all equally related to him, he will in his treatment of them follow one rule—He will justify the Jews to whom he has given his oracles, by their faith in these oracles, and the Gentiles through the law of faith mentioned in ver. 27.

31 Do we then make law of every kind useless, by teaching the justification of the Gentiles, through the law of faith? By no means, for by this doctrine we establish law, as necessary in many respects.

Summary

The justification of God is by belief, and not by deeds of law. It is a matter of favor, then, and not of merit. Consequently, no man can boast that he has deserved it or merited it. This justification is for Gentiles as well as for Jews. God is the God of both, and is ready to bless both, to bless them in the same way, and on the same conditions.

Comment

With this glorious picture before us where is the opportunity for pride and glory on the part of man? There is none; it is excluded. That it is excluded is evident, but how? What law did this? What works brought it about? Neither the law of the Jew nor of the Gentile has shut out this boasting, since through the law and obedience to it there would be reason to boast. The law that has thus effected such a state is the law of faith or "the gospel." Only through the gospel is man's boasting excluded, all glory going to God. 27.

We concluded then that man is justified by faith apart from the works of the law. If this is true then there must be some hope for the Gentiles. Then, rather ironically, Paul poses the question, "Or is God just the God of the Jews and not the God of the Gentiles?" Then he answers his own question by saying, "Yes, he is the God of the Gentiles; what other God would they have? There are not two Gods, one for the Gentiles and one for the Jews." There is one God and all have sinned against him; thus all stand equal before him

73. How is man's pride excluded by the gospel?

in need. Therefore, He will justify both the circumcised and the uncircumcised through faith. 3:28-30

Finally, since the gospel has been pointed out so clearly to be the only way of justification, what has happened to the law? Is it now of no use? No, God forbid. Shall we, simply because the law has been proven valueless in securing justification, believe that it does not serve some other good purpose? "No, not at all," says Paul. "I preach and teach the real value of the law which is to point out right and wrong; thus I establish the law's true purpose." Moses E. Lard has said, "Law may be wholly useless for one purpose and yet indispensable for others." 3:31.

Rethinking in Outline Form

III. Proposition Expounded. 3:21—5:21
  1. Justification by the Gospel Only. 3:21-31
    a. A description of this justification. vs. 21
      (1) It is apart from the law.
      (2) It is of God.
      (3) It is manifested or now present.
      (4) It was spoken of in the law (by types) and in the prophets (by prophecies).
    b. It is obtainable by all who believe, and needed by all, for all have sinned. vs. 22-23
    c. It is made possible by the propitiatory sacrifice of Christ. 24-25a
    d. This sacrifice explains why God was so lenient with the "sins done aforetime." 25b
    e. In the death of Christ we can see the basis for both justice and forgiveness. 26
    f. The following conclusions may be drawn from the fact that justification is found only in the gospel. 27-31
      (1) Boasting is excluded. 27
      (2) This justification is entirely apart from the works of the law. 28
      (3) The Jew and the Gentile are on the same footing, for there is but one God, and faith is the only means of acceptance with him. 29-30 (Sandy, p. 94)
      (4) To the objection that the law is made of no effect, we can say that the very purpose, or "work of the law," is established by the preaching of the gospel. 31

Text

4:1-8. What then shall we say that Abraham, our forefather, hath found according to the flesh? 2 For if Abraham was justified by works, he hath whereof to glory; but not toward God. 3 For what saith the scripture? And Abraham believed God, and it was reckoned unto him for righteousness. 4 Now to him that worketh, the reward is not reckoned as of grace, but as of debt. 5 But to him that worketh not, but believeth on him that justifieth the ungodly, his faith is reckoned for righteousness. 6 Even as David also pronounceth blessing upon the man, unto whom God reckoneth righteousness apart from works, 7 saying,

Blessed are they whose iniquities are forgiven,
And whose sins are covered.

8 Blessed is the man to whom the Lord will not reckon sin.

REALIZING ROMANS, 4:1-8

134. Why does Paul introduce Abraham?

135. "According to the flesh" in vs. 1 means what to you?

136. I thought James said Abraham was justified by works (Jas. 2:21-24). Here Paul says he was not. Reconcile the difference.

137. Both James and Paul refer to the Old Testament statement, "And Abraham believed God, and it was reckoned unto him for righteousness." What did he believe—i.e., about or from God? Give the circumstance of this statement.

138. How could a man be righteous if he did not keep the law of God?

139. What argument in favor of justfication "by faith" is advanced in vs. 4?

140. In what sense are we to understand the phrase "worketh not" in vs. 5a?

141. Why call David in to testify on this subject?

142. Tell the meaning of the world "blessed" as in 7a. How would David be especially acquainted with such blessedness?

Paraphrase

4:1-8. Ye Jews think ritual services meritorious, because they are performed purely from piety. But what do we say Abraham our father obtained by works pertaining to the flesh? That he obtained justification meritoriously? No.

74. If man is justified by faith and not by law, to what conclusion does this lead us?

75. How does the gospel establish the law?

2 For if Abraham were justified meritoriously by works of any kind, he might boast that his justification is of no favor, but a debt due to him: But such a ground of boasting he hath not before God.

3 For what saith the Scripture? Abraham believed God, when he promised that his seed should be as numerous as the stars, and his belief of that promise was counted to him for righteousness.

4 Now it is evident, that to one who, for a stipulated hire, worketh all that he binds himself to work, the reward is never counted as a favor, but is paid as a debt.

5 But to one who does not work all that he is bound to do, but implicitly believeth the promise of him who gratuitously justifies the sinner, his faith is counted to him for righteousness as a favor. (The words, "as a favor", are supplied from ver. 4.)

6 In like manner also, David (Psa. xxxii. 1.) declareth that man blessed, as Abraham was, to whom God counteth righteousness without his having performed works of law perfectly:

7 Not saying, Blessed are they who obey the law of God perfectly: That he knew to be impossible: But saying, Blessed are they whose omissions are forgiven, and whose commissions are covered by an atonement.

8 And, deeply affected with the goodness of God in pardoning sin, he says a second time, Blessed is the man to whom the Lord will not count sin.

Summary

Abraham was not justified by deeds. If so, he had ground to boast that he merited justification. On the contrary, his belief was counted to him for justification. Justification by deeds is like a debt, but justification by belief is matter of favor. David describes justification to be the same as the forgiveness of sins.

Comment

Realizing the fact that this thought of justification through faith apart from meritorius works would be somewhat of a shock, the inspired writer now hastens to point out that the principle of justification by faith is not new, for the great father of the faithful was so justified. That Abraham was justified was admitted by all. Now the apostle poses the question: "How did this justification take place? You say by law; I say by faith. Let us look into the case. What did Abraham obtain through the works of the flesh?" If he had fulfilled to the letter all the demands of God he would have been justi-

76. Was there any question as to whether Abraham was justified or not? If not, why not?

fied by works and would then have had reason to glory. However he did not so perform his obedience. This being true, he has no reason for self glory. Do you remember what the Scripture says about this matter? It says, "And Abraham believed God, and it was reckoned unto him for righteousness." So you can see that the faith Abraham exercised in God provided the ground for his justification, not his imperfect works. It is easy to see then that the justification granted Abraham was given because of the favor, or grace of God, through the belief of father Abraham. 4:1-3.

Just think a moment. When a man works and does all the employer asked him to do, his pay is not given because of the grace of the employer, but rather because of the merit of the employee. You have seen that Abraham was counted righteous only because of God's grace received by faith; so then your idea that he worked, and through his work, earned justification is out because it excludes the element of grace. Here is the thought:—to the man who has not fulfilled all the demands of law, but yet has a great faith in the one who can justify the ungodly, justification is made possible through his belief. It is even as David has said concerning that happy man to whom the Lord granted justification apart from works. Hear him: "Blessed are they whose iniquities are forgiven, and whose sins are covered. Blessed is the man to whom the Lord will not reckon sin." Ro. 4:4-8 cp. Ps. 32:1-2a

Text

4:9-12. Is this blessing then pronounced upon the circumcision, or upon the uncircumcision also? for we say, To Abraham his faith was reckoned for righteousness. 10 How then was it reckoned? when he was in circumcision, or in uncircumcision? Not in circumcision, but in uncircumcision: 11 and he received the sign of circumcision, a seal of the righteousness of the faith which he had while he was in uncircumcision: that he might be the father of all them that believe, though they be in uncircumcision, that righteousness might be reckoned unto them; 12 and the father of circumcision to them who not only are of the circumcision, but who also walk in the steps of that faith of our father Abraham which he had in uncircumcision.

REALIZING ROMANS, 4:9-12

143. Why mention circumcision?
144. Give the meaning of the word "reckoned" as in vs. 9.
145. Paul is going to prove something by showing that Abraham

77. How did the Jew think Abraham was justified?
78. Could Abraham have been justified by works?

was declared righteous before he was circumcised; what is it?

146. Circumcision is here called a sign and a seal—what does this indicate as to its importance—or lack of importance?

147. Abraham became the father of all who believe at the time in which he was circumcised. Explain how.

148. Abraham can be the father of those in unicircumcision. This was a terrible thought to the Jew. Why?

149. What is the meaning of the expression, "Walk in the steps of that faith . . . "?

Paraphrase

4:9-12. Cometh this blessedness, then, of the Lord's not punishing sin, on persons in the visible church [*assembly of Israel*] only? or on persons out of the visible church also? Certainly on them also. For we affirm, that faith was counted to Abraham for righteousness, in uncircumcision.

10 What state then was Abraham in, when it was so counted? When he was in circumcision or in uncircumcision? Not in circumcision, but in uncircumcision. For it happened long before he and his family were made the church of God by circumcision.

11 And instead of being justified by circumcision, he received the mark of circumcision on his body after his justification, as a seal of the righteousness of the faith which he exercised in uncircumcision, in order to his being made the federal head of all them who believe out of the visible church, to assure us that the righteousness of faith shall be counted even to them, by virtue of God's promise to him:

12 Also the federal head of the circumcised, that is, of those who are in the visible church, to assure us that righteousness shall be counted to them who do not rest contented with being of the visible church only, but who also walk in the footsteps of that faith and obedience which our father Abraham exercised in uncircumcision; that is, while he was no member of God's visible church.

Summary

The blessedness of justification by belief, is for Jews and Gentiles alike. Abraham was justified before he was circumcised, his circumcision being a seal of that fact. Hence justification does not depend on circumcision. Abraham is father to all who believe in an uncircumcised state, as well as to all the circumcised who walk in his steps.

Comment

Since the discussion has been concerned with Abraham, David also being mentioned, are we to conclude that only to the circumcised has the blessing or justification through faith been given? Or is it given to the uncircumcised also? This can be answered from the very illustration given, for we must realize *WHEN* Abraham was declared righteous. Was it when he was circumcised or before his circumcision? Ah, you know, it was before circumcision. If you will but consider for a moment you will remember that circumcision was given to Abraham as a seal or a sign of the fact that God had justified him. Then because of Abraham's submission to this rite as a token of God's covenant with him, he became the spiritual head of all in the world who have faith like his. cp. Gen. 17:11. He did become the father of all who, although not circumcised, had a belief like Abraham and through this faith were justified. And likewise he became the father of the Jew who was not only circumcised but also walked by faith, faith like that exercised by Abraham while he was yet in uncircumcision. 4:9-12

Text

4:13-22. For not through the law was the promise to Abraham or to his seed that he should be heir of the world, but through the righteousness of faith. 14 For if they that are of the law are heirs, faith is made void, and the promise is made of none effect: 15 for the law worketh wrath; but where there is no law, neither is there transgression. 16 For this cause it is of faith, that it may be according to grace; to the end that the promise may be sure to all the seed; not to that only which is of the law, but to that also which is of the faith of Abraham, who is the father of us all 17 (as it is written, A father of many nations have I made thee) before him whom he believed, even God, who giveth life to the dead, and calleth the things that are not, as though they were. 18 Who in hope believed against hope, to the end that he might become a father of many nations, according to that which had been spoken, So shall thy seed be. 19 And without being weakened in faith he considered his own body now as good as dead (he being about a hundred years old), and the deadness of Sarah's womb; 20 yet, looking unto the promise of God, he wavered not through unbelief, but waxed strong through faith, giving glory to God, 21 and being fully assured that what he had promised, he was able also to perform. 22 Wherefore also it was reckoned unto him for righteousness.

79. Why is the time of the justification of Abraham important?
80. What relation did circumcision hold to justification?
81. In what way is Abraham our father?

REALIZING ROMANS, 4:13-22

150. Circumcision has been dealt with. We are now introduced to a new refuge of the Jew. What is it?
151. Did God promise Abraham that he would be "heir of the world"? Where? When? What does it mean?
152. How is faith made void by law? Is this bad?
153. What is "the promise" of vs. 14?
154. Does law always work wrath?
155. In what possible situation could there be "no law"? cf. vs. 15.
156. Faith produces grace. In what way?
157. If the promise is predicated on faith, all can enjoy it(?) How?
158. Is Christ "the promise" of vs. 16?
159. Is Abraham our father right now? Does it mean anything to you? It should—it should be a wonderful blessing. Discover how.
160. There are five or six characteristics of Abraham's faith given in vs. 17b-21. See if you can list them.
161. When and where did God give life from the dead?
162. Isn't it wonderful to worship and serve a God who "calleth things that are not as though they were"? Why is it wonderful to you?
163. Abraham held one hope against another. What were they?
164. Why were not the physical circumstances a source of discouragement to Abraham?
165. Abraham, instead of becoming weaker in faith, actually became stronger. How?
166. How shall we reconcile this account of Paul with the account of Moses in the birth of Ishmael from Hagar?
167. Name three promises God has made to you. Do you feel vs. 21 relates to these promises?
168. What is the "it" of vs. 22?
169. Define in one sentence the meaning of faith. "Faith is _____ _____ _____ etc.

Paraphrase

4:13-22. Besides, from the scripture (ver. 3) it is evident, that not on account of a perfect obedience to any law whatever, the promise was made to Abraham, and to his seed, that he should inherit the world, but on account of a righteousness of faith. How then can the Jews expect to obtain the inheritance of heaven, on account of a righteousness of law?

14 For if they who are righteous by works of law are heirs of the world, their faith (ver. 11) is rendered useless, and the promise, by which they became heirs as a matter of favor, is made of no effect:— It does not, in reality, convey that blessing.

15 Farther, instead of conferring a title to the inheritance, the law worketh out punishment, even to the heirs who, by receiving the inheritance as a gree gift, are declared to be transgressors of the law written on their hearts; because where law is not, there no transgression is, nor treatment of persons as transgressors.

16 For this reason, the inheritance is bestowed on account of a righteousness of faith, and not of law, that it might be a free gift, in order that the promise made to Abraham concerning it might be sure to all his seed, not to that only which is his seed by the law of circumcision, but to that also which is his seed by possessing the faith of Abraham, who is the federal head of us all who believe, whether we be Jews or Gentiles; that is, persons not in the visible church of God.

17 (Agreeably to what is written, Gen. xvii. 5. Surely a father of many nations I have constituted thee); which honor of being the father of all believers, Abraham obtained when he stood in the presence of him whom he believed; even of God, who maketh alive the dead, and speaketh of things in the remotest futurity, which exist not, with as much certainty as if they existed.

18 Abraham, contrary to all the ordinary grounds on which men build their hope of offspring, believed with a strong hope, founded on the promise of God, that he should be the father of many nations, according to what was spoken, So shall thy seed be; namely, as the stars of heaven for multitude.

19 And not being weak, either in his conceptions or in his belief of the power and veracity of God, he did not consider his own body now dead, in respect of procreating children, being about a hundred years old, neither the deadness of Sarah's womb, as obstacles to his having a numerous progeny by her, though she was nintey years old.

20 Therefore against the promise of God he did not dispute through unbelief, by alleging that the thing was impossible; but having the firmest persuasion of the veracity of God, he gave the glory of that perfection to God, by waiting patiently for the performance of his promise.

21 And was fully persuaded, that what was promised, God was able even to perform; although the longer he waited, the accomplishment of the promise must have appeared, to an ordinary faith, the more difficult.

22 This strong faith, exercised by Abraham for so long a time, being highly pleasing to God, Therefore also it was counted to him for righteousness.

Summary

God promised to Abraham and his offspring that they should inherit the world. But the promise was in virtue of justification by belief, and not in virtue of law. If the inheritance depended on law, none could attain it. Therefore it is by belief that all may attain it. The power and influence of Abraham's belief is shown.

Comment

It might be well to put before us those historic events so precious to the Jew which are being discussed in these verses.

a. God promised Abraham a son in his old age. Abraham, in spite of his age, believed God, and through this belief God constituted him just. cp. Ge. 15:1-6.

b. God then made the promise to Abraham because of his faith that He would make him the father of many nations if he would continue in his faith and circumcise all the males. This Abraham did and thus received an inheritance of many peoples. cp. Gen. ch. 17.

The subject of justification and circumcision has already been settled. There yet remains the promise of God to Abraham as to his inheriting of the world. This Paul discusses beginning with vs. 13.

The plain statement is that the promise given to Abraham and his seed (Isaac, Jacob, Joseph, etc.) concerning the inheritance of the world was not given because these fathers were perfectly obedient to any law, but rather because of their faith, faith which prompted God to call them righteous. Reason is then given for the thought expressed. If the only persons who will enter into this promise are those who are obedient to law, of what use is the belief spoken of when both Moses and Paul by the Holy Spirit said, "Abraham *believed* God and it was reckoned unto him for righteousness"? What object would there be in extending to man grace and accepting him as righteous through his faith and imperfect obedience if it were possible for him to keep the law of God? Furthermore, the fulfillment of the promise could never have been realized on a basis of perfect obedience to law since all have sinned, and the only possible result is wrath. The law was not given so that man could receive the

82. State the two historic events upon which this event is based.
83. What new thought is introduced at verse 13?
84. Why couldn't the promise have been through law?

promise by fulfilling it. Yet if man had kept the law he would have inherited the world. Since, however, man did not keep the law we can see that the promise would have utterly failed on such a basis. 4:13-15a

If perchance there should be some Jew audacious enough to suggest that he could inherit by law because he had never broken it, Paul places the following principle before him: When there is no law, there is no transgression. In other words, only when no law is present can there be freedom from sin. Since no one has ever lived in this state (either Jew or Gentile) no one can claim freedom from transgression. No one can inherit through the law, for all have law and all have transgressed it; thus all have sinned. 4:15b

This promise to Abraham was given on the basis of faith for the purpose of showing God's favor. If the promise had been on the basis of law, God would have owed man the promise. Then too, the promise would not have been sure, for if it had been of law it would have failed all. But being of faith it is obtainable by all. It could thus be obtained not only by the Jews under the law but also by those Gentiles who exercised the same kind of faith in God as Abraham, who was and is father of us all. cp. 4:11b ". . . as it is written, A father of many nations have I made thee." 4:16-17a

The faith of Abraham is mentioned in verse 16b in connection with the type of faith man must have to please God. Abraham's faith in all its beauty and strength is then described from verses 17b through 22. Abraham is spoken of as standing, not only before the Jews and all men but even before God, in whom he believes, in the position of the father of many nations. Then the power of Abraham's God is illustrated in the circumstances of Jehovah's dealing with Abraham. He gave life to the dead and called the things that are not as though they were. There follow then the details of this general statement of God's power and Abraham's faith. 4:17b

"Who in hope believed against hope" are the apostle's words which further describe the faith of Abraham. In Abraham's case there was absolutely no natural ground for hope. In spite of this fact, Abraham believed in hope. Furthermore, he exercised his hope through belief, against the adverse circumstances. He held this hope for the one purpose that he might indeed be a father of many nations, that the promise of making his seed as innumerable as the stars of the heaven might be fulfilled. The end in view and his faith actuated his hope. Paul then speaks of the discouraging prospects of the fulfillment of the

85. Why would the promise have failed through law?
86. What is the meaning of 15b? What two reasons are given for the promise being "of faith"?
87. What is described in vs. 17b-22?
88. What two thoughts are discussed in connection with each other in vs. 18-21?

promise, namely, the agedness of Abraham and his wife, which made it humanly impossible to carry out the promise. Then notice the great faith of Abraham: a. He considered his own body at the age of one hundred, yet in spite of this he lost no faith in Jehovah. b. Likewise, he realized the deadness of the womb of Sarah. c. He looked to the promise of God and did not waver through unbelief; he rather became strong. d. He gave God the glory. This bespeaks his humility for he, under the circumstances, could easily have gloried in his faith (even as Job). e. His faith is again described as "full assurance" in the ability of God to perform what he promised. (cp. Heb. 11:1) 4:18-21

Let us sum up the matter. Have you seen the faith of Abraham? Have you beheld its beauty and strength? Have you noticed its separation from the law? Paul could then fittingly say: "Well, my Jewish friend, *THAT* faith was reckoned unto our father Abraham for righteousness." vs. 22

Text

4:23-25. Now it was not written for his sake alone, that it was reckoned unto him; 24 but for our sake also, unto whom it shall be reckoned, who believe on him that raised Jesus our Lord from the dead, 25 who was delivered up for our trespasses, and was raised for our justification.

Realizing Romans, 4:23-25

170. The purpose of the Old Testament scriptures is here revealed. What is it?

171. How shall we know that we have a faith like Abraham's?

172. Is our faith to be centered in God, or in Jesus?

173. Jesus was delivered up for our trespasses. In what sense is this true?

174. In what manner does the resurrection provide for our justification?

Paraphrase

4:23-25. Now it was not recorded by Moses for Abraham's honor only, that his faith was thus counted to him in his uncircumcised state; (see ver. 3.)

24 But it was recorded for our benefit also, to whom, as Abraham's children, the like faith will be counted for righteousness, even to those in every age and nation who believe on him (believe whatever he declares and promises) who raised up Jesus our Lord from the dead:

89. What is the meaning of "in hope believed against hope"?
90. Give from memory three of the five points of Abraham's faith.

25 Who, being the seed of Abraham, in which all nations are to be blessed, was delivered to death by God for our offences, and was raised again from the dead, and made universal Lord, for our deliverance from ignorance and wickedness.

Summary

The fact that Abraham's belief was counted to him for justification was written for our sake as well as his. Whom we must believe on, and what in, why Christ was given up to death, and the object for which he rose, are dealt with in this section.

Comment

We must not forget that the promise of righteousness by faith was not only written for the benefit of Abraham alone, but for our sake also. For to us God will impute this same justification if we believe in Him even as Abraham did. He, who raised Jesus our Lord from the dead, is the object of our faith. In the last verse of this chapter we find the rock upon which the whole structure of salvation by faith rests: "Who was delivered up for our trespasses and was raised for our justification." This is why God can declare us righteous through our faith. "He bare in his body" the sins we committed, both when we were in rebellion as a sinner, and now those committed in spite of our conscientious faithfulness as a Christian. Yes, he was raised and thus consummated our justification. The Jew who knew the true purpose of the Messiah could see in these remarks about Jesus the method by which Abraham and Christians are justified. 4:23-25

Rethinking in Outline Form

2. Justification Through the Gospel Illustrated and Applied. 4:1-25

    a. Abraham, the illustration. The principle of justification through faith finds a wonderful application in his life. Note:

    (1) His state of justification was obtained only through his faith, not by works. vs. 1-8

    (2) His justification had no dependence upon circumcision, for he was declared just before his circumcision. This was done in order that he could indeed be the father of the circumcised and the uncircumcised. 9-12

91. How can the faith of Abraham benefit you and me?
92. What is the rock foundation of this doctrine of salvation by faith?
93. What is the meaning of 25a?

(3) The promise made to Abraham of inheriting the world was a promise of faith, not of works.

    (a) This was true in order to include "all the nations" in the promise.

    (b) The inheritance of the world was to come through Abraham's seed. Abraham, knowing this, believed in the power of God in spite of the discouraging circumstances.

    (c) This faith of father Abraham was what God considered in declaring Abraham righteous, and it is a type of the faith that will secure justification for us today.

    (d) It must be in God through Christ and his death.

Text

5:1-11. Being therefore justified by faith, we have peace with God through our Lord Jesus Christ; 2 through whom also we have had our access by faith into this grace wherein we stand; and we rejoice in hope of the glory of God. 3 And not only so, but we also rejoice in our tribulations: knowing that tribulation worketh stedfastness; 4 and stedfastness, approvedness; and approvedness, hope: 5 and hope putteth not to shame; because the love of God hath been shed abroad in our hearts through the Holy Spirit which was given unto us. 6 For while we were yet weak, in due season Christ died for the ungodly. 7 For scarcely for a righteousness man will one die: for peradventure for the good man some one would even dare to die. 8 But God commendeth his own love toward us, in that, while we were yet sinners, Christ died for us. 9 Much more then, being now justified by his blood, shall we be saved from the wrath of God through him. 10 For if, while we were enemies, we were reconciled to God through the death of his Son, much more, being reconciled, shall we be saved by his life; 11 and not only so, but we also rejoice in God through our Lord Jesus Christ, through whom we have now received the reconciliation.

REALIZING ROMANS, 5:1-11

175. The "therefore" of vs. 1 seems to suggest past action—in what way and with whom?

176. Have we "made our peace" with God or has someone else done this for us? Explain.

177. When we accept Jesus as our Saviour, please notice He holds another vital relationship to us, "our *Lord* Jesus Christ."

178. Jesus is the door or "the access" into so many spiritual blessings. Name three of them.

179. We stand "in grace"—oh, what a privilege. What does this mean to you? What is grace?

180. What is "the glory of God" in vs. 2b?

181. Is it right for us to rejoice in the hope of heaven when we are not sure we will go there?

182. Isn't "rejoice" too strong a word in vs. 3?

183. It is not always true that tribulations work steadfastness. Sometimes the very opposite occurs. What else must prevail before tribulations will work steadfastness?

184. What is the approvedness of vs. 3b? Who does the approving?

185. I should think we would hope before tribulations began. How could tribulations—steadfastness—approvedness issue faith in hope?

186. Meaning of the little expression, "hope putteth not to shame"?

187. Please explain to your own satisfaction how the Holy Spirit can shed abroad the love of God in our hearts.

188. When was the Holy Spirit "given unto us"?

189. We were (and are) "weak" in what regard? cf. vs. 6a.

190. The "due season" speaks of God's action as of Gal. 4:4, or our acceptance of Christ. Which?

191. In what sense were we "ungodly"?

192. Is there some difference in the "righteous man" of 7a and the "good man" of 7b? If so, what is it?

193. God has commended His love toward us. Give the meaning of the expression "commended"?

194. What is a "sinner"? For what purpose did Christ die for sinners?

195. To what does the "much more" refer as in vs. 9a?

196. Notice the plain statement that we are "justified by his blood." What import does this place upon the blood—not death only, but "the blood"?

197. We are saved from the guilt of our sin in our own conscience; but not only so, we are also saved from "the wrath of God." Explain.

198. Review this section of scripture (5:1-11) and select the words and phrases descriptive of our relationship to God *before* we were Christians, of those which describe our *present* relationship, and those which describe God's attitude toward us before and after.

199. How could Christ's life save us as in vs. 10b?

200. To what in the previous verses does the phrase "and not only so" refer?

201. We rejoice in God, as well as tribulations. Is this a fair deduction?

202. Has God ever been our enemy? Who produced this relationship?

Paraphrase

5:1-11. Wherefore, being delivered from the power of sin by faith, and having laid aside our enmity to God, we the spiritual seed of Abraham, have peace with God, through our Lord Jesus Christ.

2 Through whom also we have been introduced by faith into this gracious covenant in which we stand, and boast, not in seeing the glory of God in any tabernacle or temple on earth, as the natural seed do, but in the hope of beholding the glory of God in heaven.

3 And this is not our only boasting, for while the Jews boast of the earthly felicity promised in the law, we even boast of afflictions knowing that affliction worketh out patience in us;

4 And patience, approbation from God, and approbation, hope of enjoying eternal life.

5 And this hope will not make us ashamed, as the hope which the natural seed of Abraham entertain of salvation, on account of their descent, will make them ashamed; because a convincing proof of the love of God is poured out into our hearts by the Holy Ghost, who is given to us.

6 Besides, we being still so weak through sin, that we could not deliver ourselves, in the proper season Christ died for the idolatrous Gentiles, as well as for the Jews.

7 Now, Christ's dying for all mankind appears a most astonishing instance of love, when we consider that scarcely for a just man, who only gives to every one his due, will any one die, though, for a beneficent man, some one perhaps would even dare to die.

8 But his own love of men God hath raised above all human love, because, we being still sinners, Christ died for us, to procure us a temporary life on earth, under a better covenant than the first.

9 Much more then, being now allowed to live under the new covenant through the shedding of his blood, we shall be saved from future punishment through him, if we behave well under that covenant.

10 For if, being enemies under sentence of death, we were respited, and made to lay down our enmity to God, through the death of his Son; much more, being thus reconciled, we shall be saved from

73

punishment through his life in the body, which he regained, that he might govern us now, and acquit us at last.

11 And not only do we hope to be saved from wrath by Christ's life, but we believers, the spiritual seed, even boast in God as our God, through our Lord Jesus Christ, by whom we have now received an opportunity of being pardoned.

Summary

Being justified by belief, we have peace with God. Through Christ we have access into our present state of favor, and through him, are filled with hope. God's love is poured out in our hearts by the Holy Spirit given to us. While we were helpless and wicked, Christ died for us. Be a man ever so good no one will die for him; yet Christ died for us when we were sinners. Hereby God showed his love for us. Since Christ died for us when sinners, we may feel sure of being saved now that we are justified by his blood. We are reconciled to God by the death of Christ, by whom we are to be saved.

Comment

The inspired author has given ample proof that: a. Man needs justification; b. Man can be justified only by faith; c. Man to be justified by faith must follow the example given of Abraham. Therefore he feels free to make this positive, unqualified assertion, "Being therefore justified by faith . . ." There is no further doubt as to its truth. Then follow the glorious results that emanate from this position. 5:1a

When we stand justified before God we have peace. Of course, this peace is given through the Prince of Peace, Jesus Christ. Through this superlative Prince we have been given our access by faith into this covenant of grace wherein we stand. Again, when we stand through this grace justified, we are prompted to rejoice. We rejoice when we contemplate the glories of God in the eternal home we are now prepared to enter. Still further, we can say that our rejoicing is not alone found in contemplation of the glory to come but that it even springs from that which causes others to sorrow—"we also rejoice in our tribulations." This is true because of our knowledge of the circumstances. We know that tribulations (borne like a Christian should bear them) will work out in our characters that valuable element known as "steadfastness." While we are thus continuing stead-

94. Why is the positive unqualified statement in 5:1 appropriate?
95. Name three results of justification as mentioned in verse two.
96. Why can the Christian rejoice in tribulations?
97. Show the connection between steadfastness and approvedness.

fastly, there will arise within our hearts the knowledge that we must surely be pleasing God with our conduct. Thus we can know we are approved. Associated with this sense of approvedness, and arising out of it, is "hope." This hope will not be frustrated, for the knowledge that God loves us and thus will keep his promise is manifested in his act of giving to us that great gift, the Holy Spirit. Our hearts are full of the knowledge of God's love because of this fact. 5:1-5

4. A Review of our state before justification. 5:6-11

The positive side of the position "in Christ" has been given and a great appreciation has been aroused through considering its benefits. But it is equally true that gratitude can arise in the heart through a look into "the pit from whence we have been digged." This is the burden of the next five verses. Verse 6 refers back to the love of God mentioned in verse five. This love is expressed here in a most touching manner. While we were ungodly, having been too weak to resist Satan's suggestions, and in the very time when all looked hopeless, Christ provided our pardon by his substitutionary death. The love of God expressed in sending Christ for this purpose is brought more clearly to mind when we realize that it is hard to find a man who would give his life for a righteous man. Once in a while, you might find here and there a man who would give his life for a good man (one who had all the loving attributes of goodness). But one look at the cross and its purpose persuades us that God has there portrayed the greatest expression of his love toward mankind. We are not righteous nor good, but sinners, wilful transgressors of God's law, and yet Christ gave himself for us. There is yet "much more," for this truth proceeds from glory unto glory. We have seen that the justification provided by Christ through faith releases us from the guilt of sin. There yet remains the thought of punishment. This too is removed and through Him we are saved, not only from the guilt of sin, but also from the "wrath of God." 5:6-10

The final word of victory is found in the thought that we not only realize our blessed position in reconciliation, but that our hearts are full or rejoicing in God through our Lord Jesus Christ through whom we have now received the reconciliation. 5:11

98. Show the connection between approvedness and hope.
99. What do you believe is the purpose of vs. 6-11?
100. How is the love of God shown in the death of Christ?
101. To what do the words "much more" refer as found in vs. 9?
102. What is the final word of victory found in this section?

Text

5:12-19. Therefore, as through one man sin entered into the world, and death through sin; and so death passed unto all men, for that all sinned:—13 for until the law sin was in the world; but sin is not imputed when there is no law. 14 Nevertheless death reigned from Adam until Moses, even over them that had not sinned after the likeness of Adam's transgression, who is a figure of him that was to come. 15 But not as the trespass, so also is the free gift. For if by the trespass of the one the many died, much more did the grace of God, and the gift by the grace of the one man, Jesus Christ, abound unto the many. 16 And not as through one that sinned, so is the gift: for the judgment came of one unto condemnation, but the free gift came of many trespasses unto condemnation, but the free gift came of many trespasses unto justification. 17 For if, by the trespass of the one, death reigned through the one; much shall they that receive the abundance of grace and of the gift of righteousness reign in life through the one, even Jesus Christ. 18 So then as through one trespass the judgment came unto all men to condemnation; even so through one act of righteousness the free gift came unto all men to justification of life. 19 For as through the one man's disobedience the many were made sinners, even so through the obedience of the one shall the many be made righteous.

REALIZING ROMANS, 5:12-19

203. How does this section connect with the preceding one?
204. In what way is it true that through Adam sin entered the world? He did not originate it, did he?
205. Did death enter at the same time sin did? What death? i.e., what type of death?
206. The same death which Adam brought by his sin spread to all men. Would you agree with that thought?
207. The reason "death passed to all men" is that when Adam sinned they sinned. Or would you say they are to die for their own sins?
208. Please note the past tense in "sinned" of vs. 12b. What significance does it have?
209. "The law" of vs. 13 is obviously the law of Moses—"sin was in the world"—in what sense? Specify.
210. The most difficult passage for interpretation in the whole book of Romans is the little phrase, "but sin is not imputed when there is no law." What do you believe about it? Remember, you are obligated by God to attempt to know His will. The next phrase is a key to understanding. Read it.

211. What death reigned from Adam to Moses?
212. In what way has no one sinned like Adam?
213. In several comparisons we can say we do sin like Adam. Mention two or three.
214. Adam is like Christ. Specify two ways in which this is true.
215. What are "the trespass" and "the free gifts" of vs. 15? Surely you know what "the trespass" is.
216. "The gift" superceded "the trespass" in overcoming the results of the trespass. How so?
217. The gift brought "much more." In what way?
218. In vs. 16 is yet another comparison. This one has to do with judgment. What is it?
219. What is the "condemnation" and "justification" of vs. 16? Be careful. You could be wrong.
220. Once again: what death reigned because of Adam's sin? **Notice** please, the persons of vs. 17 are those who have accepted Christ. Are some going to be lost, "condemned," who never came to the age of accountability?
221. Notice please in your attempt to understand vs. 17 that Christ's gift does *more* than merely overcome Adam's transgression and its effects. How is this true?
222. Does vs. 18 teach that Adam caused all men to be lost, and Christ saved all men? In what sense? Remember, what you ascribe to Adam you must also ascribe to Christ.
223. "The many were made sinners" (vs. 19a). How did we define the word "sinner"? By Adam's sin *all* were made sinners. How can this be understood?
224. The same connotation you place upon "sinners" must apply to the anthithesis "righteousness." What will it be?

Paraphrase

5:12-19. All mankind are brought into a state of salvation through Christ, for this reason, As by one man Adam, sin entered into the world, and by his sin death, and so death passed through the world to all men, because all have sinned; even so, by one man Christ, righteousness entered into the world, and by his righteousness life, and so life passed through the world to all men, because all have obeyed.

13 Death hath come on all men for Adam's sin; for, from the fall until the law, sin was counted to every person in the world; it was punished with death: but sin is not counted, when there is no law transgressed.

14 Nevertheless, death, the punishment of sin, reigned from Adam

to Moses, even over infants and idiots, who, being incapable of law, had not sinned actually like Adam; who, because he brought death on all, may be called, by way of contrast, the representation of him who was to come and restore life to all.

15 However, the resemblance is not exact; for, not as the fall by Adam, so also is the gracious gift by Christ. They differ in their power, the one to kill, and the other to make alive: for if by the fall of the one man Adam, all mankind died, much more the goodness of God and the gift of life by that goodness, which is bestowed on account of the one man Jesus Christ, hath abounded to all mankind, by giving them life under the new covenant, and by raising them from the dead at the last day.

16 Secondly, Not like the sentence passed through the one who sinned, is the free gift of pardon which is bestowed through the one who obeyed. They differ in their causes and consequences: for verily the sentence was for one offence only, and issued in condemnation to death; but the gracious gift of pardon is of all offences, issuing in righteousness counted to the pardoned person, whereby he is entitled to the reward of eternal life.

17 Thirdly, If, consistently with justice, (as was shown ver. 12), by the fall of one man Adam, death hath reigned over all mankind, through that one man; much more is it consistent with justice and goodness, that they who receive the overflowing of grace, in the glorious resurrection of the body, (ver. 15), and of the gift of righteousness, (ver. 16) shall reign in the happy life which they are to regain through the one man Jesus Christ.

18 Well then, as it pleased God, through one offence committed by Adam, to pass sentence upon all men, condemning them to death temporal; even so, it pleased God, through one act of righteousness performed by Christ, to pass sentence on all men, justifying, that is, delivering them from immediate death, and allowing them to live a while on earth, and declaring that, after death, they shall all be raised from the dead.

19 And as through the disobedience of one man, all were made liable to sin and punishment, notwithstanding many of them never heard of Adam, or of his disobedience; even so, through the obedience of one man, all have been, are, and shall be made capable of righteousness and eternal life, notwithstanding many of them never heard of the person through whom these blessings are bestowed.

Summary

By one man sin entered into the world, and death by that sin. Sin was in the world before the law, but not counted. From Adam to

Moses men died, though guilty of no sin like Adam's. Adam was a type of Christ, but not in all respects. The sin not like the gift. By the sin of one all died. The favor of God and the gift of Christ abound to all. Nor was the sentence like the gift. The sentence was because of one sin; the gift consists in being justified from many sins. Through one sin death reigns over all; yet all who are justified will reign in life through Christ. As by one sin all have been condemned, so by Christ's death all are to be so far justified as to live. By the sin of Adam all are constituted sinners; by the death of Christ all are constituted just.

Comment

5. Adam and Christ contrasted. 5:12-21

Since the subject of sin had been introduced along with its results, Paul now thought it only logical to offer the explanation of the existence of sin, and at the same time show how Christ completely answered every need man incurred through sin. The facts presented concerning Adam and his part in the circumstances must have been common knowledge to the Jew. The Jew must have known from ages past that "through one man sin entered into the world." John tells us that "sin is lawlessness" (A. R. V.), or the "transgression of law is sin" (K. J. V. I Jn. 3:4). God gave a law to Adam. He said, "Of the tree of the knowledge of good and evil thou shalt not eat of it." (Gen. 2:17a). Adam, through the influence of his wife, transgressed this law and thus sin entered the world. Where there is no penalty there is no power in the law; hence we find Jehovah not only giving a law, but also pronouncing punishment for disobedience—"for in the day thou eatest thereof thou shalt surely die." (Ge. 2:17b). Hence we see the twofold result of Adam's act—sin and death.

Now we come to those few words that have occasioned so much discussion and controversy. Here they are; read them carefully and think upon them as we make a few observations. ". . . and so death passed unto all men for that all sinned . . ." The literal translation of Moses E. Lard is good: ". . . and thus it (death) spread to all men, because all sinned." What is the death spoken of? It must surely be the same type of death associated with Adam, for it is so used in this verse. The same death that Adam suffered is the death that spread to all men. What type of death then did Adam suffer? The only death spoken of in the life and experience of Adam was the

103. Show the reasonableness of introducing the thought of the section 5:12-21.
104. Explain in your own words how "through one man sin entered the world."
105. What is the twofold result of Adam's act?
106. What is the thought of Lard's literal rendering of verse two?

cessation of physical life described in Gen. 5:5 where it says, ". . . and he died." While it is probably true that Adam also died spiritually, the subject of physical or natural death is the main one under discussion in this passage. We hope to clear this up by further study. Until then please keep it in mind. 5:12a

How can it be explained that Adam did not die *"in the day"* that he first sinned? The first answer is that he did begin to die then for he was cut off from the tree of life. Corruption and enfeeblement of his body immediately resulted which ultimately brought death. The second is that he was granted an extension of life because of the promise of God (Gen. 3:15) concerning the death, burial and resurrection of Jesus, which as we shall see counteracted the physical death resulting from Adam's sin.

Adam suffered physical death for this one sin of his and this death "spread to all men, because all sinned." When and how did all men sin so as to bring death into every life? Is death the result of the wilful sin in the life of each individual? Surely not, for how then can we account for the death of babies who have no reasoning power and are not yet responsible? The only explanation seems to lie in the fact that when Adam sinned all men sinned also. McGarvey says: ". . . one act of sin brought sentence of condemnation unto death upon all because all were in sinful Adam as their forefather, thus sharing his act." Moses E. Lard said, God decreed beforehand that if Adam sinned, both he and all his posterity should die." Thus we see according to the justice of God how the sentence of death passed to all men. Though God has not clearly revealed just why Adam's descendants had to die for his one sin, the following statements may throw a little light on the answer. The answer seems to be based on this one fact, that at the time of Adam's sin he had no children. Had the full death penalty been inflicted upon Adam and Eve in the day of their sin, their descendants would have effectively received the penalty also seeing that they (the descendants) would thus have been denied the chance to live at all. Thus, because God's justice would have extended to both Adam and his posterity, also must God's mercy in lengthening Adam's life extend to his offspring in giving them a limited physical life. There also was given to man the opportunity to counteract his personal sin and to receive eternal life after death by availing himself of God's pardon and all the benefits of the promise (Gen. 3:15) fulfilled. 5:12b*

107. Give your reasons for believing the death spoken of in the case of Adam was physical.
108. How can we say that Adam died "in the day" that he ate?
109. Why do you believe Adam's descendants had to die for his sin?

After Adam's sin until the law of Moses, sin as a transgression of God's will was in the world. There were laws of sacrifice (consider Cain and Abel) and there was a law against murder (Gen. 9:6) and also other laws of right and wrong. (Gen. 26:5). If there had been no law the people of this period could not be held responsible before God for their deeds. That the people of this period sinned personally as well as in Adam is evident. 5:13

"Nevertheless" (in spite of their personal sins) they all died. Their personal sins had nothing to do with the fact that physical death at some time overtook each of them. They died even though they had not sinned as Adam did. The natural consequence of Adam's sin both to him and his posterity was physical death. Though for some sins men might be put to death at the hands of society, such a death is not a natural result of their sin as is death from Adam's sin. Since, then, there was no law (and still is none), the breaking of which would bring physical death, we can see that it would be impossible to sin just as Adam did. Their sin which did bring death to them was unlike Adam's in that they sinned in him and were not personally responsible, while Adam was personally responsible. 5:14a

The last part of verse 14 points out that Adam is a type, "a figure of him that was to come," Christ (cp. V. 15b). The comparison and contrast of Adam and Christ is not so much a personal likeness or unlikeness, but rather a viewing of their respective acts and the consequences of their acts. The similarity between them is seen only as far as the scope or range of their work is equal. Where the scope of Christ's work exceeds that of Adam, there is no longer a likeness but a contrast. Also a contrast is seen in the nature of the respective accomplishments of Adam and Christ. 5:14b

*It is interesting to notice that there are three exceptions to the statement, "death passed to all men": Enoch (Gen. 5:24), Elijah (II Ki. 2:1, 11-12) and the living Christians at the time of Christ's coming (I Co. 15:51-52; I Thess. 4:16-17).

In verse 15a the work of Adam (his first sin) is referred to as "the trespass," and the work of Christ (the benefits of his death, burial and resurrection) as "the free gift." The contrast is seen in that "the trespass" and "the free gift" are opposite in nature and also in that the latter superseded the former. Paul continues on (vs. 15b) to say that if because of Adam's one sin physical death came to all, then the

110. Explain verse 13.
111. What is the meaning of the term "nevertheless" in vs. 14?
112. What two exceptions are there to the statement, "death passed to all men"?
113. What is compared and contrasted in Adam and Christ?
114. What is the meaning of the term "free gift"?

sacrificial act of Christ not only counteracts physical death but "much more." Adam's sin brought physical death to all without any hope of a resurrection and still less hope of immorality. Christ by His "obedience unto death" redeems all men from physical death by accomplishing for them the resurrection of the dead. Thus far the range of their accomplishments are the same; the work of Christ has only cancelled the work of Adam.

Now we come to explain the "much more" of verse 15b. Christ's accomplishments did not stop at merely cancelling the effect of Adam's sin but far superseded it by making available to all a means whereby forgiveness of personal sins and eternal life could be obtained. Christ's act unconditionally accomplished for all the resurrection from the dead which will release them from the penalty of their sin in Adam. This, however, is not sufficient, for all have committed other sins than the one they committed in Adam, and for these there are other punishments beside physical death. Though Adam and his descendants will all be freed from physical death there is spiritual death with which all must reckon. Here we see the "much more" in that the work of Christ surpasses in scope that of Adam by bringing release from spiritual death also. Adam and his offspring receive *physical* death as a result of *his one* sin. They also receive *spiritual* death as a result of *their personal* sins. "The free gift" counteracts the former unconditionally and the latter conditionally, through faith and obedience. Adam's act condemned many to physical death. Christ's act rescues all from physical death. Christ's act does more; it also saves from spiritual death those who have faith in Jesus Christ. 5:15b

Further contrast is seen in verse 16. Through Adam's first sin he only was condemned to spiritual death. But through "the free gift" the "many" personal sins of all who believe and obey Christ are forgiven. Those who are thus forgiven are justified from their "many trespasses" and at the same time saved from spiritual death. Christ's death atoned not just for our sin in Adam, which brought physical death, but also for our many personal sins, which brought spiritual death. 5:16

In verse 17 the apostle gives us two graphic word pictures. In the first, he describes death as a tyrant king reigning over the world because of Adam's sin. In the same picture, he also describes those who "receive the abundance of grace and the gift of righteousness" as kings who "reign in life" because of Jesus Christ. The second pic-

115. What is the meaning of the words "much more" in vs. 15b?
116. Explain vs. 16.
117. What is the word picture in vs. 17?

ture shows how far the effect of the "abundance of grace" and "the gift of righteousness" surpasses in scope that of "the trespass." Here again we see the words "much more." The thought undoubtedly is that in Christ we are not only saved from physical death but also from spiritual death. God's grace unconditionally cancels the effect of Adam's sin (physical death) in the lives of all. But the "abundance" of God's grace cancels the effect of personal sins (spiritual death) in the lives of those who will receive it through faith and obedience.

5:17

In summary of the previous words, we have verse 18. The inspired writer simply says: "through one trespass (Adam's sin) the judgment (or we could say "the sentence") came unto all men to condemnation (that is, all men had to suffer the penalty of the sentence which was physical death); contrariwise, even so through the one act of righteousness (the death of Christ) the free gift came unto all men (the provision of forgiveness in His blood) to justification of life (the full result of the free gift)."

In verse 19 we find the reasons given for the statement made in verse 18. In verse 18 we have the plain statement made that sentence was passed upon all men and all men died, but that all could live through Christ. No reasons were given for these conclusions but now we are informed of the circumstances. All die because through the disobedience of Adam they were "made" (or constituted) sinners." Likewise the many are to be given life because through the obedience of the one the many were "made" (or constituted) "righeous." In what sense were they sinners and in what sense were they righteous? Surely it would be without reason to say that any man had a part in the personal guilt of Adam's sin except Adam. The very thought of the word "constitute" or "made" has to do with an act not of man himself but of an objective accomplishment. If man was to be held accountable in a personal way for Adam's sin the text would read, "through the one man's disobedience the many *were sinners*", thus placing the guilt upon them and suggesting personal participation and responsibility. Again the same reasoning used to show personal guilt or responsibility in Adam's sin would provide universal salvation with no personal effort on the part of man. If through the one act of disobedience all men had a personal participation in that act without any act of volition upon their part at all, then through "the second Adam's" act of obedience all men could and would be saved or constituted righteous with no act of choice upon their part. This is a parallel and such would have to be the conclusion. The only pos-

118. What is the thought of "condemnation unto all men in vs. 18?
119. What is the import of the thought "made sinners" in vs. 19?

sible sense in which all men could be constituted sinners through Adam's disobedience would be that they sinned "in Adam" and in this sense were constituted sinners, and hence suffer physical death. 5:18-19

Text

5:20-21. And the law came in besides, that the trespass might abound; but where sin abounded, grace did abound more exceedingly: 21 that, as sin reigned in death, even so might grace reign through righteousness unto eternal life through Jesus Christ our Lord.

REALIZING ROMANS, 5:20-21

225. The law made sin abound. In what sense? Isn't it wrong to associate sin with God's law?
226. Grace overcame sin by what process? In what sense is grace superabounding?
227. Sin reigned through its king. Grace reigned through its king. Name the kings. Explain.
228. What "law" is meant by 20a? Try to be as sure as possible in your answer. This will require thinking through the section. Do it!

Paraphrase

5:20-21. But when Adam was allowed to live, law secretly entered into the world as the rule of man's conduct, even the law written on his heart, so that the offence hath abounded. However, where sin hath abounded, through the entrance of law, the goodness of God in the new covenant hath superabounded, through the gift of pardon granted to all penitent believers:

21 That as sin, both original and actual, hath tyrannized over mankind by introducing and continuing death in the world, with its train of sorrows and miseries; so also the goodness of God might reign, that is effectually exercises its power, through righteousness, (ver. 16.), even the righteousness of faith, followed with eternal life, through Jesus Christ our Lord.

Summary

The law entered that sin might increase. But the law did not increase sin by creating it. It increased it merely by discovering to men certain acts as sins, which before they had not known to be sins. But the more sin thus increased, the more favor to those committing it abounded. Sin, like a monster, reigned formerly and still reigns unnaturally in death. Favor, on the contrary, now reigns chiefly through or by means of justification. Hereafter it will reign in and through eternal life.

Comment

This whole section has discussed but one thought: the analogy of Christ and Adam. The Jew had ever before his mind "the law", so Paul answers the question of the Jewish mind and shows the relation of the law to this circumstance. Sin entered the world and the results of sin immediately followed. Now, in addition to sin and its results, the law came. For what purpose was it given? Well, we have been discussing sin, so what relation does the law have to sin? It came that "the trespass might abound." It came, not to cause men to sin, but to emphasize the sinfulness of transgression and to lay before the mind and conscience of man many more prohibitions or laws, the violation of which would be sin. In stepping across God's law, man did sin, and after the giving of the law sin surely did abound *in the number of violations*. Thus did the law cause the trespass to abound. "But where sin did abound grace did abound more exceedingly." Thus does the apostle point out the answer of God through Christ to man's sin. (In this case it was most especially pointed out to those under the law.) 5:20

Once more the view of the two kings is brought to our attention. This time it is the personification of "sin" and "grace." Sin could occupy the throne of the world and hold sway over each individual upon the earth, for into his hand had been given the power of death. This sentence had been pronounced upon every man; thus were all his slaves. But there is another king, "King Grace." In his scepter he holds the power of "righteousness", which means that God has provided to free man from the guilt of Adam's sin and to deliver him from physical death; yes, much more, to free man from his personal sins and deliver him from spiritual death into eternal life. This king (King Grace) reigns only because of Jesus Christ our Lord; yes, he reigns "through" him. 5:21

Rethinking in Outline Form

3. Results of Justification. 5:1-5
    a. Peace with God through our Lord Jesus Christ. vs. 1b
    b. Access into the covenant of grace. 2a
    c. Rejoicing in the hope of the glory of God. 2b
    d. Rejoicing in tribulations, since they will result in steadfastness, approvedness and hope. 3-4. This hope will be fulfilled because:
    e. God loves us. This love of God for us is shown by the gift of the Holy Spirit. 5

120. What is the alternative to the interpretation that we give?
121. Explain verse 20.
122. Name the two kings of vs. 21 and describe briefly the reign of each.

4. A Review of our state before justification. 5:6-11
   a. *We were weak and ungodly*, yet Christ died for us. vs. 6
   b. While yet *sinners* Christ expressed the love of God in dying for those for whom no man would think of risking his life. 7-8
   c. *We were under the guilt and punishment of sin.* Through the death of Christ are released both from the guilt and punishment. 9-10
   d. *We were desperately in need of reconciliation.* Now that we have received it, our hearts are full of rejoicing. vs. 11

5. Adam and Christ Compared and Contrasted. 5:12-21
   a. A description of Adam and his work. 12-14
      (1) Sin entered the world through Adam. 12a
      (2) Death came as a result of his sin. 12b
      (3) Death spread to all men, for all were in Adam when he sinned.
      (4) Sin was in the world before the law, but no penalty of death was attached to sin. vs. 13
      (5) Even so, death did reign from Adam to Moses, not because of the sinfulness of individual persons, but because of Adam's sin. vs. 14

   b. The Comparison and Contrast. 5:15-19

ADAM	CHRIST
Brought the trespass. vs. 15a	Brought the free gift.
Through the trespass the many died 15b	Through the free gift "much more" given—life physical and eternal.
One sinned and brought the judgment of condemnation upon himself. 16	Through the free gift of Christ justification was provided for the many who trespassed.
Death reigned through the trespass. vs. 17	"Much more" was g i v e n through Christ's abundant grace.
Through one came the judgment to condemnation — i.e., physical death, for all men. vs. 18	Through the free gift came justification to physical life for all men.
Through one act of disobedience the many were made sinners; i.e., they had to pay the physical death penalty f o r Adam's sin. vs. 19	Through the obedience of the one the many were made righteous, i.e., were freed from the penalty of death and given an opportunity for justification.

c. The purpose of the law in its relation to the above comparison and contrast. vs. 20-21

Text

6:1-11. What shall we say then? Shall we continue in sin, that grace may abound? 2 God forbid. We who died to sin, how shall we any longer live therein? 3 Or are ye ignorant that all we who were baptized into Christ Jesus were baptized into his death? 4 We were buried therefore with him through baptism into death: that like as Christ was raised from the dead through the glory of the Father, so we also might walk in newness of life. 5 For if we have become united with him in the likeness of his death, we shall be also in the likeness of his resurrection; 6 knowing this, that our old man was crucified with him, that the body of sin might be done away, that so we should no longer be in bondage to sin; 7 for he that hath died is justified from sin. 8 But if we died with Christ, we believe that we shall also live with him; 9 knowing that Christ being raised from the dead dieth no more; death no more hath dominon over him. 10 For the death that he died, he died unto sin once: but the life that he liveth, he liveth unto God. 11 Even so reckon ye also yourselves to be dead unto sin, but alive unto God in Christ Jesus.

REALIZING ROMANS, 6:1-11

229. How would grace abound by our continuing in sin?
230. Who believes that sin makes grace abound?
231. Is this belief a temptation today? Why?
232. When did we die to sin? Did we die when Christ died? cf. Gal. 2:20. Did we also die later?
233. What is the point of the argument of vs. 2?
234. In what sense could we say the saints in Rome were ignorant?
235. In what sense were we baptized into Christ?
236. How does being baptized into the death of Christ hinder sinning?
237. Into what were we buried? Is there any objection to saying this represents Holy Spirit baptism?
238. In what way (specify) is the Christian life new?
239. We were united with Christ. Where and when?
240. What resurrection is discussed in vs. 5?
241. What is "the old man" of vs. 6? Where was he crucified with Christ?
242. What is "the body of sin"?
243. We are in bondage to sin when we continue in it, but we cannot continue in sin, for we are dead. Is that the argument of vs. 7?

244. What circumstance of living with Christ is discussed in vs. 8—here or hereafter?

245. The type of death and resurrection Christ experienced is an example for us. How so?

246. We are dead and alive at the same time. Explain.

Paraphrase

6:1-11. We who have declared the malignity of sin in killing men, what do we say when we teach the superabounding of grace? Do we say, Let us continue in sin, that grace may abound in our pardon?

2 No. We who have died by sin corporally and spiritually, can we hope to live eternally by continuing in it? The thing is impossible, unless the nature of God and of sin were changed.

3 Our baptism teaches us, that we have died by sin. For are ye ignorant, that so many of us as have by baptism become Christ's disciples, have been baptized into the likeness of his death, (ver. 5.) have been buried under the water, as persons who, like Christ, have been killed by sin? ver. 10.

4 Besides, we have been buried together with Christ by baptism, into the likeness of his death, (ver. 5.), to teach us this other lesson, that though we have been killed by sin, (ver. 6), yet like as Christ was raised up from the dead by the power of the Father, to live forever, (ver. 9), even so we also, by the same power, shall enjoy a new and never-ending life in heaven with him.

5 For seeing Christ and we have been planted together in baptism, in the likeness of his death as occasioned by sin, certainly, by being raised out of the water of baptism, we are taught that we shall be also planted together in the likeness of his resurrection.

6 Ye know this also to be signified by baptism, that our old corrupt nature was crucified together with him, that the body, with its affections and lusts, (Gal. v. 24), which sin has seized, might be rendered inactive, in order that we may not any longer as slaves serve sin in the present life.

7 Sin has no title to rule you; for, as the slave who is dead is freed from his master, he who hath been put to death by sin is freed from sin.

8 Since then we have died with Christ by sin, we believe, what our baptism likewise teaches us, that we shall also rise and live together with him in heaven, to die no more.

9 For we know that Christ being raised from the dead, dieth no more: death no more lordeth it over him; but he will live eternally in the body, as we shall do also after our resurrection.

10 I say, dieth no more. For Christ who died, died by the malignity of sin once, that being sufficient to procure our pardon; but Christ who liveth after having died, liveth in the body for ever by the power of God:

11 So then, from Christ's death and resurrection, conclude ye yourselves to have been dead verily by sin, but now made alive by God, who at present delivers you from the spiritual death by regeneration, and will deliver you from the bodily death by a blessed resurrection, through Jesus Christ our Lord.

Summary

We are not to continue in sin that favor may abound. On the contrary, as we died to sin before our immersion, it would be inconsistent to still live in it now. By being immersed into Christ we were immersed into his death, and so were buried with him; and as he rose to live a new life, so we also, being risen like him, are to live in newness of life. We became united with Christ by being buried with him; and we are to remain united with him by doing as he does, not living our former, but a new life. We were crucified with Christ in order to render inactive our sinful bodies, and this is to the end that we might not serve sin. As we died with Christ and rose with him, so we must now live like him—we must live a new life free from sin. Christ being raised from the dead, is to die no more; and so with us. We have died to sin once, and this must be the end of our dying. In order to this we must sin no more. In dying, Christ died to sin once for all, but now lives to God; so our death to sin must be a finality; we must now constantly live to God, and consequently commit no more sin.

Comment

1. Objection as to the Abundance of Grace. 6:1-14

The Objection stated. From what Paul had said about sin and grace ("where sin did abound grace did abound more exceedingly") it would seem to some that they would be encouraged to go on sinning. If more sin means more grace, why not "continue in sin that grace may abound"? 6:1

The apostle is horrified at such a suggestion. He cries out, "God forbid." Then follow the reasons for the denial. 6:2a

The whole answer to this objection is associated either directly or indirectly with the true meaning of baptism. Note:

a. We cannot continue in sin any more than a corpse could con-

123. State the first objection to the proposition.
124. Give the first answer as found in 2b.

tinue in its former life. Just as the dead man has died to his former life, so we have died to sin. Just as he cannot live any longer in his former life because of his death, we cannot live any longer in sin because of our death. This condition was brought about by our belief and repentance preceding our baptism. 6:2b

b. Then follow comments upon that act that brought about our separation from sin. Since the thought of death to sin in repentance and the separation from sin in baptism were always so closely associated (cp. Acts 2:38; 3:19) the author places this comment in a self explanatory question. Being baptized, we were baptized "into Christ" and at the same time baptized "into his death." This gives abundant reason for not continuing in sin. Not only have we died to sin through our repentance, but in our baptism we have become identified with Christ in his death. The thought of the impossibility of a dead man still manifesting life is developed from a twofold position: (1) our death to sin; (2) our union through baptism with Christ's death. 6:3

c. We find next a description of that act in which we came into the death of Christ. How did we find union with Christ? How did we become associated in his death? The answer is by being buried with him through baptism into his death. But that is not all, for even as Christ did not remain in the tomb, but was raised by "the glory of the Father" to that new life, even so, we who have met his death in baptism and have thus been buried with him must also be raised to walk in a new life. Here we see a further reason for not continuing in sin. How could we think of continuing in sin following our burial and resurrection any more than Christ could have continued in his former life following his burial and resurrection? The fifth verse expresses this very thought: "For if we have become united with him in the likeness of his death, (this has been thoroughly described) we shall be also in the likeness of his resurrection." (In other words, we are to follow Christ in this point also; even as Christ's life was not the same after his resurrection, so ours is to be "like" his. Following our resurrection from the waters of baptism we are to live and walk in a resurrected life.) 6:4-5

d. Verse six carries a word picture of what has already been said. "Our old man" so often spoken of as "the animal nature," or as Paul calls it, "the flesh," has been nailed to the cross. When we were being immersed we were thereby signifying that we had died to sin and were now being buried. In the act of baptism we came into his crucifixion. This was carried out for the purpose of nullifying "the body

125. Give the second answer as found in vs. 3. (This answer is twofold.)
126. Give the third answer as in vs. 4-5.
127. State in your own words the fourth answer as in 6-7.

of sin" or "the flesh" so we could be given freedom from the bond-age in which we were held by the animal nature. The method of attaining the crucifixion of self and thus being released from the bondage of the flesh is by way of faith and repentance before baptism, and repentance and prayer following baptism. This all, of course, presents a further reason for not continuing in sin, for if the whole purpose of our salvation was to free us from the bondage of sin, through self, we would be defeating the very economy of God to continue in sin. The final word of proof on this point is offered in the seventh verse which speaks of a legal fact. There can be no legal claims made on a man who is dead; his death has released him from any such claims. Just so with the Christian and sin, since he is dead, sin can lay no claim to him; through his death he is free from its power. 6:6-7

e. "But if we died with Christ, we believe that we shall also live with him" (v. 8). It must be kept in mind that the apostle is still answering the objection. He has beautifully portrayed our death with Christ, and in this portrayal we saw many reasons why we could not continue in sin. Now he adds one further thought, and that is that if we were "in Christ" when he died, surely we would be in him when he arose; hence we must *live like him*, like he now is in his resurrected state. Being "in Christ" means something; it means living as a transformed "new creature in Christ Jesus." 6:8

f. A parallel is formed in the next three verses which serves to illuminate, illustrate and enlarge what has just been said. We have been told that when Christ died and arose again we were "in him" and thus were to participate in the benefits of his death (by our re-pentance and baptism) and to walk in the glories of the resurrected life. Notice now the description given of his death and resurrection. See the completeness of his death; behold the glories of his victory over the grave. Well, Christians of Rome, your death to sin is to be like his death. He died unto sin "once"; even so, you are not to fall back into sin and then have to die all over again. And your new life is to be like his: "the life that he liveth he liveth unto God." vs. 11

Rethinking in Outline Form
Objections to the Proposition 6:1—7:25

1. Objection as to the Abundance of Grace. 6:1-14

   Objection Stated: If more sin means more grace, why not continue in sin that grace may abound? vs. 1

   Objection answered, or reasons for not continuing in sin. vs. 2a-11

128. What is the fifth reason for not continuing in sin as found in vs. 8?

a. We cannot continue in sin because we have died to sin. We are as dead to sin as a corpse is to its former life. 2b

b. We cannot continue in sin, for we are in union with Christ and his death.
Being "in" the sinless one, we cannot continue in sin. Being in his death, we can no more live in sin than he could while he was dead. 3

c. We have been raised into a resurrected life, a new life. If we have been raised, how can we think of walking in our former lusts? vs. 4-5

d. The very purpose of our crucifying the old man was that the body of sin (or the flesh) might be done away. Now, if that was the purpose of our death, burial and resurrection, would we not be nullifying the purpose of our redemption if we continued to live after the desires of the flesh? vs. 6

e. It is a legal fact that there can be no claim brought against a man after his death. We are dead to sin. Would it not be a ridiculous spectacle to allow sin to lay claim to our hearts and lives? vs. 7

f. If we were in Christ when he died, surely we would be in him when he arose; hence we must live "with him" now or "like him"—like he now is in his resurrected state. vs. 8

g. Note the death of Christ to sin: he died "once"; he lives unto God. Imitate him . . . die once to sin, be alive and live unto God in Christ Jesus. vs. 9-11

Let us describe what happens when we continue in sin. Our members become instruments in the hands of Satan. A call comes to present ourselves to God as alive from the dead and use our members as his instruments for righteousness. vs. 12-13

We can know that we are under grace and can be forgiven any time we might stumble, so there is really no reason why sin should have dominion over us. vs. 14

Text

6:12-14. Let not sin therefore reign in your mortal body, that ye should obey the lusts thereof: 13 neither present your members unto sin as instruments of unrighteousness; but present yourselves unto God, as alive from the dead, and your members as instruments of righteousness unto God. 14 For sin shall not have dominion over you: for ye are not under law, but under grace.

REALIZING ROMANS, 6:12-14

247. Sin or Satan can reign like a despot in our clay tabernacle. Why? How?

248. When serving under a king, we give complete service. All we have belongs to him. Who is our king? What is our service?

249. Being "under grace" gives us assurance of victory over sin. Does it? How is it we so often find it very much otherwise?

Paraphrase

6:12-14. Wherefore, since God hath made you spiritually alive, and is to raise you with immortal bodies, let not sin reign in your present mortal body, so as to obey him [*Satan*] by fulfilling the lusts of the body.

13 Neither present ye to sin your bodily members, to be used as instruments of unrighteousness, but present the faculties of your mind to God, as persons whom he hath made alive from the death of sin: your bodily members present to God as instruments of righteous actions, which is the work he requires from his servants.

14 Besides sin shall not lord it over you, for this reason, that ye are not under a dispensation of law, which gives no assistance against sin; but under grace, which affords all the aids necessary for subduing sin.

Summary

We are not to allow sin to reign in our bodies by obeying bodily desires. Nor must we use our members in the service of sin; but, as persons alive from the dead, we must be devoted to God, and use our members as instruments in exclusively working righteousness. Sin is not to lord it over us in the end, by having us condemned, for we are now under favor, and will be forgiven, and not under law which knows no forgiveness.

Comment

Yes, brethren, "even so reckon ye also yourselves to be dead unto sin (in repentance and baptism) but alive unto God (through the new life begotten within you) in Christ Jesus." 6:12

g. In the last two verses of this section we find the conclusion to the whole matter of continuing in sin. Reasons have been given for not living in sin, so the inspired writer feels free to say, "Let not sin therefore reign in your mortal body that ye should obey the lusts thereof." Sin in this verse is personified as a tyrant reigning in and through the body of man. This tyrant has certain lusts or desires, and we will surely fulfill them. Next we see the weapons that King Sin

129. Give the sixth reason as found in vs. 9-12.

reigning in our bodies uses to further his kingdom of darkness. His weapons are none other than the members of our own bodies: our hands, our feet, our tongues, etc. But away with this thought! We have died out to sin; we have dethroned sin and have placed Jesus on the throne of our hearts; we are alive unto God and therefore we will present the members of our bodies as his weapons to be used in the battle against sin and for righteousness. The last triumphant thought is that sin will not *finally* be the victor. Even though we do yield to Satan from time to time, we can be forgiven, for we are not governed by law (which would demand absolute obedience) but by grace which offers forgiveness to those who fall through temptation. Thus we know that if we are faithful to Christ, on that last day when the books are balanced, we will be the victors over sin because of the grace bestowed upon us in Christ. 6:13-14

Text

6:15-23. What then? shall we sin, because we are not under law, but under grace? God forbid. 16 Know ye not, that to whom ye present yourselves as servants unto obedience, his servants ye are whom ye obey; whether of sin unto death, or of obedience unto righteousness? 17 But thanks be to God, that, whereas ye were servants of sin, ye became obedient from the heart to that form of teaching whereunto ye were delivered; 18 and being made free from sin, ye became servants of righteousness. 19 I speak after the manner of men because of the infirmity of your flesh: for as ye presented your members as servants to uncleanness and to iniquity unto iniquity, even so now present your members as servants to righteousness unto sanctification. 20 For when ye were servants of sin, ye were free in regard of righteousness. 21 What fruit then had ye at that time in the things whereof ye are now ashamed? for the end of those things is death. 22 But now being made free from sin and become servants to God, ye have your fruit unto sanctification, and the end eternal life. 23 For the wages of sin is death; but the free gift of God is eternal life in Christ Jesus our Lord.

Realizing Romans, 6:15-23

250. Being free from the law could offer license to sin. How?
251. We cannot continue in sin even though free from the law because we belong to the one whom we serve. Who is this?
252. Not only do we belong to our master, but we receive wages from him. Tell what wages each master gives.

130. Who are the two kings described and what relationship to them do we hold?
131. What relation do verses 13-14 bear to the rest of the section?

253. What is the "righteousness" of vs. 16b?
254. What "obedience from the heart" is described in vs. 17?
255. We were obedient to "a form of teaching." What was it?
256. In what sense are we "free from sin", as in vs. 18a?
257. Are we to be slaves to righteousness?
258. What portion of this discussion was spoken "after the manner of men"? In what way?
259. Explain the expression, "infirmity of flesh," as in 19a?
260. Is it possible to offer ourselves as servants to Satan even after we have become Christians?
261. Notice in vs. 19b that sin never lessens its hold on man, it rather grows. What warning is in this?
262. What is the outcome of serving righteousness? What is sanctification?
263. Give the meaning of the word "free," as in 20a.
264. Paul seems to place the subject of service to Satan on a practical level in vs. 21. Can you explain how?
265. What marvelous advantage do we have in Christ? See it and believe it—yea, live it!—as in vs. 22.
266. How does vs. 23 sum up the whole section? Or does it?

Paraphrase

6:15-23. What then do we teach? That we will sin, because we are not under law but under grace? By no means. Our account of law and grace demonstrates, that we cannot possibly teach any such doctrine.

16 This however we say, that even under the gospel ye may be the slaves of sin or of righteousness, as ye choose: only ye should consider, that to whatsoever master ye make yourselves slaves to give him obedience, ye are his slaves whom ye obey, and must be contented both with his work and with his wages, whether it be of sin, whose service ends in death, or of the obedience of faith, whose service ends in righteousness.

17 By thus speaking, I do not insinuate that ye have made yourselves slaves to sin; on the contrary, I thank God, that although formerly ye were the slaves of sin, ye have willingly obeyed the mould of doctrine into which ye were cast at your baptism:

18 And that being set free from the slavery of sin by your faith, ye have voluntarily become the slaves of righteousness, whom therefore ye ought to obey.

19 I speak according to the customs of men respecting slaves, on account of the weakness of your understanding in spiritual matters, that I may give you a just idea of the influence which sinful lusts

have had over you formerly, and of the influence which holy affections ought now to have. Wherefore, as in your unbelieving state ye presented your members servile instruments to unclean affections, and to unjust desires, to work wickedness; so now present your members servile instruments to righteousness, to work holiness.

20 To devote yourselves to the service of righteousness, without serving sin at all, is reasonable: For when ye were slaves of sin, ye were free men as to righteousness; ye gave no obedience to righteousness.

21 And what advantage did ye then reap from those base actions with which ye served sin, and of which ye are now ashamed? Instead of being profited, ye have been hurt by them; for the reward of all such things is death eternal.

22 But now being set free from sin, both in respect of its power and punishment, and having become the servants of God, your state is entirely changed; ye are real free men, and ye have holiness as your service, and, as the reward thereof, everlasting life.

23 For the wages which sin gives to its slaves is eternal death; but the gracious gift which God bestows on his servants is everlasting life; a reward gratuitously bestowed through Jesus Christ our Lord.

Summary

It is not true that we may sin because under favor, and not under law. We are to sin in no case and for no end. If we attempt to serve sin we become slaves to it, and in the end will be condemned to eternal death; but, on the other hand, if we are obedient to Christ, the effect will be release from all our sins. Though formerly sinners, we have now sincerely obeyed the gospel; and the consequence is freedom from all sins. Being thus freed, we are now living in holiness. When slaves to sin we were, in a sense, free from righteousness; and so now, being servants to righteousness, we are free from sin. We owe it nothing, and cannot serve it. Indeed as we derived no benefit from our former sins, it would be manifest folly to return to them again. The end would be death, and by this we must be restrained. But we can no longer serve sin; for we are now servants of God, and are living holy lives. We cannot serve both. The result of serving God will be everlasting life, which we cannot afford to forfeit. The end of serving sin is eternal death.

Comment

2. Objection Concerning Freedom from the Law. 6:15-7:6

Objection Stated: Since you have said we are not under law (6:14) but under the favor of God, what is to restrain us from continuing in sin?

The soundness of this thought is repudiated (vs. 15). Then follow the reasons for the disavowal:

a. Reason Number One. 6:16-19

(1) The first answer to the objection is found in verses 16 through 19. The thought of this answer is, "Shall we continue in sin simply because we are free from the law, continue in unrighteousness because we are now living under the covenant of God's grace? God forbid." Do you realize the application of a very well known fact to this situation? You are acquainted with the fact that when you become a bond-servant of another that you are bound to your master. When you obey, you are obeying your master. In a very real sense you belong to this man and as long as you remain in his service and obey him you are his property. Well, now, apply this thought to sin. If you obey the lusts or desires of sin are you not then a bondservant to sin? Remember too, that if the master of any slave were to suffer any disaster the slave suffers with him. If the master were to move the slave would move with him; they abide together in whatever place the master occupies. Now think a moment: what is the end of Satan and sin? You know it is the lake of fire, the second death. If you are then the slave of sin, what will be your final end? If on the other hand you choose not to obey sin but rather to obey Christ you will be given the end of obedience to him, i.e., justification here and eternal life hereafter. 6:16

(2) "But thanks be to God" this is not the situation at all (giving the persons addressed the greatest benefit of the doubt), for the picture I have just drawn is a portrayal of your former condition and action. You were one time indeed the bondservants to sin, yet you escaped this bondage by dying out to sin and being baptized for the remission of your sins. Yes, you became obedient from the heart to that form of teaching of which we have just been speaking (6:1-4); and thus having become free from sin you have become bondservants to righteousness. Just as your bondservice to sin was a voluntary service, so is your righteousness. 6:17, 18

(3) "I have used words which describe the everyday things of your life in metaphorically portraying this spiritual truth," so says the apostle. "But I have only done so because you in your present state of weakness in comprehending spiritual matters would not have understood it if I spoke to you in any other way." 6:19a

132. State the second objection.
133. Give the first answer.
134. What bearing do verses 17, 18 have to the objection?
135. What is the thought of 19a?

(4) One final word in this answer comes from the apostle. Still using the metaphor of the slave, Paul says: "As you formerly came to the tyrant sin and offered him your hands, your feet, your mind, as his servants to be used in acts and thoughts of uncleanness and iniquity, so now come to Christ and present these same members as his servants in acts of righteousness to the end that you may be holy. In so doing, you will be set aside as God's possession." 6:19b

b. Reason Number Two. 6:20-23

(1) While yet maintaining the thought of the relationship of a slave to his master, Paul introduces another reason why freedom from the law does not give license for sin. He suggests this thought: "It is true that while you were living in sin you were free from any obligation to live a righteous life. (I see by your thinking that you would fain return to that position and yet have the hope provided by Christ.) Yet, what pleasure did you derive from your life of sin? Did it yield any peaceable fruit? In participating in those things of which you are now ashamed, did Satan give you any real satisfaction? The answer is self-evident. And after all, the end of such rebellion is eternal death. 20, 21

(2) But now let us lift our eyes from our past and look at the present. We are free from sin and are servants of God. What fruit do we have in *this* service? Ah, yes, the blessed fruit of sanctification, the benefits of a Christian that are to be found in the sanctified or holy life he lives. All of those elements of character that come as a result of living wholeheartedly for Christ are the fruit of holiness. cf. 6:1-5; II Pe. 1:5-8. The end of this life of joy and peace is eternal life. 6:22

(3) How true it is in viewing the whole subject of living in and for sin that "the wages of sin is death." After we have faithfully served sin and Satan, suffering all the time under the galling yoke, we will finally be paid for our service with eternal death. But the "free gift" of God, not something for which we must work, no, "not by works" but the "free gift" freely bestowed, is eternal life. But this gift is only given through Jesus Christ and in obedience to him. 6:23

We cannot continue in sin even if we are delivered from the law, for a life of sin pays off with eternal death.

136. How does 19b relate to the answer found in verses 16-19?
137. What is the second answer as found in verses 20-23?
138. How does vs. 22 relate to what is said in 20, 21?
139. Show how vs. 23 is a conclusion to the answer given in verses 20-22.

Text

7:1-6. Or are ye ignorant, brethren (for I speak to men who know the law), that the law hath dominion over a man for so long time as he liveth? 2 For the woman that hath a husband is bound by law to the husband while he liveth; but if the husband die, she is discharged from the law of the husband. 3 So then if, while the husband liveth, she be joined to another man, she shall be called an adulteress: but if the husband die, she is free from the law, so that she is no adulteress, though she be joined to another man. 4 Wherefore, my brethren, ye also were made dead to the law through the body of Christ; that ye should be joined to another, even to him who was raised from the dead, that we might bring forth fruit unto God. 5 For when we were in the flesh, the sinful passions, which were through the law, wrought in our members to bring forth fruit unto death. 6 But now we have been discharged from the law, having died to that wherein we were held; so that we serve in newness of the spirit, and not in oldness of the letter.

REALIZING ROMANS, 7:1-6

267. Please, notice that this section is only a small part of a larger one. Relate it to the whole. How does it relate?

268. A principle is stated in vs. 1 that is applied later. What is it?

269. In the example presented, are we to understand Paul to say there is no reason at all for divorce? What did Jesus say about divorce? Please remember that the thought of divorce and remarriage was *not* the subject under consideration in 7:1-6.

270. Is the man whom the adulteress marries guilty also?

271. The law was our first husband, but our husband died. What law was this? cf. vs. 1.

272. We are now married (in a figure of speech) to Christ. How will this keep us from sin?

273. The fruit of our relationship to Christ is in what?

274. Give the meaning of the little expression, "in the flesh"? cf. vs. 5.

275. Please note the progress of Satan's work in man: (1) sinful passions; (2) through the law; (3) wrought in our members; (4) fruit unto death. Explain each step.

276. We are discharged from what law? We also died in what sense?

277. "We serve in newness of spirit." Explain this expression.

278. It *is not* true that all who have accepted Christ are free from the power of sin and the law. Why not? How is this answered in this very section?

Paraphrase

7:1-6. Ye Jews think the law of Moses is of perpetual obligation; but know ye not, brethren, (for I speak to them who know law), that the law of Moses, as the law of God's temporal kingdom among the Jews, hath dominion over a man only so long as he liveth; its obligation being that of a marriage?

2 For a woman who hath an husband, is bound by the law of marriage (Gen. ii. 21-24) to her husband while he liveth: but if her husband die she is loosed from the law of marriage, which bound her to her husband, and hindered her from marrying any other man.

3 So then such a women shall be reputed, both by God and man, an adulteress, if, while her husband liveth, she be married to another husband: but if her husband die, she is freed from that law which bound her to her husband, and hindered her to marry any other man; so that she is no adulteress, though, after his death, she be married to another husband.

4 Wherefore, my brethren, since marriages are dissolved by the death of either of the parties, ye Jews, who were married to God as your king, and thereby were bound to obey the law of Moses, are loosed from that marriage and law, because ye also, as well as the Gentiles, (chap. vi. 6), have been put to death by the curse of the law in the person of Christ, that ye may be married to another, even to him who died for you, but is now raised from the dead; and that we should bring forth fruit to God.

5 Besides, the law of Moses never was intended as the rule of our justification; for when we were the subjects of God's temporal kingdom, the sinful inclinations which we had under the law, wrought effectually in the members, both of our soul and body, to bring forth such evil actions as, by the curse of that law, subjected us to death without mercy.

6 But now we Jews are loosed from the law of Moses, having died with Christ by its curse in that fleshly nature by which, as descendants of Abraham, we were tied to the law, and are placed under the law of the gospel; so that we now should serve God in the new manner of the Gospel, and not in the old manner of the law.

Summary

The law rules over a man so long as he lives. As an example, take the married woman. She is bound by law to her husband while he lives. As proof that she is thus bound, if while her husband is alive, she marries another man she will act the adulteress. But when her husband dies she is released from the law which bound her to him. If she then marries she is no adulteress. And so you, my brethren, died to the law by the body of Christ when he died. You thus became released from the law, and consequently are at liberty to obey the risen Savior. When we were under the flesh, which we were before we obeyed the gospel, those sinful desires which are discovered to be such by the law, worked in us to produce fruit to death. But we are now released from the law, by dying to it, so that at present we serve God in a renewed spirit, through the gospel, and not in the old fashion prescribed in the law.

c. Reason Number Three. 7:1-6

Comment

(1) Paul felt that he had established this premise in the minds of all Jews who would be honest in their consideration of what he had said. But to seal the argument beyond a word of retaliation, he strikes upon his readers' minds the truth that in the law was found the very principle for which he was pleading. Notice his words: "Or are ye ignorant, brethren (for I speak to men who know the law), that the law hath dominion over a man for so long time as he liveth?" There is the principle. Then follows the illustration of this principle. The illustration given is that of a woman who, while married, is bound by the law to her husband, but if the husband dies she is free from the law that bound her to him. Now, of course, if she were to marry another while her husband lived she would be called an adulteress, but not so if she were to marry after her husband's death. 7:1-3

(2) "Well," answers the Jew, "how does that apply to the objection I have raised? How does that demonstrate that although we are free from the law we cannot continue in sin?" Ah, yes, here is the wonderful application, that at the same time we were released from the law through the death of Christ (cp. Col. 2:13-16), we were joined to another, even to him who was raised from the dead. While we were married to the law, Paul says that we were bound to obey it because of the responsibilities of the married state, and now that we are married to Christ we are equally bound to obey him. In our obedience to him we will "bring forth fruit unto God." 7:4

Continue in sin? How can we while we are joined in spiritual marriage to Jesus Christ?

(3) Speaking of our bearing fruit unto God in our new marriage, contrariwise, we can look back to our old marriage and remember the wicked desires of Satan, coupled with a yielding of our wills. This

140. What is the third answer to the second objection?
141. How does the answer demonstrate that we cannot continue in sin?

transgression of God's will only resulted in the fruit of death. 7:5

(4) "But now we have been discharged from the law." How did this take place? The answer is found in the fact that we were in Christ when he died, and since he in his death blotted out the law, we too have thus died with him to the law. In coming into Christ we are delivered from the bondage of the law. We now serve God with a renewed spirit, a spirit made new by God's Spirit indwelling our bodies. We do not serve God in the old letter of the Mosaic law, but by the renewed spirit of a Christian. 7:6

Rethinking in Outline Form
Objections to the Proposition Continued

2. Objection concerning freedom from the law. 6:15—7:6
Objection Stated: Since you have said we are not under law (6:14) but under the favor of God, what is to restrain us from continuing in sin?
Objection Answered:

a. Reason number one. 6:16-19

(1) If you continue in sin you are a slave to sin. Being a slave of sin, your final destiny will be the same as your master—eternal death. vs. 16a

(2) However, you need not choose to act this way, for you can become the bondservant of Christ through obedience to him and can enter into the benefits of sanctification. vs. 16b

(3) Indeed, this is what you did once when you threw off the bondage of sin through your obedience to the gospel. So now even as you once gave yourselves body and soul to Satan, give yourselves to your new master. In doing this, you will be God's own possession. vs. 17-19

b. Reason number two. 6:20-23

(1) What fruit did you find while living in sin? You found none. Well, why do you long to return to this fruitless existence? vs. 20-21

(2) There is a wonderful reward for those who serve Christ . . . joy and peace here (which is the fruit of sanctification) and eternal life hereafter. vs. 22

(3) The wages of a life of sin is eternal death, but the free gift of God is eternal life through Jesus Christ our Lord. vs. 23

142. What fruit is brought forth by continuing in sin?
143. Show how we have been discharged from the law.

c. Reason number three. 7:1-6

(1) It is a well known fact of the law that a woman is bound to the man she marries as long as her husband lives. You were once married to the law; the law died in the body of Christ, so you are free from the law. And since you have obtained your freedom you have been joined to another; this time your husband is Christ. Continue in sin? How can we while joined in spiritual marriage to Christ Jesus? 7:1-4

(2) While in this new state, we are to bring forth fruit, not unto Satan as in times past, but unto God. vs. 5

(3) We serve God now, not like we did once, from the letter, but from our spirits. vs. 6

Text

7:7-12. What shall we say then? Is the law sin? God forbid. Howbeit, I had not known sin, except through the law: for I had not known coveting, except the law had said, Thou shalt not covet: 8 but sin, finding occasion, wrought in me through the commandment all manner of coveting: for apart from the law sin is dead. 9 And I was alive apart from the law once: but when the commandment came, sin revived, and I died; 10 and the commandment, which was unto life, this I found to be unto death: 11 for sin, finding occasion, through the commandment beguiled me, and through it slew me. 12 So that the law is holy, and the commandment holy, and righteous, and good.

Realizing Romans, 7:7-12

279. If the power of sin is the law, why not do away with all law so we would have no sin?

280. If the law causes sin, is it not itself some form of sin?

281. In just what way does sin or Satan find an occasion in the law?

282. There *must* be a very personal Devil, for how else would he be able to approach our spirits through the law? Do you believe this is a fair deduction?

283. When was Paul ever "alive apart from the law"?

284. In what sense did the commandment "come" to Paul?

285. What death did Paul die as a result of his personal sin?

286. In what sense did "sin revive"? cf. vs. 9b.

287. Verse ten states the purpose of the law. What was it?

288. Just what was, or is, "the occasion" of vs. 11a?
289. Paul was "beguiled" or deceived by sin through the commandment. How?
290. In what sense are we to understand vs. 12? The law is holy. In what respect?
291. Is the commandment different from the law? Explain. Answer *all* of these questions with your *present* knowledge. You are directly responsible to God and directly responsible to the word of God. These words were written to the Christians in Rome, who had no more ability to understand than you do, yet God expected them to understand by reading and thought. He expects the same thing of each of us.

Paraphrase

7:7-12. What then do I say when I affirmed, ver. 5. that, under the law, our sinful passions wrought in our members to bring forth fruit unto death? Do I say that the law is a bad institution? By no means. Nay, I could not have known sin in its extent and demerit, unless through law. For even strong desire of things sinful, I could not have known to be sin punishable with death, unless the law of Moses had said, thou shalt not covet.

8 But I say that sin, taking opportunity under the law to kill me by its curse, wrought effectually in me the strongest desire of things forbidden, and thereby subjected me to death, (ver. 5) For without the law, sin is dead; hath no power to kill the sinner.

9 Accordingly, I was in my own imagination entitled to life, while without the knowledge of law formerly: but when the commandment, with its curse, came to my knowledge in their full extent, sin, which I fancied had no existence in me, lived again, and I died by the curse.

10 And so the commandment written on the hearts of men, and published in the law of Moses, which was intended for giving life, the same was found by me, in my present state, to be the occasion of death.

11 For as law neither remedies the weakness of human nature, nor subdues its evil appetites, sin, taking opportunity while I was under the commandment to kill me, deceived me into the commission of evil actions by its specious allurements, and through the commandment slew me.

12 Wherefore, the law indeed, as it restrains us from sin by the fear of punishment, is holy even in its curse, and the moral commandment is holy, and just, and good.

Summary

The law is neither sinful nor the cause of sin. On the contrary, sin becomes known by the law. As proof, I had never known desire to be sin, but for the precept of the law forbidding it. But so soon as the precept was given, sin took advantage of the circumstance to work up desire in me, the very thing the law forbade; and thus I fell under the condemnation of the law. Without law sin is dead or powerless to kill. Accordingly, before the law I was alive or uncondemned, but when the precept came I broke it. Thus sin arose, and for it I was condemned to die. It was in this way that a precept which was designed for life turned out to end in death. The law then is not sin; but is holy in all its parts.

Comment

a. The Objection Stated: Since it is so desirable to be released from the law, is the law a form of sin? 7:7a

b. The answer is given. 7:7b-12

The apostle, in this instance as in the former two, first states the objection then immediately denies it. Then follow the reasons for his refusal to accept the validity of the objection. 7:7b

Since the subjects of sin and law have been brought together, Paul takes this opportunity to explain the relationship of the law to sin and vice versa.

(1) His first observation is that although the law of itself is not sin, it does make sin known. In other words, it defines sin. As an illustration of this thought Paul says, "I would never have known it was a sin to covet unless the law had been given. In the law I was informed that a condition of covetousness was a condition of sin." 7:7c

(2) His second thought is to describe the work of sin (or Satan, as sin is here personified) in its relation to the commandment. When the commandment was given it afforded an occasion to Satan for temptation. Even as Satan took the command of God in the garden and, appealing to the power of choice, tempted Eve, so now he comes to you and me and says, even as of old, "Yea, *hath* God said?" In the case cited by the inspired writer he would have said: "Yea, *hath* God said, 'Thou shalt not covet'?" Thus when man makes the wrong choice, all manner of coveting is given entrance to his heart. We can see then indeed that "apart from the law sin (or Satan) is dead" or powerless. 7:8

144. State in your own words the thought of the objection concerning the law in respect to sin.

145. What is the relationship of the law to sin (cp. I Cor. 15:56)?

146. Describe briefly the work of Satan in respect to the law.

(3) The third point in this discussion recalls the days of innocent childhood, before the demands of the law were comprehended or ere the light of reason shone upon its penalties. Regarding his childhood state Paul could truly say, "I was alive (or happy, living in blissful unconsciousness of moral responsibility) apart from the law. But when I became conscious of God's demands upon my soul, when I understood God's will for my life, no sooner had this taken place, than sin (or Satan) came alive and I died." How his death took place has already been described. 7:9

(4) Further describing the work of the commandment: it was given to point men to a life in God. But tragic as it may sound, I found it to result only in death. It is even as I have already observed, that Satan found an occasion through and by the commandment to beguile me, even as he in his craftiness did beguile Eve. Thus we see that Satan actually used the commandment as a death weapon in his hands to slay me. 7:10-11

(5) So, in conclusion, and in direct answer to your objection, I can say that the law is not a form of sin. The commandment bears no vestige of sin. "The law is holy, and the commandment holy, and righteous, and good." From what I have said, you know the true relation of the law and sin. 7:12

Text

7:13-25. Did then that which is good become death unto me? God forbid. But sin, that it might be shown to be sin, by working death to me through that which is good;—that through the commandment sin might become exceeding sinful. 14 For we know that the law is spiritual: but I am carnal, sold under sin. 15 For that which I do I know not: for not what I would, that do I practise; but what I hate, that I do. 16 But if what I would not, that I do, I consent unto the law that it is good. 17 So now it is no more I that do it, but sin which dwelleth in me. 18 For I know that in me, that is, in my flesh, dwelleth no good thing: for to will is present with me, but to do that which is good is not. 19 For the good which I would I do not: but the evil which I would not, that I practise. 20 But if what I would not, that I do, it is no more I that do it, but sin which dwelleth in me. 21 I find then the law, that, to me who would do good, evil is present. 22 For I delight in the law of God after the inward man: 23 but I see a different law in my members, warring against the law of my mind, and bringing me into captivity under the law of sin which is in my members. 24 Wretched man that I am! who shall deliver me out of the body of this death? 25 I thank God through Jesus Christ our Lord. So then I of myself with the mind, indeed, serve the law of God; but with the flesh the law of sin.

REALIZING ROMANS, 7:13-25

292. God had several purposes in giving the law, or we might say there were several results forthcoming. Another is stated in vs. 13. What is it?

293. The nature of sin or Satan is also revealed. How?

294. Is Paul here describing an experience before or after he became a Christian?

295. In what sense was the law "spiritual"? In what sense was Paul "carnal"?

296. Who sold Paul under sin?

297. How could it be true that Paul did not know what he was doing in the matter of sin?

298. How could man be held responsible if sin has such a power over man? cf. vs. 15. Please do not be superficial in your answer.

299. What is the reason for all this emphasis upon the goodness and spirituality of the law?

300. Sin does it, but I am responsible. Is this true? Explain.

301. Paul makes a confession in vs. 18. Have you ever made such an admission? Have you found a solution?

302. What is "the inward man" of vs. 22?

303. The power of Satan seems to be "in our members." cf. vs. 23. In what sense is this true?

304. The law of the members is contrasted with the law of the mind. Define each.

305. This is indeed a most wretched state. Why?

306. Paul was living in or with "a body of death." Explain.

307. Does vs. 25 say that we *can* overcome this terrible bondage through Jesus Christ? Just how complete and final will this overcoming be?

308. Does vs. 25b describe a state or a principle? Explain.

Paraphrase

7:13-25. The good law, then, which you praise so much, to me hath become the cause of death? I reply, It is by no means the law, but sin, which hath become the cause of death to sinners. And God hath so appointed it to be, that sin might be seen to work out death to sinners, through the good law; that is, that sin might become known to all God's subjects, as a thing most exceedingly destructive, through the commandment, forbidding it under the penalty of death.

14 Besides, we know that the law is agreeable to our spiritual part, but that I am led by my carnal part, being enslaved to sin.

15 The spirituality of the law we know; for what evil things in an unregenerate state I habitually work, I do not approve: and our slavery to sin we know; for I practise not the things which reason and conscience incline, but what they hate, that I do.

16 And if, as often as I obey the law, I do that which reason and conscience incline not; by thus condemning these actions, I acknowledge the law to be good.

17 Now, therefore, it is not reason and conscience which work out these evil actions, but they are wrought out by the sinful inclinations which prevail in my animal nature.

18 These evil actions I justly ascribe to the prevalence of fleshly appetites: For I know that good is not predominant in me, that is, in my flesh. Indeed, to have an inclination to what is good, is easy for me, or any one whose conscience is not wholly seared; but to practise what is excellent I do not find easy.

19 Therefore I and others do not the good which reason and conscience incline; but the evil which these higher parts of our nature are averse to, that we practise; we omit many duties, and commit many sins, contrary to the dictates of reason and conscience.

20 Now if I omit good, and commit evil, contrary to the inclination of my reason and conscience, which constitute my higher part, it is no more I who practise it, but sin dwelling in my carnal part.

21 Well then, what experience discovers [*reveals*] to me, and to every one, is, we find, this law in us inclining to do what is excellent, that evil lies near at hand; is easy to be practised, being agreeable to our strongest passions.

22 For I am well pleased with the law of God, according to the dictates of my inward man, or better self.

23 Yet I, and all other men, while unregenerated, find in ourselves a variety of lusts, whose influence is so strong and constant that it may be called another law in our animal part, warring against the law of our mind, and making us abject slaves to the law of sin which is in our animal part.

24 In this miserable situation, having from law no assistance to subdue my lusts, nor any hope of pardon, I, in the name of mankind, cry out, O wretched man that I am, who will deliver me from the slavery of the body, ending in this death!

25 Our deliverance from these evils does not come from the law but from the gospel: therefore I thank God, who delivers us through Jesus Christ our Lord.

Being thus delivered, Do I myself, then, or any delivered person, as slaves, still serve with the mind the law of God, by ineffectual approbations of good and disapprobations of evil, but with the body the law of sin, (ver. 23), performing wicked actions habitually? No, as becomes delivered persons, we serve God both with the mind and with the body.

Summary

Did then a holy law become death to me? No. But sin did, in order that by effecting my death by a just law, its true nature might become known. The law is no source of death, because it is spiritual; but I am fleshly, and therefore at times under the dominion of sin. As evidence that I am fleshly, and consequently under evil influences, I often do what I do not approve, that is, I do wrong, and practise what I do not wish to practise. If now I do what I do not approve, I agree with the law that it is right; for the law requires just what I wish to do, and condemns only what I do not wish to do. Now when, under these circumstances, I sin, it is not I alone that of my own accord do it, but it is the sinful influences which I am under that impel me to it. There is no good dwelling in my flesh; for while I can wish to do right, I am unable, because of the flesh, to do it. Indeed, I find it the rule with me, that whenever I wish to do right, evil is present, because the flesh is ever ready to prompt me to do wrong. In the inner man I delight in the law of God, but then there is another law in my members— this strong tendency to sin; and under its power I often sin. I am toil-worn in this strife between wishing to do right and not doing it, and hating to sin and yet sinning. Who shall deliver me from it? Thanks to God, he will. So then with the mind at least, I serve the law of God which is the great matter; but with the flesh I at times serve the law of sin.

Comment

4. Objection as to the law in respect to death. 7:13-25

a. Objective Stated: "Did then that which is good become death unto me?" This, of course, refers to the commandment which is called good in verse 12b.

b. Objective answered: God forbid that such a condition should exist; no, it does not exist. The answer to this objection entails in it some of the same considerations that are found in Paul's answers to the law in respect to sin. However, the answers, though necessarily similar in content, are given to answer two different problems. The other problem was the act of sin but this one is in regard to the result of sin. 7:13a

(1) The first comment is a direct answer to the question, "Who

147. What is the thought of the objection of the law in respect to death?
148. What is the difference between this objection and the preceding one?

brought this spiritual death if the commandment didn't?" It is answered in the statement: sin, or Satan brought it. If Satan took that which was good and used it wrongly, why did God choose such a procedure? This reason is that the true evil nature of Satan could be shown. So it is that through the use Satan made of the commandment his exceeding wickedness is clearly shown. 7:13b

(2) When we think of the law Satan used we must confess that it is from God, spiritual; but when we examine ourselves we see that we are fleshly. Paul says of himself that he is "carnal, sold under sin." This we take to mean as an ordinary Christian, not as an apostle; he was tempted by Satan through his flesh, and struggle as he would against it he could not completely free himself from the bondage in which sin, through the flesh, held him. Please remember that he is describing here a circumstance to which there is a deliverance through Jesus Christ. The extent of the deliverance depends entirely upon the willingness of the individual to avail himself of it. 7:14

(3) In verse 14 the apostle states a condition, that the law is spiritual, but "I" am fleshly. In verses 15-25 he discusses the results of this condition.

(a) "That which I do I approve not." (We render the word "know" as "approve", since it is one translation of the Greek word and fits more easily into the sense of the passage.) Here is the situation: I practice not what I wish, but rather I do the very things I hate. 7:15

(b) But of course in doing this if I hate the things I do because they are contrary to God's law, I thus consent to the law that it is good. 7:16

(c) So you can see that of myself, as a Christian, I would not do these things; hence there must be some other force at work. That power is sin (or Satan) which is dwelling in me. (Of course this dwelling would only be in the sense that Satan is a spirit and thus could associate with our spirits and exert his influence upon our flesh.) 7:17

(d) As a further conclusion to this matter I can see that in me alone (apart from Christ), as an individual, a mere creation of the dust, there dwells no good thing. It is not that I do not want to do right, for I do, but the power to do it just is not there. For when I decide to do good, somehow I never get it done; and the evil which

149. What is the thought of 13b?
150. What does Paul mean "the law is spiritual"; "I am carnal"?
151. What would be a better translation of vs. 15?
152. How does Paul consent that the law is good?

I have decided not to do, lo, I find myself practicing. But it is even as I have said that this practice of sin is not carried out by me alone but rather by sin taking over my will through the flesh. 7:18-20

(e) The law says to do good. That is fine; I consent to it and I would do it, but evil is present. Why, I delight in the law in my very soul; with my spirit I revel in the beauty of God's will; but there is another law, or power, or tendency in my flesh, in my nature, or in my being, and since the members of my body are directed by my mind I can say that this tendency to do evil is a veritable part of my members. This tendency, which becomes a lust when excited by temptation, wars against the "law of my mind," the desire, the tendency to do good, of which I have already spoken. Hence there is a terrible conflict between the tendency to do evil and the tendency to do good. "Wretched man that I am (or as Lard words it, 'Toilworn man that I am',) who shall deliver me out of this body of death?" What is the body of death? In answer, we might inquire, what body was it that was being used by Satan to cause sin and spiritual death? Was it not the "body of flesh," the "mortal body" in which sin could reign? (6:12) So then, the cry of Paul is for release from the power of the flesh, a cry for deliverance from the thralldom in which the flesh can hold a man. We can see clearly now who caused spiritual death. It was not the law, but Satan using the law to beguile man through the tendency to sin which is in man's flesh. Is there an answer? Is there a deliverer? Yes, thank God, Jesus Christ our Lord can effect our deliverance. He can release us from spiritual death. He can through his Spirit give us victory over the flesh. The extent of this victory is dependent solely upon the willingness of the Christian to give himself, body, soul and spirit, into the hands of Christ. We can indeed say that only by a denial of self, coupled with a commitment of our bodies as a "living sacrifice," can we hope to be delivered from the power of Satan through the flesh. 7:21-25a

(f) In review of the whole situation, we have the words of Paul: "So then I of myself with the mind, indeed, serve the law of God. I of myself apart from any thought of the power of Christ, I of my natural self as a Christian, assent to the worthiness of obedience to the law of God, but with the flesh the law of sin. There is also with me "the flesh," and under the influence of this nature I serve the law of sin, or yield to the tendency to sin." This choice is before us and we know how to become the conqueror rather than the victim. 7:25b

153. In what way could sin dwell in Paul and in us?
154. What is it we need in order to practice the things we know are right?
155. Explain in your own words 21-23.
156. What is the "body of death"?

Rethinking in Outline Form
Objections to the Proposition Concluded

3. Objection as to the law in respect to sin. 7:7-12
   Objection Stated: Since it is so desirable to be released from the law, is the law a form of sin?
   Objection Answered:
   (1) The law is not sin, but defines sin. vs. 7c
   (2) Satan uses the law as an occasion for temptation and sin. vs. 8
   (3) The personal experience of Paul is given, from his childhood of innocence, to his subsequent death through the efforts of Satan. vs. 9
   (4) The commandment was given to bring life, but Satan used it to bring death. vs. 10-11
   (5) The law of itself, apart from the use made of it by Satan, is holy, righteous, and good. vs. 12

4. Objection as to the law in respect to death. 7:13-25
   Objection Answered:
   (1) God forbid. The law of itself brings about the death of no one. Satan uses it as an occasion, and through it spiritual death makes its advent. vs. 13-14
   (2) The law is from God, but man is fleshly and through the weakness of man's flesh Satan occasions his death. Our spirits are willing, but the flesh is weak. This circumstance results in great inward pain, and we are moved to cry out, "Who will deliver us?" The answer and deliverance comes through Christ Jesus. vs. 15-25

Text

8:1-11. There is therefore now no condemnation to them that are in Christ Jesus. 2 For the law of the Spirit of life in Christ Jesus made me free from the law of sin and of death. 3 For what the law could not do, in that it was weak through the flesh, God, sending his own Son in the likeness of sinful flesh and for sin, condemned sin in the flesh: 4 that the ordinance of the law might be fulfilled in us, who walk not after the flesh, but after the Spirit. 5 For they that are after the flesh mind the things of the flesh; but they that are after the Spirit the things of the Spirit. 6 For the mind of the flesh is death; but the mind of the Spirit is life and peace: 7 because the mind of the flesh is enmity against God; for it is not subject to the law of God,

157. Where can we obtain the victory over the flesh?

neither indeed can it be: 8 and they that are in the flesh cannot please God. 9 But ye are not in the flesh but in the Spirit, if so be that the Spirit of God dwelleth in you. But if any man hath not the spirit of Christ, he is none of his. 10 And if Christ is in you, the body is dead because of sin; but the spirit is life because of righteousness. 11 But if the Spirit of him that raised up Jesus from the dead dwelleth in you, he that raised up Christ Jesus from the dead shall give life also to your mortal bodies through his Spirit that dwelleth in you.

Realizing Romans, 8:1-11

309. What a marvelous encouragement in vs. 1! Amplify the words "no condemnation"—no condemnation from what, to what, in what, etc.

310. In what sense are we "in Christ Jesus"?

311. What is "the law of the spirit of life," as vs. 2? Show how appropriate this title is.

312. We are indeed separated and delivered from the power of Satan and the law. Do you believe this statement? Experimentally or theologically? Have we entered the fullness of salvation if we do not now have this testimony?

313. The law was good and not weak. The evil and weakness was located elsewhere. Where?

314. What the law and man could not do, God could and did do. What was it?

315. Explain the little expression, "in the likeness of sinful flesh"?

316. In the previous question you discussed the nature of Christ. Now we ask for the purpose of Christ. He came "for sin." Explain.

317. Give a careful explanation of the thought of "condemning sin in the flesh."

318. Did Jesus fight Satan with weapons we do not have? If not, why do we fail to "condemn sin in the flesh"?

319. What did God fulfill in us? Note the marginal reading of "ordinance."

320. Does our walking after the spirit instead of the flesh have anything to do with the requirement of the law being fulfilled in us? If so, what?

321. Just how can we know when we walk by the Spirit?

322. Explain the phrases, "minding the things of the flesh," and "minding the things of the spirit."

323. Give three good reasons for minding the things of the Spirit instead of the flesh.

324. What "death" is referred to in vs. 6?

325. Wouldn't it be wonderful to have the life and peace spoken of in vs. 6b? It will never be real to us until we know the meaning of "the mind of the Spirit." Do you know? Do I? Who is responsible if we do not?

326. "The mind of the flesh" must be that inspired and educated by Satan. Can we have both minds at the same time? Explain.

327. The mind of the flesh can never be subjected to God or his law. Are we not then foolish to attempt to overcome it? How can it be overcome?

328. Are we not all "in the flesh"? Explain.

329. We have the victory not of ourselves but by him who loved us and came to make his abode within. In what sense are we to understand vs. 9a?

330. What is "the Spirit of Christ" of vs. 9b? Is this a disposition or a person?

331. Verse 9a states that the Spirit of God dwelleth in us; verse 10a says Christ dwells in us. Explain and compare.

332. What "body" is meant in vs. 10a? Is this literal or figurative?

333. What is the spirit that is "life" or "alive"?

334. Whose "sin" and whose "righteousness" are discussed?

335. Now in vs. 11 we are told that someone else dwells in us. Who is it? Harmonize vs. 11 with other references to the indwelling presence.

336. What "life" is referred to in vs. 11b? Is this in reference to the resurrection of the last day?

337. Please try to gather an outline of each section (of your own) as you study these verses. What would be the main and subdivisions of this section?

Paraphrase

8:1-11. Mankind under the new covenant being delivered from the curse of the law, there is therefore now no condemnation to those Christians who walk not according to the inclinations of their flesh, but according to the inclinations of their spirit, enlightened and strengthened by the Spirit of God.

2 We the disciples of Christ are able so to walk, because the law of the gospel, which promises eternal life by Jesus Christ, has delivered us from the power of sin in our members, and from the curse of death.

3 For God sending his own Son is the likeness of sinful men to teach us, and of a sin-offering to procure pardon for us, hath destroyed the power of sin in the flesh, so that it can neither enslave nor kill believers, (which is the thing impossible to be done by the precepts and threatenings of the law, because it was weak through the corruption of our nature).

4 This destruction of sin in our flesh God accomplished, that the righteousness enjoined in the law of the gospel, (ver. 2) may be fulfilled by us, who walk not according to the flesh, the law in our members, (chap. vii. 23), but according to the Spirit, the law of our mind.

5 Now, they who live according to the flesh, employ themselves in enjoying sensual pleasures, and in making provision for these enjoyments; and they who live according to the Spirit, employ themselves in the things which reason and conscience dictate: (Gal. 5:16-26.)

6 But whatever wicked men may think, the minding of the body, to the neglect of the soul, is eternal death; and the minding of the soul, is the road to eternal life.

7 The minding of the body to the neglecting of the soul, will be justly punished with death: First, Because to mind the body in that manner, is enmity against God; secondly, Because this temper of mind is not subject to the law of God, neither indeed can be; it is actual rebellion against God.

8 Wherefore, they who live after the flesh cannot be the objects of God's favor, in any dispensation whatever.

9 Now ye live not to the flesh, but to the Spirit, because the Spirit of God dwells in you. But if any one have not the Spirit of Christ dwelling in him, and forming him into the temper and behavior of Christ, whatever such a person's profession may be, he is none of Christ's disciples.

10 And if the Spirit of Christ be in you, the body, with its lusts, which formerly governed you, (chap. vii. 18), will certainly be dead with respect to sin; but the spirit, your rational powers, will be alive, or vigorous, with respect to righteousness.

11 For, if the Spirit of him who raised up Jesus from the dead abide in you by his influences, he who raised up Christ from the dead, will make even your dead bodies, (ver. 10), your animal passions, together with the members of your mortal bodies, alive, that is, subservient to the spiritual life, through his Spirit who dwelleth in you.

Summary

There is no condemnation to them that are in Christ, for by him the gospel freed me, when I first became obedient to it, from the law of sin and death. This the law could not possibly do, because of its weakness through the flesh. But what was impossible for the law, God did, by sending his Son into the world in a body of human flesh, and as a sin-offering. Moreover in this body he condemned all sin committed under influence of the flesh, by showing that such influence can be resisted. He came as a sin-offering that the justification of the law, remission of sins, might be accomplished in us who live not in obedience to the flesh, but to the spirit. To live according to the flesh is to be led by it into sin; to live according to the spirit is to be led by it to do right. They that do the former will die; they that do the latter shall live. Attending to the flesh is continued hostility to God; and he that does it is never obedient to his will; nor can he be so long as he thus acts. We are in the spirit, under its control, provided the Holy Spirit dwells in us; and if it dwells not in us we are not Christ's. If the Holy Spirit dwells in us God will one day make our bodies alive by it.

Comment

1. Freedom in the Gospel. 8:1-11

Introductory Remarks

There has been no little discussion over this chapter as to whether it is a conclusion of the closing remarks of the seventh chapter or a conclusion of the whole preceding treatise. It seems to me that both thoughts could well be held in viewing this chapter. It develops in a wonderful way the thought of deliverance from the bondage of the flesh expressed in 7:24-25a, as well as bringing forth a conclusion for all that has been said of the power of the gospel over the law and the flesh.

a. "There is therefore now no condemnation to them then that are in Christ Jesus." The heart cry of the apostle when he said, "Wretched man that I am! Who shall deliver me from the body of this death?" was answered in the deliverance provided by God through Jesus Christ. So now he can say while considering this happy state, "There is therefore now no condemnation to them that are in Christ Jesus." It would be well to point out that to be free from condemnation we must first of all be "in Christ Jesus". How this is

158. State in your own words the review of the entire situation just discussed.
159. Do you believe Ch. 8 is a conclusion to Ch. 7 only, or to Ch. 1-7? Give your reasons.

achieved was thoroughly discussed in 6:1-4. And after we are "in Christ" we must "abide in him" (Jn. 15:1-12) in order to escape from the tragic victory of the flesh over the spirit described in 7:13-25. But once we are placed "in Christ" through immersion, and we continue in him by denying self daily (Lu. 9:23), truly there is "no condemnation." God does not demand sinless perfection, but he does demand absolute sincerity. 8:1

In considering this passage in a broader scope we can say there is no condemnation to those who "are in Christ Jesus," in the sense that God has provided through the death of his Son an escape from "the stroke that was our due," for it fell upon him. Jehovah made him our substitute as an offering for sin. 8:1

b. Now follow the words of the inspired writer as to how this glorious position was achieved. It is like this: "The law of the spirit of life in Christ Jesus made me free from the law of sin and death." In other words, the gospel (the preaching of the death, burial and resurrection of Christ) freed me from the condemnation of the law under which I was living. The law was a law of sin, for it gave the definition of sin, and also because it became, by the use Satan made of it, a means of bringing sin into my life. When I sinned, the penalty of death was passed. But it is wonderful to know that all that is lifted from my heart; the Son through his gospel has made me free and I am free indeed. 8:2

c. There was only one other provision made by God for man's justification. That was the law. If man had kept the law he would indeed have stood justified before God, but the law was weak; its weakness lay not within itself but in the flesh of man. Man's spirit was indeed willing to obey the law, but his flesh was too weak to carry out the demands of the law. But our Father of love did not leave us to the power of the evil one through the law, for what the law could not do the law-giver could, and what he could, this he did through sending his Son. We know how it took place; the eternal word was made flesh, that is, inhabited a body in which there was as much tendency to sin as in any other mortal creation. But this one did not only come "in the likeness of sinful flesh," but he came to be offered "for sin." He came knowing no sin that he might be made to

160. What "condemnation" is spoken of in 8:1?
161. How can we retain this sense of "no condemnation"?
162. What is "the law of the Spirit of life"?
163. What is "the law of sin and death"?

be sin for us that we through him might stand justified before God. Further, in coming in this body of flesh and being tempted in all points like as we are tempted, and yet not yielding to Satan's suggestions, he condemned the idea that because we are "in the flesh" we must of a necessity yield to sin. 8:3

But back to the thought of how God through Christ did what the law could not do. What was the purpose of the law? Was it not justification, that man through keeping the law was to be made just before God? But this the law failed to accomplish. What the law failed to provide, God provided through his Son. "In us" the requirement of the law finds its fulfillment by Jesus Christ. Of course the persons discussed are Christians who are to walk according to the leading of the Spirit of God. Only by thus continuing in a life lived unto God can we hope for final justification on the day of judgment. 8:3-4

There is a connecting thought between the discussion of verse 4 and verse 5. The thought of justification is the burden of verse 4, whereas we find the course of the Christian's life to be the thought of verse 5. How are they connected? Simply by realizing that although we were brought into this glorious position of justification at our conversion, we will not finally be acquitted unless we follow the life of the spirit. This life of the spirit is discussed in the following verses.

d. The first observation in this life of the spirit that will lead to final justification is a perfectly obvious fact. If our spirits are led by Satan to go after the flesh then we will be giving our attention to the activities of the flesh. (These would be synonymous with the "works of the flesh" mentioned in Gal. 5:19). If on the other hand we allow Jesus to be the leader and captain of our spirits we will be led into the fruitful life of the Christian. There is good reason to choose to follow the life of the spirit rather than the life of the flesh, for the end of a life of sin is death, but the life led for Christ brings peace here and eternal life hereafter. 8:5-6

The reason God has to be so severe with some persons is found in the fact that a mind and heart filled with the desires of the flesh is a mind and heart filled with that which is exactly contrary to God's

164. In what way was the law weak?
165. How is the law fulfilled?
166. What thought connects verses four and five?
167. What is discussed in 8:5-11?

will; that person is at enmity with God, and while thus giving himself to the lusts of the flesh he is not subject to the law of God, neither indeed can he be while so continuing. It is impossible for sweet and bitter waters to flow from the same spring. While living for the flesh, you may as well know that "you cannot please God." 8:7-8

e. "But," remarks the apostle, "this is not your situation for you are not following a course of fleshly desire, but rather you are following the dictates of your spirit which has been educated to do God's will in Christ. This is true providing the Holy Spirit abides in you, for you could not hope to live a life pleasing to God just of yourself (Cf. 7:13-25); hence the Holy Spirit has been sent to strengthen and energize your spirit to the end that we might live after the spirit and not after the flesh." 8:9a

f. Here is a plain statement of fact:—To be a Christian we must have Christ's spirit or the Holy Spirit. How did we obtain the Holy Spirit? Let Peter answer that question for you in Acts 2:38. "And Peter said unto them, Repent ye, and be baptized every one of you in the name of Jesus Christ unto the remission of your sins and ye shall receive the gift of the Holy Spirit." So it follows we cannot be counted as children of God without first obtaining as a gift from God the Holy Spirit. And further, that we cannot continue in a life pleasing to God without the help of the Holy Spirit. Truly, how important does the Comforter become to man! 8:9b

g. Speaking of the Holy Spirit, Paul now brings to our minds that to have the personality of the Holy Spirit, is to have "Christ in us." When we examine ourselves in the light of God's Word we find ourselves to be temples of the Holy Spirit. We also find that although our physical bodies are the sanctuary of God's presence, they nevertheless must die because of Adam's sin. But our spirits will not die. No, they will live eternally with God because of the justification provided by Christ. We need not even despair of the loss of our physical bodies for "if the Spirit of him that raised up Jesus from the dead dwelleth in you, he that raised up Christ Jesus from the dead shall give life also to your mortal bodies through his spirit that

168. What strong reason is presented for following the spirit as in vs. 6?
169. Why is God so severe with some persons?
170. How does the Holy Spirit help us?
171. What is essential for one to possess in order to be a Christian?
172. How did we come into possession of this great essential?

dwelleth in you." This word of course points to that glad resurrection morning when he will fashion anew the body of our humiliation (Phil. 3:21). 8:10-11

Text

8:12-15. So then, brethren, we are debtors, not to the flesh, to live after the flesh: 13 for if ye live after the flesh, ye must die; but if by the Spirit ye put to death the deeds of the body, ye shall live. 14 For as many as are led by the Spirit of God, these are sons of God. 15 For ye received not the spirit of bondage again unto fear; but ye received the spirit of adoption, whereby we cry, Abba, Father.

REALIZING ROMANS, 8:12-15

338. We are indeed debtors to the lost world, (cf. 1:14,15) and also to the Holy Spirit. What is our debt and how shall we pay it?

339. There is a call upon us by one who claims we owe him something. Who is it and what is it? We *do not* owe him a thing— not one minute or one ounce of energy or one cent of money. We often pay what we do not owe.

340. To live after the flesh is to die. Explain this. Be specific.

341. By the help of the Holy Spirit we can put to death the deeds of the body. Explain how this takes place.

342. In what particular manner are we "led by the Spirit of God"?

343. Our sonship is revealed in what action? cf. vs. 14.

344. What "spirit" is discussed in vs. 15?

345. Where and when do we cry, "Father, father"?

Paraphrase

8:12-15. Well then, brethren, having such assistances, we are not constrained by the corruptions of our nature to live according to the flesh: we may overcome our evil inclinations.

13 Wherefore, I say a second time, if ye live according to the lusts of the flesh, ye shall die eternally; but if, through the Spirit of God, (ver. 9) ye put to death the lusts of the body by continually restraining them, ye shall live eternally with God.

14 Because, in every nation, as many as are habitually guided by the Spirit of God, these are the sons of God: they partake of his nature, and are heirs of immortality.

173. What are two present results of having Christ in us (8-10)?
174. What is a yet future result of having the Holy Spirit in us (8:11)?

15 That ye Romans are the sons of God, appears from your dispositions. For ye have not received the spirit of slaves again to serve God from fear; that disposition the law produces; but, through the discovery [revelation] of the mercy of God in the gospel, ye have received the spirit of children, by which in our prayers we call him Father, each in our own language.

Summary

We owe the flesh nothing, that we should live according to its evil inclinations. Besides, to live thus will end in death. But if by aid of the Holy Spirit we put an end to the deeds of the body, we shall live. As many, and no more, as are led by God's Spirit are his sons; and we have this Spirit, for we received it at our baptism; and in it we now cry to him, calling him Father.

Comment

2. New Life in Christ. 8:12-17

a. With the thought of our wonderful deliverance found in Christ comes the thought of the new life in Christ. What responsibilities do we have as we thus live? Our responsibilities are expressed here in the words of Paul: "We are debtors." To what are we debtors? We owe nothing to the flesh; we have died out to its bondage. We are debtors to the spirit. We know if we live out the desires of the flesh we will reap the penalty or wages of sin, which is *death*. But contrariwise, if we, although in the flesh, do not yield to Satan's efforts but rather "put to death," by the help of God's Spirit, the suggestions and actions of the flesh we can indeed live—live unto God. Thus our debt is paid to the spirit. 8:12-14

b. The result of such a life lived after the desires of God through the Spirit is to make us know that we are sons of God. There is no thought here of the Holy Spirit imparting knowledge apart from the word to enable man to be led by the Spirit. God leads us through his Spirit by the Spirit's word in the sacred scriptures, and by his Spirit's leading in providence. 8:14

c. The Spirit we received was not a spirit that would lead us into bondage, bringing fear of punishment upon our hearts, like the condition as found under the law, which did truly lead into bondage and fear. But the Holy Spirit is the sign of adoption. He is the "seal" (Eph. 1:13), the "earnest" or "down payment" (2 Cor. 1:22) of our

175. Why are we *not* debtors to the flesh to live after the flesh?
176. Compare the results of living after the flesh and after the spirit?
177. How are we led by the Holy Spirit?
178. Explain 8:15.

inheritance. Thus while letting the Holy Spirit have his way and living a life directed by the Spirit we can truly call out to God as Father. 8:15

Text

8:16-17. The Spirit himself beareth witness with our spirit, that we are children of God: 17 and if children, then heirs; heirs of God, and joint-heirs with Christ; if so be that we suffer with him, that we may be also glorified with him.

REALIZING ROMANS, 8:16, 17

346. Does the Holy Spirit tell us that we belong to God? Notice the use of the word "with" in vs. 16.
347. The child will have his father's inheritance. When God is the father and we are the children, what an inheritance it will be! Describe the inheritance.
348. If we are to enjoy along with Christ the wonders of the Father's house, we must also be willing to pay the price. What is it?
349. Define the word "glorified."

Paraphrase

8:16-17. Also the Spirit itself, bestowed on us in his extraordinary operations, beareth witness along with the filial dispositions of our own minds, that we are children of God.

17 And if children, then we are heirs; heirs, verily, of God, heirs of immortality and of the felicity of God's house, jointly with Christ; if we jointly suffer with him what afflictions God appoints, that also we may be jointly rewarded.

Summary

The Holy Spirit testifies with our spirit that we are children of God, and if children, then joint-heirs with Christ, provided we suffer with him.

Comment

d. The testimony of the Holy Spirit with our spirit affirms that we are the children of God (8:16). There are many and varied remarks upon this passage but those remarks which seem best to explain the witness of the Spirit with our spirit are as follows:

The Holy Spirit has spoken in the form of the written Word, which is his "testimony". He has told us what to do to become a Christian, or a child of God, and what to do to continue as a child of God. Please notice the all-important fact that the Holy Spirit and our spirit are said to stand side by side in voicing the testimony that we

179. How does the Holy Spirit bear witness with our spirit that we are children of God? Explain fully.

are children of God. The Holy Spirit has already given his testimony. Anyone who will comply with what he has said can become and stay a Christian. We come now to the testimony of our spirit. Can our spirits stand, as it were, alongside of the Holy Spirit and witness to the fact that we are God's children? This testimony could be given by our spirits, if we have done what the Holy Spirit commanded to become a Christian, and are now doing what the Holy Spirit asks to remain a Christian. Thus our spirits can testify "with the Holy Spirit that we are children of God", and the "Spirit himself" can bear witness "with" (not "to") our spirits, that we are children of God. 8:16

e. It follows then that if we are children of God we will surely inherit in the Father's family. Not only are we heirs of God, but having Jesus as our elder brother, we are joint heirs with him. The glories of our inheritance cannot be comprehended with mere mortal mind; only heaven itself will reveal the riches of the heirs of God and joint heirs with Christ Jesus.

There is yet one further word on this matter of inheritance. We can only be counted worthy of being glorified with Christ if we are also willing to suffer with and for him. 8:17

Text

8:18-25. For I reckon that the sufferings of this present time are not worthy to be compared with the glory which shall be revealed to us-ward. 19 For the earnest expectation of the creation waiteth for the revealing of the sons of God. 20 For the creation was subjected to vanity, not of its own will, but by reason of him who subjected it, in hope 21 that the creation itself also shall be delivered from the bondage of corruption into the liberty of the glory of the children of God. 22 For we know that the whole creation groaneth and travaileth in pain together until now. 23 And not only so, but ourselves also, who have the first-fruits of the Spirit, even we ourselves groan within ourselves, waiting for our adoption, to wit, the redemption of our body. 24 For in hope were we saved: but hope that is seen is not hope: for who hopeth for that which he seeth? 25 But if we hope for that which we see not, then do we with patience wait for it.

REALIZING ROMANS, 8:18-25

350. Paul knew something about suffering. Read II Cor. 11. List some of his sufferings.

351. The glory will be beyond compare. Do you think many believe this?

180. What must we endure if we are to be glorified with Christ?

352. The sufferings of this present time *are* compared with the total lack of any tangible evidence of God's glory in the lives of many people. As a result, they become bitter and cynical. Why?

353. How could "expectation" wait? cf. vs. 19.

354. What "creation" is referred to in vs. 19?

355. Are not the sons of God now known? Explain: "The revealing of the sons of God".

356. Is the "creation" of vs. 20 the same as in vs. 19?

357. Define the word "vanity" as here used.

358. Is verse 20 saying that the inanimate creation of God such as the vegetation is hoping and yearning for a deliverance? If so, explain.

359. Is "the liberty of the glory of the children of God" the same as "the revealing of the sons of God"? Now all of this might seem too hard for you, but it is not. It was written for you and me by the Holy Spirit through the Apostle. Do not depend on others. Find out for yourself. Read the verses again—and again.

360. Could it be that "the creation" is man, even as Jesus used the word when he said, "Preach the gospel to the whole creation"? In that case, how does that relate it to verse 23?

361. If our adoption is the redemption of our bodies (not our souls), this must have reference to a different redemption than we ordinarily consider. What is it?

362. In hope were we saved, and by hope we are saved full many a time. What hope is here referred to? Be specific here.

363. One day hope will be turned into reality. What part does patience play here?

Paraphrase

8:18-25. However, the thoughts of suffering with Christ need not terrify you. For I reckon, that the sufferings of the present time are not worthy to be compared with that glorious resurrection which is about to be revealed to the whole universe, in the persons of us the heirs thereof.

19 What a blessing a resurrection to immortality is, may be understood by this, That the earnest desire of mankind hath ever been to obtain that glorious endless life in the body, by which the sons of God shall be made known.

20 Nor is their expectation without foundation; for mankind were subjected to misery and death, nor by their own act, but by God, who, for the disobedience of the first man, hath subjected all his offspring to these evils:

21 In the resolution that, on account of the obedience of the second man, even the heathens themselves shall be set free from the bondage of the grave, and those who believe be brought into the full possession of the happiness which belongs to the children of God.

22 Besides, we know that every human creature hath groaned together under the miseries of life, and hath undergone together sharp pain, like that of child-bearing, till now, on account of their uncertainty with respect to a future state.

23 And not only do they groan under these evils, but ourselves also, who are the sons of God by faith in Christ, and who have the chief gifts of the Spirit as the earnest of eternal life, even we ourselves groan within ourselves, while we wait for that great event by which our sonship will be constituted and manifested, (ver. 19.), namely, the deliverance of our body from corruption, by raising it glorious and immortal.

24 The redemption of the body is not bestowed at present; for we are saved only in hope, that our faith and patience may be exercised. Now hope which hath obtained its object, is no longer hope; for what a man possesses, how also can he hope for it?

25 But if we hope for what we do not possess, we wait with patience for it, and so display our faith in the promises of God.

Summary

But the sufferings we are to undergo are not worthy to be named with the future glory which awaits us. So great is that glory that even creation, or as much of it as was affected by the fall, is waiting for and anxiously expecting the day when the children of God shall realize it. Creation was, by the curse, subjected to frailty much in the same way as man, and, like him, awaits deliverance from it. Under this curse, creation groans together and is in pain till now, and not only creation, but we too who have the earnest of the Spirit groan with it, while waiting for the deliverance of our bodies from the grave. In hope of this deliverance we were saved, and we are cherishing that hope still. Although we have not yet attained what we hope for, we are waiting in confidence that we shall attain it.

Comment

3. Encouragement to Endure Suffering. 8:18-39

The concluding words of Paul in verse 17 suggest the topic for this section.

a. The first encouragement is found in the realization that as trying as may seem the tribulations we are now undergoing, as much as we sometimes make of our ills and heartaches, that it is not even reasonable to think of comparing them with the glories of the world to come. If we attempted a comparison in order to ascertain whether the glories of heaven would recompense our sojourn amid "this vale of tears," the glories to come would so far outweigh "the sufferings of this present time" that there would really be no comparison. Paul ought to know for we believe he caught a glimpse of those things when he departed from his body and returned again (cp. 2 Cor. 12:1-6.). 8:18

(1) Concerning the event and the time of the event spoken of in verse 19: The greatness of this event can be appreciated when we realize that the very creation itself is waiting expectantly for "the revealing of the sons of God." There are many and detailed remarks upon the meaning of the term "creation." We take it to mean all that which was affected by Adam's sin, both animate and inanimate. The creation is personified in this passage and is pictured as a man earnestly waiting out the time until the sons of God will be revealed. What is the meaning of "revealing of the sons of God"? We know because of the context that it refers to the same time and event as "the glory which shall be revealed" spoken of in verse 18. The sons of God are spoken of as being concealed and awaiting a time when they shall be "revealed," and truly they are. There are literally thousands upon thousands who have departed this life and are thus concealed to us and the world. Those sons of God who are upon the earth are not now revealed in glory. The humble estate of the minority will in the resurrection day be changed to the proud state of the majority. 8:19

(2) The questions might be asked, "Why is the creation waiting in expectancy for the resurrection day? For what does it wait?" The whole creation waits to be "delivered from the bondage of corruption into the liberty of the glory of the children of God." (vs. 21). The creation did not come under this bondage of its own will (for it has no will), but was subjected to frailty and corruption through the sovereign will of him who subjected it, even God (vs. 20). But he did not thus place it in bondage with no hope of release, for even at the time of the curses pronounced upon earth (Gen. 3:17b), God was looking forward to his great plan for man's redemption, and the consequent resurrection of his children, and the deliverance of the creation from its frailties (Gen. 3:15). 8:20-21

(3) Again, speaking figuratively, Paul portrays both the animate

181. What is the subject of 8:18-39?
182. What is the first encouragement given?
183. What is the meaning of "creation" in verse 19?
184. To what event does "revealing of the sons of God" refer?
185. What can "creation" expect to receive in the resurrection day?

and the inanimate creation as groaning and travailing in pain as a woman with child, looking to that time when a new life will be brought forth. The thought of a "new heaven and a new earth wherein dwelleth righteousness" (2 Pet. 3:13) is herein suggested. The thought of a purified, renovated heaven and earth is at least intimated. It is not our purpose to discuss it pro or con; let it suffice to say that this thought is not unreasonable. 8:22

(4) Speaking of the expectation of the creation reminds the writer of the expectant longings of his own spirit, yes, the desire of every child of God: "And not only so, but ourselves also, who have the first fruits of the Spirit, even we ourselves groan within ourselves, waiting for our adoption, to wit, the redemption of our body." Even though we have the earnest payment on heaven with us, the Holy Spirit, we yet groan while waiting within this earthly tabernacle. Our groanings take the form of desires to be rid of this body of flesh which is subject to much suffering and temptation and to be adopted into that glorified family. This act of adoption into that new world will simply be the deliverance of our bodies from the grave on the resurrection day. 8:23

(5) We find the closely associated truth that all this revelation of the future glory was comprehended in our salvation. When we were converted we considered this fact; the hope spoken of was before us when we accepted Christ. This is true, but we must ever keep before us the true nature of hope. Hope is only hope when it is directed toward something as yet unseen. If the object of hope is seen then hope gives place to realization. We must not, as Christians, grow discouraged because we do not immediately possess heaven. But if we really have our hope set on our goal (firmly established because of the great and glorious reasons for hoping), then we can with patience and confidence wait for the fulfillment of our fondest hopes. 8:24-25

Text

8:26-27. And in like manner the Spirit also helpeth our infirmity: for we know not how to pray as we ought; but the Spirit himself maketh intercession for us with groanings which cannot be uttered; 27 and he that searcheth the hearts knoweth what is the mind of the Spirit, because he maketh intercession for the saints according to the will of God.

186. How is the creation in bondage today?
187. Discuss briefly 8:22.
188. What is the "adoption" spoken of in 8:23?
189. Explain 8:24-25 and tell what lesson is taught.

REALIZING ROMANS 8:26, 27

364. Our infirmities have been helped by what has preceded verses 26, 27. Explain.
365. We *do* know how to pray in some matters. How then are we to understand the expression in 26a?
366. I thought Christ was our only intercessor. How then can it be so said of the Spirit?
367. Who does the "groaning" as in vs. 26b?
368. Explain the word "uttered".
369. Please spend some time and thought and prayer on this passage. It is too important and helpful to give up. Who is the one who searches hearts?
370. How does knowing what is in the mind of the Spirit relate to the Spirit's intercessory work?
371. The intercession of the Spirit is limited to the will of God. Explain.

Paraphrase

8:26-27. And likewise, for your encouragement to suffer with Christ know that even the Spirit helpeth our weaknesses, by strengthening us to bear. For what we should pray for as we ought we do not know, being uncertain what is good for us; but the Spirit himself, who strengthens us, strongly complaineth [pleads] for us, by those inarticulate but submissive groanings which our distresses force from us.

27 And God, who searcheth the hearts of men, knoweth what the design of the Spirit is, in strengthening us to bear afflictions, that to God he complaineth [pleads] for the saints, by these submissive groanings, that he may deliver them when the end of their affliction is attained.

Summary

While in the flesh we are weak, and know not what we should pray for as we ought. But the Holy Spirit, which dwells in us, helps this weakness by interceding for us in inarticulate groanings. God who searches our hearts knows their true state. He also knows what the Spirit's mind is in these groanings, aware that the Spirit always pleads for his children as he wishes.

Comment

b. The Second Encouragement to Endure Suffering is found in the aid the Holy Spirit gives to the Christian. 8:26-27

The hope just expressed in the foregoing verses is a great help to the heart of the child of God. There is yet another help; it is that which is found through the personal contact of the Holy Spirit. For one example of the way the Spirit aids our weaknesses, we can consider his work in our prayers. We do not know many times how to pray as we ought. It is not that we do not know how to pray at all, but there are occasions when words fail us. We may have a great burden upon our hearts which we bring to God. Our spirits are drawn out to him in prayer. It is then that the Holy Spirit's ministry of help takes up its work. Our groanings and inarticulate sighs are directed by the Holy Spirit and have within them the real and right expression of our needs before God.

The Holy Spirit takes the message of these groanings before God for us. The way these petitions are borne to God is described in verse 27. "He (God) that searcheth the hearts (that is, the inmost being of man—his spirit) knoweth what is the mind of the Spirit, because he maketh intercession for the saints according to the will of God." Jehovah looks into the inner man, the abiding place of the Holy Spirit, and also looks into the mind or understanding of the Spirit. He there sees and understands the petition the Holy Spirit has helped to express, thus receiving the intercession of the Spirit on behalf of the saints. This is all according to the will of God, for the Holy Spirit would not inspire any message that was not in God's will. 8:26-27

Text

8:28-30. And we know that to them that love God all things work together for good, even to them that are called according to his purpose. 29 For whom he foreknew, he also foreordained to be conformed to the image of his Son, that he might be the firstborn among many brethren: 30 and whom he foreordained, them he also called: and whom he called, them he also justified: and whom he justified, them he also glorified.

REALIZING ROMANS, 8:28-30

372. Consider carefully that vs. 28 does *not* say that all things are good for the Christian. What is good?
373. If we do not love God, we cannot see the good. Is that the thought here?
374. Do "things" just "work out" by themselves?
375. When and by whom were we called?
376. Study very, very carefully the meaning of the word "purpose" in vs. 28. It is the key word.
377. Who is involved in the foreknowledge of God, as in verses 28a

190. What encouragement is found in 8:26-27?
191. Explain the Holy Spirit's intercession for us.

and 29a? Does this mean God has no foreknowledge of others? Are others in his purpose, too?

378. You have a dictionary. Look up the meaning of the word "fore-ordained." Note please the several synonyms given.

379. Christians are not foreordained to everything, but rather to one thing. Read verse 29b and determine what it is.

380. In verse 29b we learn Jesus is our "elder brother" in what respect?

381. Attempt to discover the position and progress of the expressions: "foreordained—called—justified—glorified." Relate them to your own salvation and hope. Show the progress in God's dealings with you. What happened first, second, etc., first from God's view, then from yours?

382. If we are already glorified in God's plan, could we ever be otherwise? In other words, does this verse teach eternal security?

Paraphrase

8:28-30. Besides, we patiently suffer, because we know, from God's love and from Christ's power, that all things, whether prosperous or adverse, co-operate for the salvation of them who love God, whether they be Jews or Gentiles, even to them who are called the children of God according to his purpose.

29 For those whom God foreknew were to be called his sons, he also predestinated to be conformed to the image of his Son, by having their minds adorned with his virtues, and their bodies fashioned like to his glorious body, that he might be the first-born of many brethren, the children of God.

30 Moreover, whom he predestinated to be conformed to the image of his Son, them he also called his sons, (ver. 28.): and whom he called his sons, them he also justified, by counting their faith for righteousness: and whom he justified, them he also glorified, by putting them in possession of the eternal inheritance.

Summary

All things work together for good to those that are called according to God's ancient purpose, to those that are called by the gospel. Those who would obey him, he predetermined to be, when raised from the dead, of like form with that of his Son. Those whom he predetermined, he also called; and those whom he called, he justified; and those whom he justified, he glorified. The perfection of God's ancient purpose, or plan, is evident.

Comment

c. Encouragement Number Three is found in consideration of God's eternal purpose for his children. 8:28-30

The encouraging words have all been addressed "to them that love God." We find now this word of conclusion, that "all things work together for good" to these persons. We know that all things which come into the experience of the Christian are not good. God in his infinite wisdom, however, by his everlasting love, works all things together in such a way that they will result in our good. This life may not even see the final good for the child of God (although many times it does), yet in the eternal realm we will know that God has kept his word. There is yet another descriptive comment to be made about those persons who are the objects of God's love. Not only do they "love God," but they are "called according to his purpose." This is the very reason why God works all things together for their good.

The phrase, "called according to his purpose," says Lard, is the clue to understanding all that is said in verses 28b-30. The one word "purpose" is the most important word of the whole section. We quote from Moses E. Lard concerning the meaning of this word. " 'Prothesis' here rendered 'purpose' is from 'protithimi,' which means 'to place out' or 'set before.' Accordingly, 'prothesis' means a placing or setting before. 'Purpose,' from the Latin 'propono,' 'to place before,' literally and exactly translates it. But 'prothesis' is not predicated of men, but of God, and it denotes not his physical act of placing things locally before or in front of him, but his act of placing them before his mind so as distinctly to see them. The placing is before his mind, and the seeing is mental seeing." Lard, p. 280.

When did this setting before his mind take place? The answer cannot be given as to the exact time, but we know it to be "before the foundation of the world" (Eph. 1:4), at some time before the material universe (including man) came into existence.

What was involved in this setting before? What was comprehended in it? Again we quote from Lard: ". . . . *man*, including this world with all that in any way pertains to it, from his conception on,

192. What encouragement is found in 8:28-30?
193. To whom is this encouragement directly addressed?
194. How do we harmonize this scripture with the fact that all things that come into a Christian's life are not good?
195. What special fact is stated about those that love God in addition to the fact that all things work together for good.)
196. What special key word opens our understanding to the verses 28b-30?
197. What does this word mean?
198. Whose purpose is here considered?

to say the least, until his glorification. Beyond this period, for the present, we need not attempt to look. God, as it were, set before him the whole human race with their entire destiny. All that man is or shall be stood before him—sin, redemption, glorification—all were naked and open to his eye. It was there that the Logos was foreordained before the foundation of the world (I Pe. 1:20) to be the lamb of God that takes away the sin of the world; and from that point forward he was ever viewed as slain. There the whole gospel was ideally perfected; in a word, the whole of time, with all that shall transpire in it, was in vision as completely before God as it will ever be in fact when it is past. To us this is utterly incomprehensible, and yet we cannot conceive how it could possibly have been otherwise. In that prothesis, accordingly, each man was as distinctly before God, as saved or lost, as he will be when the judgment is past, not because God decreed that this man should be saved and that one not, but because, leaving each absolutely free to choose his own destiny, he could and did as clearly foresee what that destiny would be, as though he himself had fixed it by unchangeable decree. To assume that God must foreordain what a man's destiny shall be, in order to foresee it, is a profound absurdity. He can as unerringly forecast the end of a perfectly free agent as he can that of a being to whom his decree has left no more of volition than belongs to the merest machine. Can any one be found so daring as to deny that he can do this?" Lard, pp. 280-281.

It yet remains to say that the calling of those who love God was accomplished even as Paul said elsewhere—"through the gospel." (II Thess. 3:13-14)

With these thoughts in mind, we can approach verse 29 with the preparation necessary to understanding.

"For whom he foreknew." The "fore" refers back to the thought that this is the reason we know all things work together for good. The sense in which God foreknew has already been stated: he did foreknow all things regarding the Christian from before his birth to his glorification. His foreknowledge had nothing to do with the choice of man. "He foresaw in the 'prothesis' that certain persons would, of their own choice, obey him or his Son.

199. What act of God does the word "purpose" here denote?
200. At what time did this act of "setting before" take place?
201. What was involved or comprehended in this "setting before"?
202. Is there any conflict between the thought of God's foreknowledge and man's free will?
203. What connection is there between foreknowledge and foreordination?
204. How is the calling of them that love God accomplished?
205. What is the only thing mentioned that God foreordained?

"He also foreordained to be conformed to the image of his Son."

There is no need to be alarmed at these words if we but remember that the conditions here spoken of were spoken of as if they had occurred long before they actually took place. So, to say that God foreordained or predetermined certain persons to be conformed to the image of his Son is to speak of the conclusion without comment as to what could have occurred between the time they were called and the day they were ushered into eternal presence. It is our conviction that God does not foreordain the life or actions of anyone. He foreknows, it is true, but the shaping of life is done by free choice in obedience to God's will. Because God foresaw that certain persons would of their own volition be faithful to him, he foreordained such individuals to be his. "In other words, their obedience was not determined by his act of predetermination; but his act of predetermination was determined by their voluntary act of obedience." Lard, p. 282

Please notice that the only thing God foreordained (according to the text) is that those "whom he foreknew" would "be conformed to the image of his Son." The words "to be conformed to the image of his Son" have reference to the resurrection day when we will indeed be transformed into his likeness. ". . . . who shall fashion anew the body of our humiliation, that it may be conformed to the body of his glory . . ." (Phil. 3:21) Since Jesus was the first to receive this resurrection body, and since he also is our elder brother, we can consider him "the first-born from among many brethren." We then can give him due honor and praise. As the elder brother, the first-born was to be honored by all others of the family; so is Jesus to be honored who will give us his likeness on the resurrection morn. 8:29

Still viewing the "prothesis" of God, we can say of those that have been predetermined that they were first called by the gospel, then through their surrender and obedience to Christ they were justified, and finally, viewing the matter as if it had already occurred, we could say, "Them he also glorified."

In conclusion we can say that the help given to the child of God which will enable him to bear up under any circumstance is found in the bold statement: "We *know* that to them that love God all things work together for good, even to them that are called according to his purpose." The reasons why we know then follow. We know because of the knowledge we have of God's eternal purpose or "prothesis." 8:28-30

206. To what does "conformed to the image of his Son" refer?
207. Name the steps to glorification as mentioned in these verses.
208. In conclusion, what reason is given to show that "to them that love God all things work together for good"?

Text

8:31-39. What then shall we say to these things? If God is for us, who is against us? 32 He that spared not his own Son, but delivered him up for us all, how shall he not also with him freely give us all things? 33 Who shall lay anything to the charge of God's elect? It is God that justifieth; 34 who is he that condemneth? It is Christ Jesus that died, yea rather, that was raised from the dead, who is at the right hand of God, who also maketh intercession for us. 35 Who shall separate us from the love of Christ? shall tribulation, or anguish, or persecution, or famine, or nakedness, or peril, or sword? 36 Even as it is wirtten,

For thy sake we are killed all the day long;
We were accounted as sheep for the slaughter.

37 Nay, in all these things we are more than conquerors through him that loved us. 38 For I am persuaded, that neither death, nor life, nor angels, nor principalities, nor things present, nor things to come, nor powers, 39 nor height, nor depth, nor any other creature, shall be able to separate us from the love of God, which is in Christ Jesus our Lord.

Realizing Romans, 8:31-39

383. "What shall we say to these things?" What "things"? Note the outline of the whole section.

384. We know who is against us, but in a very real sense no one is against us when God is for us. Explain.

385. We are encouraged to believe that God was and is not only concerned in our redemption but also in our preservation and perseverence. How is this so?

386. We know Satan and sinners will attempt to lay many things to our charge. How are we to understand vs. 33?

387. Christ at God's right hand as our intercessor shall "keep us saved." Explain. cf. vs. 34.

388. In verses 35-37 are we to understand that God sends "tribulation, anguish," etc? Is this a discussion of our love for God, or God's love for us?

389. How can we be "more than conquerors"?

390. What is the difference in the list in vs. 38, 39 from those of 35-37? Is the point the same in the conclusion as in 37 and 39?

Paraphrase

8:31-39. What shall we say then to these things, whereby believers are proved to be the sons and heirs of God?. Since God, who hath the whole power of this matter in his hand, is for us, since he sustains our claim to these honors, who can be against us?

32 He certainly who spared not his proper Son, but delivered him up to die for us all, for believers among the Gentiles as well as among the Jews, how, do ye think, will he not with him also gratuitously give us all the other blessings promised to the children of God?

33 At the judgment, who will bring an accusation against the elect of God? Since it is God who justifieth them by faith, neither angel nor man can frustrate his sentence.

34 Who is he who can condemn us believers? Since it is Christ who died to obtain pardon for us, or rather who hath risen from the dead to take possession of the government of the universe for our benefit; who is also at the right hand of God as ruler, and who maketh intercession for us.

35 Elated with our privileges, we cry out, Will any thing induce us to renounce our faith, and make us no longer the objects of Christ's love? will affliction in body, or distress in our affairs, or persecutions, or famine, or nakedness, or danger, or deadly weapons, be able to do this?

36 Sufferings have always been the lot of God's people: As it is written, Psal. xliv. 22. Truly for thy sake we are put to death in a lingering manner; we are accounted as sheep for the slaughter, by our persecutors.

37 These evils have not hitherto made us forfeit the love of Christ. Nay in all these things we do more than overcome, through the aid of him who hath loved us.

38 For I am persuaded, that neither the fears of death, nor the allurements of life, nor all the different orders of evil angels, against whom we fight, (Eph. vi. 12.) nor things present, nor things to come, whether good or evil,

39 Nor prosperity, nor adversity, nor anything else made by God, will be able to make us, the elect, (ver. 33) through apostasy, forfeit the love of God, which is bestowed on us, through Christ Jesus our Lord.

Summary

What now shall we say to these things? God is for us; no one then can successfully be against us. After giving his Son for us, he will withhold from us no other good. He will give us every good thing. No one can bring a charge against us, no one condemn us, for we have Christ to plead for us, and God to acquit us. Not only so, but nothing can separate us from God's love, neither persecution nor anything else, and although we may pass through sufferings, as we certainly shall, still over them all we shall be more than victors through Christ who gave himself for us.

Comment

d. Encouragement Number Four (which forms also a conclusion to what has been said). 9:31-39

"What shall we say to these things?" What things? Why, the hope of the Christian, the help of the Holy Spirit and the eternal purposes of Jehovah. There is only one thing to say, only one conclusion that can be drawn, and that is, "God is for us." When we consider our own hearts and then behold "all his benefits," we are moved to cry out, "God is love." Then follows the thought, "God is for us" —that is, all that can be done for frail man by a loving father has been and is being done. If that be so, then who is there who could successfully bring anything against us? This thought is based upon the truth of the superior strength and authority of Jehovah. If he is for us, then through him we can triumph over any adversary. 8:31

The conclusion here formed is to the effect that because of all the great and glorious benefits God has bestowed upon us we can be assured of our glorification (providing, of course, we are faithful). Verse 32 emphasizes this very point by bringing to our minds the greatest of our gifts from the hand of Jehovah—the gift of his son. If God was willing to give us his own son, will he now hesitate to add to this unspeakable gift "all things," that is, all and any of those things that would help us in attaining a life of approval before him? Is this not a great source of encouragement to the child of God? This encouragement is based on the hope of heaven even as was the first thought of this section, but it is approached from a different viewpoint. Section one discusses the glories of the new earth; this section discusses the basis for the certainty of our hope. 8:32

There are many things that might arise from time to time to cause us to wonder. There are those who will attempt to lay something to our account so as to prevent us from attaining our reward. But let us think a moment—if our hearts are right before God, if we are living a life of faithfulness, who will be able to "lay anything to the charge of God's elect?" If God through his son has pronounced us just, who could successfully condemn us? No one can, for if the supreme authority of right and wrong declares us right, then there can be no further appeal in the case. More than this, Christ Jesus has died; yes, rather it should be said that he arose from the dead and is

209. To what does the "these things" of 8:31 refer?
210. What is the only conclusion that can be drawn from "these things"?
211. Show how verse 32 is a great source of encouragement to the child of God.

now at the right hand of God, acting as our intercessor. What an array of encouragements as to the certainty of our glorification! Since the hope of the eternal inheritance is ours because of Christ's love, Paul thought it well to give the marvelous foregoing description of Christ's love. 8:33-34

Now follows a conclusion based upon the fact that Christ does love us. There are many circumstances which arise in the Christian's experience which must be explained in their relationship to the love of Christ. There is tribulation, anguish, persecution, famine, nakedness, peril and sword. When these things come upon us, what are we to say of the love of Christ? 8:35 Perhaps our sufferings could best be expressed by the words of the psalmist when he spoke of the children of Israel in Babylon (Psalms 44). They were God's children, and yet because of the very fact that they were his children they were being killed day by day as sheep in the shambles.

This is even our experience, for we indeed suffer many things. What then shall be our answer? Does Christ love us and still permit these things to so press us? Has he not somehow forgotten us? "No in all these things we are more than conquerors." How so? Ah, it is easy to see, for we not only overcome these things through the strength divine, but we actually use them to work out in our character those elements which enhance us in the sight of man and God (cf. 5:3-5). We are more than conquerors, for we not only can overcome our adversaries but can make them to fight on our side. The final note of victory will be struck when we one day pass from the presence of these earthly trials to be crowned above them in the presence of the one who loves us. 8:35-37

So we can indeed say with Paul that we are going to hold to our persuasion that God loves us in Christ, that nothing is going to separate us from this persuasion: neither death, nor life, nor angels, nor principalities, nor things present, nor things to come, nor powers, nor height, nor depth, nor any other creature. 8:38-39

212. Discuss briefly 8:33-34.
213. How do we reconcile the trials of a Christian with the love of Christ?
214. How are we more than conquerors over trials of faith?
215. Why did Paul believe that we should hold fast the thought that God loves us in Christ?

Rethinking in Outline Form

Complete Redemption Through the Proposition. 8:1-39

1. Freedom in the gospel. 8:1-11
   a. Freedom through "the law of the spirit of life in Christ Jesus", from the condemnation which was the penalty of our sin. 8:1-4
   b. Freedom from condemnation on that final day, for we are called to walk by the spirit and thus be led to our eternal home. 8:5-11

2. New Life in Christ. 8:12-17
   a. A new position—no longer in debt to sin. vs. 12
   b. A new power which will enable us to overcome and live in a new life. vs. 13
   c. A new father, and a new sense of our relationship to God. vs. 14-15
   d. A new witness, a new inheritance, if we suffer with him. vs. 16-17

3. Encouragements to Endure Suffering. 8:18-39
   a. We are greatly encouraged when we think "that the sufferings of this present life are not even worthy to be compared with the glory which shall be revealed to usward." vs. 18-25
   b. The second encouragement is found through the help of the Holy Spirit in our infirmities. vs. 26-27
   c. Encouragement number three is found in a consideration of God's eternal purpose for his children. vs. 28-30
   d. Encouragement number four forms also a conclusion to what has been said: "What shall we say to these things?" What things? Why, the hope of the Christian, the help of the Holy Spirit and the eternal purposes of Jehovah. There is only one thing to say, only one conclusion that can be drawn, and that is, "God is for us." He being for us, there is no one who can bring anything against us, no one or no circumstance that can separate us from God's love or can persuade us that God does not love us. vs. 31-39

Text

9:1-13. I say the truth in Christ, I lie not, my conscience bearing witness with me in the Holy Spirit, 2 that I have great sorrow and unceasing pain in my heart. 3 For I could wish that I myself were anathema from Christ for my brethrens' sake, my kinsmen according to the flesh: 4 who are Israelites; whose is the adoption, and the glory, and the covenants, and the giving of the law, and the service of God and the promises; 5 whose are the fathers, and of whom is Christ as concerning the flesh, who is over all, God blessed for ever. Amen.

6 But it is not as though the word of God hath come to nought. For they are not all Israel, that are of Israel: 7 neither, because they are Abraham's seed, are they all children: but, In Isaac shall thy seed be called. 8 That is, it is not the children of the flesh that are children of God; but the children of the promise are reckoned for a seed. 9 For this is a word of promise, According to this season will I come, and Sarah shall have a son. 10 And not only so; but Rebecca also having conceived by one, even by our father Isaac—11 for the children being not yet born, neither having done anything good or bad, that the purpose of God according to election might stand, not of works, but of him that calleth, 12 it was said unto her, The elder shall serve the younger. 13 Even as it is written, Jacob I loved, but Esau I hated.

REALIZING ROMANS, 9:1-13

391. We enter a new section here. Check carefully to see what it is.

392. Why is Paul so emphatic? Who needs convincing?

393. Why does Paul repeat himself? If he were telling the truth he would not be lying.

394. There is in vs. 1 a most wonderful truth concerning the work of the Holy Spirit and the human conscience. There is an inter-relationship. Explain what it is.

395. Paul had a true "burden for souls," a burden like our Savior's. Mark carefully the two characteristics as seen in vs. 2.

396. Do you know the meaning of the word "anathema"? To what does it here refer?

397. Would you be willing to make the same sacrifice for the salvation of sinners? Be careful: "Lie not."

398. Paul is now to describe the Jews as he did once before, (3:1-9a) this time for a somewhat different reason. What is it?

399. You will refer to the history of the Hebrews to know the meaning of some of these expressions. Give the meaning of the name "Israel."

400. When was the nation of Israel "adopted"?
401. Does "the glory" refer to any one time or place? If so, what?
402. Name three covenants given to the Jews.
403. Here seems to be an indication that the law was only given to Israel. Is this a fair conclusion?
404. What "service" is meant in vs. 4b?
405. Name three promises of God to Israel.
406. Paul wanted to lead his kinsman to Christ. This he did in his description of them. Why does Paul relate Christ to "the fathers"?
407. Who is here called "God blessed forever"? Is this a reference to God or Christ?
408. In what sense could some of the Jews say that "the word of God has come to nought"?
409. Verse 6b does appear contradictory. If being "of Israel" or a descendant of Jacob does not make one an Israelite, what would?
410. Did Abraham have other children besides those from Isaac? Who? What is the point?
411. There is a principle being developed here that is made to apply to the rejection of the Jews. What is it?
412. Was it arbitrary on God's part to choose Jacob instead of Esau before they were born? Explain. How can this be applied to accepting Christ?
413. In verse 11 the word "election" is troublesome only because we either make it say more than it should, or less. By God's grace and wisdom, (Jas. 1:5) cause it to say only what it should.
414. Could God "hate" a man before he was born? In what sense?

Paraphrase

9:1-13. I speak the truth in the presence of Christ, and do not lie, my conscience bearing me witness in the presence of the Holy Ghost, when I assure you,

2 That I have great grief and unceasing anguish in my heart, because the Jews are to be cast off, the temple is to be destroyed, and the nation to be driven out of Canaan.

3 For I myself could wish to be cut off from the church [people of God] instead of my brethren, my kinsmen by descent from Abraham; and therefore, in what I am going to write, I am not influenced by ill-will towards my nation.

4 They are the ancient people of God: theirs is the high title of God's sons, and the visible symbol of God's presence, and the two covenants, and the giving of the law, which, though a political law,

was dictated by God himself, and the tabernacle worship, formed according to a pattern showed to Moses, and the promises concerning the Christ.

5 Theirs are the fathers, Abraham, Isaac, and Jacob, persons eminent for piety, and high in favor with God; and from them the Christ descended according to his flesh, who is over all, God blessed for ever. Amen. The Jews, therefore, by their extraction and privileges, are a noble and highly favored people.

6 Now, it is not possible that the promise of God hath fallen to the ground; nor will it fall, though the Jews be cast off. For all who are descended of Israel, these are not Israel; they do not constitute the whole of the people of God.

7 Neither, because persons are of the seed of Abraham according to the flesh, are they all the children to whom the promises belong; otherwise Ishmael would not have been excluded from the covenant, (Gen. xvii. 20, 21) But God said, In Isaac shall thy seed be called:

8 That is, the children of Abraham by natural descent, these are not all the children of God, and heirs of Canaan of whom God spoke to Pharaoh, Exod. iv. 22: But only the children given to him by the promise are counted to him for seed.

9 Now, the word of promise was this: I will return to thee according to the time of life, and lo, Sarah thy wife shall have a son. Wherefore, Isaac is the only seed whom God acknowledged for his son and heir.

10 And not only was there that limitation of the seed to the promised son, but to prevent the Jews from thinking Ishmael was excluded on account of his character, when Rebecca also had conceived twins by the one son of Abraham, even by Isaac our father,

11 And these twins verily not being yet born, neither having done any good or evil, that the purpose of God, in making the one twin the root of his visible church rather than the other, might stand by an election, made, not on account of works, but from the mere pleasure of him who called Isaac the seed preferably to Ishmael, (see ver. 7.).

12 It was said to Rebecca, 'Two nations are in thy womb, and two manner of people shall be separated from thy bowels; and the one people shall be stronger than the other people, and the elder shall serve the younger.'

13 This election proceeded from God's own pleasure, as it is written, (Mal. i. 2,3.), I loved Jacob and I hated Esau, 'and laid his mountain waste.'

Summary

The Apostle solemnly declares that he speaks the truth in what he is going to say of his countrymen, his conscience being his witness. He has great grief and sorrow on their account, preferring that he himself be cut off from Christ rather than his kinsmen according to the flesh. Enumerating the things that distinguished them, the chief is that from them Christ came as to his flesh. But although the great body of Israel is cut off, God's word of promise respecting them has not failed. Some of them will be saved. His word of promise related to the true Israel only, and all are not true that are descended from Jacob. God counts only the children of promise as his. Accordingly, Isaac and his offspring were chosen, while Ishmael and his were rejected. This was also true in the case of Jacob and Esau. In these choices God was governed by reasons within himself, not by the acts of the persons chosen.

Comment

Proposition Reconciled with the Rejection of Israel. 9:1–11:36

1. Paul's interest in his own nation. 9:1-5

The introduction to this section is very beautiful in its approach to the subject. Lest some Jewish friend should judge Paul's motives in a wrong manner, the apostle introduces the subject in this way. He says in essence: "Perhaps you think that I take a certain delight in the lost estate of the Jewish nation; that when I realize that I am in Christ and thus saved, and you are out of Christ, and thus lost, that I glory a little in my position and gloat over your blindness. God forbid, this thought has never entered my mind. Such a motive is utterly false." He makes a strange assertion concerning his intense love for his "kinsmen according to the flesh." He declares: "As I am in Christ and thus bound to tell the truth, I lie not" (both a positive and negative assertion). My conscience is a witness to what I say. This conscience of mine which is educated by God and prompted by the Holy Spirit (cf. 2:15) commends what I say. I have great sorrow and unceasing pain in my heart for lost Israel. This concern of mine goes beyond mere feeling. I could wish and even pray that I myself were cut off from Christ for my brethren's sake, my kinsmen according to the flesh. If it were possible for me

216. What reason can we ascribe to the apostle for the way in which he has introduced the rejection of Israel?
217. What is strong about the assertion made in 9:1?
218. What type of sacrifice does Paul suggest he would willingly make for the salvation of Israel?

to take their place, and they mine, I would most gladly give myself for them."

When we understand this to be the exact expression of the apostle's heart, we are moved to realize that he, above all, would be loath to accept the conclusion from the gospel that Israel was rejected; but accept it he must, for God has declared it to be so.

As to Paul's estimation of Israel, though he had already spoken before (2:17-20), he again describes the glorious heritage of God's former children. Notice the list: (1) "Israelites," so called for Israel, whose name means "a prince who prevailed with God." They would be "princes who prevailed with God"—a proud name. (2) ". . . . whose is the adoption." That is, they were in times past the children of God by adoption. (3) ". . . . and the glory"—the "Shekinah" or glory of God's presence with them at the ark of the covenant. (4) ". . . . and the covenants." They had the benefits of all the agreements that Jehovah had made with his children from Noah to Christ. (5) ". . . . the giving of the law"—the magnificence of God's presence at the giving of the law, and their possession of the law. (6) ". . . . the service of God." All the beauties and meaning of the Levitical worship service was their peculiar right. (7) ". . . . and the promises." Those promises relating to Christ and the gospel. (8) ". . . . whose are the fathers"—that is, all of those great men of God: Abraham, Isaac, Jacob, Joseph, yes, and crowning the whole list, the Christ himself, for it was through the tribe of Judah that the Messiah came. The greatness of this one can break upon our understanding when we realize that he is "over all, God blessed forever. Amen." 9:1-5

2. Why God was Just in Rejecting Israel. 9:6-29

The Jew would naturally object to the idea of Israel being rejected, so the Holy Spirit, through Paul, presents and answers all such possible objections.

a. The first objection stated and answered. 9:6-13

(1) Objection stated. 9:6a "Why, Paul," some Jew is heard to say, "what you have just said regarding our position is exactly true, for it is thus found within the pages of God's holy Word. And yet, in view of all you have attributed to us, you have the audacity to say that we are rejected of God, that we are accursed. If then you are right, then the Word of God in which he describes the glories of Israel has come to nought. If Israel is rejected, then all that was said of them was said for nought." 6a

219. State from memory five of the eight attributes of Israel given in 9:4-5. Explain each in your own words.
220. Give the first objection of the Jew to his rejection.

(2) "Not at all," says the inspired writer, "for you have in your haste and pride forgotten one thing, one all-important truth: that 'they are not all Israel, that are of Israel.'" Paul here takes the construction that God places upon the word "Israel" and shows the Jew that outside of Christ he could not possibly be included in it. What did the Jew believe about Israel? Simply that all who were born from Israel were to be saved because they bore the name "Israelite". Now God had made certain promises to those of Israel just as he had to those of Abraham. But did he mean all those who were of the *flesh* of Israel or, of the *spirit* of Israel? To any thinking Jew it would immediately be apparent that it would necessitate more than mere fleshly descendancy to inherit in the Israel God spoke of in his promise. If then faith was the requirement for the promises made to Israel, then truly it could be said, "they are not all Israel that are of Israel" (i.e., of Jacob or his descendants). Who then is the Israel of God? It is not answered here (cf. Ga. 6:16); it is only inferred that the true Israel to obtain the promises of salvation were those in Christ. 9:6b

But this is not enough. There is further proof that God's word has not come to nought. In the Word we have the statement that the children of Abraham would be considered children of God. What did this mean? Did it mean that simply because you happened to be of the lineage of Abraham that you were thereby a child of God? Well, every Jew knew better than that, for they could remember Jehovah had said that only those who were in Isaac could enter the covenant of promise. Abraham had many children who were of his seed, but they were children of Ishmael. There was no one among the nation of Israel who did not know "It is not the children of the flesh (i.e., children of Abraham through Ishmael) that are children of God, but the children of the promise are reckoned for a seed." But how does this apply to the thought of salvation in Christ? The Jews would very easily see the apparent application, but perhaps we, who do not have their background, will need a few words of explanation. The hidden application of what has been said is found in the method of determining God's children. How was it accomplished in the experience of Abraham? We know simply by divine determination, ". . . . in Isaac shall thy seed be called." Why did God make this selection? It is not revealed, nor indeed is there a

221. How does the statement, "For they are not all Israel that are of Israel," answer the first objection?

222. How did the fact that only those of Isaac's seed were to be called children of God demonstrate that the word of God had not come to nought?

need for revealing. It was his choice; his choices are always good and never to be called in question by man. What he did then could he not also do now? Yes, he has, for he now as then demands more than mere fleshly descendancy. He demands that we be in the great son of Isaac—in Christ. Further describing this eternal decision, Paul says, "For this is a word of promise, 'According to this season will I come, and Sarah shall have a son'." To emphasize the divine choice, we might say that at almost the same time Isaac was born Ishmael was cast forth. We do not mean to suggest that God determined the eternal destiny of either Ishmael or Isaac. All that is said in Genesis relates only to the choice or selection of God. The lives of Isaac and Ishmael were determined by their own volition. 9:7-9

Not only in the case of Isaac do we see God's sovereign will being exercised, but it is equally manifested in the circumstances of the birth of Jacob and Esau. Shortly after Rebecca conceived by Isaac, the Lord said to her, "The elder shall serve the younger" (Gen. 25:23). This was done before the children were born, before either one of them did anything either good or bad. Why did God thus deal with this case? There can be only one answer, which is this: He did it so that man might understand that the reasons for making certain choices are wholly bound up in the mind of Jehovah and are not to be contested nor questioned by man. And that is the very point under discussion. The Jew felt the word of God had failed because God had spoken too highly of them, and yet he would not grant them salvation upon the basis of their high standing, but rather demanded that they accept Christ to be saved. Why did he do this? Paul answers, "He did it for the same reason he chose Jacob instead of Esau. The reason is in the eternal purpose of God. But are you, the Jews, going to reject it because you cannot understand it? If you are, why didn't you reject the decisions of Jehovah in respect to these other two cases?" Looking back upon the history of Jacob and Esau, we could sum it up in the words of the prophet (Mal. 1-2), "Jacob I loved, but Esau I hated." "The extent to which God loved Jacob was shown in preferring him to his brother; and the extent to which he hated Esau, in rejecting him from being one of the heads of his chosen people. The words used may have had different connotations then than what they have now. 'Hatred', especially, we may assume to be used in the bold, exaggerating sense so common with the prophets." Lard, pp. 302-303. 9:10-13

223. What does the case of Jacob and Esau emphasize in this section?
224. Explain in your own words in a short paragraph why the word of God did not fail in the case of Israel.

Rethinking in Outline Form

Proposition Reconciled with Rejection of Israel. 9:1—11:36

1. Paul's interest in his own nation. 9:1-5
   a. His love goes so far as to wish that he could be anathema from Christ if in being cut off they could be saved. vs. 1-3
   b. Paul is proud of the heritage of the Israelites, the most glorious portion of their heritage being the Messiah. vs. 4-5
2. Why God was just in rejecting Israel. 9:6-29
   Objection Stated: "If God has rejected Israel, then the word of God has failed." vs. 6a
   Objection Answered: 6b-13
   a. Not all are the Israel to which God promised eternal life that are of the nation of Israel. You have failed to understand God's word; it has not failed. 6b
   b. Neither will being Abraham's seed save you, for God promised that only in Isaac were the seed to be called children of God. Likewise, he has now determined that only those "in Christ," those of his seed, shall be called children of God. vs. 7-9
   c. Also God made choice in the case of Jacob and Esau. He thus manifested his sovereign power of choice. Just so he has determined of his own will that man shall be saved through his son, Jesus Christ vs. 10-13

Conclusion: The word of God has not failed, for the action of God in this case is perfectly consistent with his past actions, as we have illustrated.

Text

9:14-18. What shall we say then? Is there unrighteousness with God? God forbid. 15 For he saith to Moses, I will have mercy on whom I have mercy, and I will have compassion on whom I have compassion. 16 So then it is not of him that willeth, nor of him that runneth, but of God that hath mercy. 17 For the scripture saith unto Pharaoh, For this very purpose did I raise thee up, that I might show in thee my power, and that my name might be published abroad in all the earth. 18 So then he hath mercy on whom he will, and whom he will he hardeneth.

Realizing Romans, 9:14-18

415. To accuse God of arbitrariness is not new. The Jews did it long ago. See vs. 14. Just what type of arbitrariness was meant?
416. Look up the reference in Numbers in which God spoke to Moses. It will help you to understand the point of Paul.
417. Please remember the point in this section. What is it?

418. In what matters does the sovereignty of God operate? In all matters?
419. Man's will or efforts have nothing to do with God's decisions. Is this the teaching of vs. 16?
420. God raised up Pharaoh for a purpose. What was it? What was the point of this illustration as it applied to the saints in Rome?
421. Explain God's responsibility in the hardening of Pharaoh's heart. Explain Pharaoh's responsibility.

Paraphrase

9:14-18. What shall we say, then, concerning the election of Isaac preferably to Ishmael, and of Jacob preferably to Esau, to be the seed to whom the temporal promises were made? Is not injustice with God? By no means.

15 For, to show that God may bestow his favors on whom he pleases, he saith to Moses, I will be gracious to whom I will be gracious, and I will show mercy on whom I will show mercy. In conferring favors on nations, and in pardoning those who deserve destruction, I act according to my own pleasure.

16 So then, the election did not depend on Isaac, who willed to bless Esau, nor on Esau, who ran for venison, that his father might eat and bless him; but it depended on God, who may bestow his favors as he pleaseth.

17 Besides, the punishment of nations is sometimes deferred, to show more conspicuously the divine justice and power in their after punishment; for the scripture saith to Pharaoh, even for this same purpose I have raised thee and thy people to great celebrity, and have upheld you during the former plagues, that, in punishing you, I might show my power, and that my name, as the righteous Governor of the world, might be published through all the earth.

18 Well, then, from the election of Jacob, it appears that God bestows his favors on what nation he will; and from the destruction of Pharaoh and the Egyptians it appears, that whom he will he hardeneth, by enduring their wickedness with much long-suffering. ver. 22.

Summary

Is it not unjust in God to choose one and reject another, as in the case of Jacob and Esau? Not at all, for in doing so, he acts according to his own avowed principles of conduct, which must be assumed to be right. Accordingly, he said to Moses, "I will make my own sense of right my rule in showing mercy." It was on this principle that he set up Pharaoh to be king. But all these choices create mere worldly distinctions. They are not choices relating to eternal life.

Comment

b. The second objection stated and answered. 9:14-18

(1) Objection stated: 9:14a. We come now to a new thought. It is connected with what has been said, but it is yet another thought. Paul has answered the question found in verse 6 concerning the word of God coming to nought. His reply was based upon the sovereign will of God, and although it would in itself answer the objection about to be raised, the apostle nevertheless raises this question: "Is there unrighteousness with God?" From what has been said, could we not imagine that God was a little too arbitrary, and would not his actions injure our sense of justice? 9:14a

(2) Objection answered. 9:14b-18. "God forbid." Then follow the principle and illustration which most completely answer this objection. First we have the principle stated. God stated it to Moses when Moses desired to see Jehovah (Ex. 33). He let Moses know that it would make no difference as far as his decision was concerned that Moses wanted to see him since Moses had done nothing that would merit a viewing of God. But because of God's own choice, he decided to let Moses catch a glimpse of him. Notice, please, that the matters wherein these choices are made never involve salvation of a man's soul. When the eternal destiny of man is involved, God acts in accordance to the principles he has laid down for their salvation, and these principles have ever been the same: faith, repentance and obedience. Nevertheless, Jehovah chooses both the occasion and the object of mercy, and he is not regulated by anything external to him. Likewise the stronger element of compassion (mercy with the heart in it) is also shown to those persons chosen by God. I deem it imperative that we understand one principle right here, and that is that this free reign of God's mercy and compassion is all related as occurring in the Old Testament and must not be carried over into the New Testament dispensation. We find in the new covenant no such free reign of sovereign decision relating to that great host whom God calls to be his children. "God was free, but in his goodness he chose to provide salvation to those who would accept it on his conditions. Thus the Lord, being free, chose to be bound by his covenants and promises, even as the Lord Jesus, being rich, chose to be poor (2 Cor. 8:9). Paul proves God's past freedom;

225. State in your own words the second objection.
226. What was the principle stated in the case of the Moses which answered the objection?
227. In what matters does God make choices? In what matters is he regulated by his own covenant?

no one save the Jew of his day ever denied it; but to say that Paul establishes a present freedom and absolute sovereignty in God, which robs man of his freedom to do right or wrong, repent or continue in sin, accept Christ or reject him, etc., is to dynamite the gospel, and blast to shivers the entire rock of New Testament Scripture. Calvinism denies to God the possibility of making a covenant, or giving a promise, for each of these is a forfeiture of freedom, a limitation of liberty. According to Calvinism, God is absolutely free; according to the Scripture, he is free save where he has pledged himself to man in the gospel." McGarvey and Pendleton, p. 397. 9:14b-15

In conclusion concerning the exercise of God's power of choice, we have a negative statement with a positive conclusion: "So then it is not for him that willeth, nor of him that runneth, but of God that hath mercy." "It is not of him that willeth" means that the desires of man have nothing to do with the decisions of God. Man's will has everything to do with his salvation, but nothing to do with the eternal decisions of God's economy. "Nor of him that runneth" is another figure of speech describing the same thought, suggesting that man could not influence God any more than a runner who has won a race could influence the judges (Man does influence God in some things, but not in the subject discussed). In other words, the reasons for showing mercy by making a choice between Isaac and Ishmael, Jacob and Esau, are all of God, not through anything that either Isaac or Jacob did to influence God in his choice. 9:16

There is yet one more scriptural example of God's independent selection of men to occupy certain positions on earth. This had to do with his choice of Pharaoh. The choices we have discussed were confined to the Hebrew nation, but we now find an example of God's supreme authority in the life of a Gentile ruler. This would surely further strengthen the point under discussion that the Jew need not wonder that "it behooved the Christ to suffer" and that "by him everyone that believeth is justified from all things, from which he could not be justified by the law of Moses" (Acts 13:39). If God could and did make these inexplicable choices, and especially the one in respect to Pharaoh, if these were not questioned, then neither should his choice be questioned in respect to salvation in Christ. 9:17

We do not wish to appear to be reproducing the works of another, but the words of McGarvey and Pendleton (pages 398-401) speak

228. What one principle is of import in a discussion of this section? Prove the principle by examples.
229. What is the predominant difference between Calvinism and the Scripture?

so well upon these verses that we feel a reproduction of their words would greatly enhance this section. " 'For this very purpose did I raise thee up (cause thee to occupy a time and place which made thee conspicuous in sacred history), that I might show in thee my power, and that my name might be published abroad in all the earth.' (For the publishing of God's name, see Ex. 15:14-16; Josh. 2:9, 10; 9:9). The dispersion of the Jews and the spread of Christianity have kept God's name glorified in the history of Pharaoh to this day. Paul is still establishing by Scripture God's freedom of choice. He chose the unborn in preference to the born; he chose between unborn twins; he chose between the shepherd Moses and Pharaoh the king. In this last choice Moses was chosen as an object of mercy, and Pharaoh as a creature of wrath, but his latter choice in no way violates even man's sense of justice. Instead of raising up a weak and timid owner of the Hebrew slaves, God exalted Pharaoh, the stubborn, the fearless. And who would question God's right to do this? Having put Pharaoh in power, God so managed the contest with him that his stubbornness was fully developed and made manifest, and in overcoming his power and stubbornness through the weakness of Moses, God showed his power. The transaction is very complex. God starts by stating the determined nature of Pharaoh (Ex. 3:19) and follows the statement with the thrice-repeated promise, 'I will harden his heart' (Ex. 10:1). Thrice it is said that his 'heart was hardened as Jehovah had spoken' (Ex. 7:13; 8:19; 9:35). Once it reads that his 'heart was hardened, and he hearkened not unto them, as Jehovah had spoken' (Ex. 7:22). Five times we read that 'Jehovah hardened' his heart (Ex. 9:12; 10:20; 10:27; 11:10; 14:8). Thus thirteen times (with Ex. 8:15, fourteen times) Pharaoh's hardness of heart is said to be the act of God. (cf. Deut. 2:30; Josh. 11:20; Isa. 63:17; John 12:40; 9:39; Mark 4:12.) Inexorably so? By no means: God would have gotten honor had he relented before matters reached extremes. Hence Pharaoh is called upon to repent (Ex. 10:3), and several times he is near repenting, and might have done so had not God been too ready to show mercy (Ex. 8:28; 9:27; 10:24). So there was sin in Pharaoh. We read that his 'heart is stubborn' (Ex. 7:14); 'was stubborn' (Ex. 9:7). 'Pharaoh hardened his heart, and hearkened not unto them, as Jehovah had spoken' (Ex. 8:15). 'Pharaoh hardened his heart' (Ex. 8:32; I Sam. 6:6). 'Pharaoh sinned yet more, and hardened his heart' (Ex. 9:34). As the hardening

230. What is the meaning of 9:16?
231. In what sphere or in what realm were the choices of God confined?
232. Why would the example of Pharaoh be a particularly appropriate one to convince the Jew?

was the joint work of Pharaoh and God, and as Pharaoh sinned in hardening his heart, God's part in the hardening was not an absolute, overmastering act. It was not even a persuasive act, as in cases of conversion. God hardened Pharaoh's heart by providing opportunity and occasion, as the narrative shows, and Pharaoh did the rest by improving the opportunity in the service of the devil. The same act of patience, forbearance and mercy which softens one heart hardens another by delaying punishment, as we may see every day. The same sunshine that quickens the live seed rots the dead one. The Jews approved God's course toward Pharaoh, but resented the same treatment when turned upon themselves, ignoring the natural law that like causes produce like effects. God found Pharaoh hard and used him for his glory negatively. He found Israel hard and made the same negative use of them, causing the gospel to succeed without them, thus provoking them to jealousy. (Rom. 10:19) 'So then (see verse 16) he hath mercy on whom he will, and whom he will he hardeneth.' (This does not mean that God arbitrarily chooses the worst people upon whom to shower his mercies and chooses those who are trying hard to serve him and hardens them that he may punish them.) The point is that, in the absence of any promise or other self-imposed limitation, God is free to choose whom he will for what he will. As applicable to Paul's argument, it means that God's freedom of choice is not bound by man's judgment or estimation, for he may prefer the publican to the Pharisee (Luke 18:9-14) and may choose rather to be known as the friend of sinners than the companion of the rulers and chief priests, and he may elect the hedgerow Gentile to the exclusion of invited but indifferent Jews (Luke 14:23, 24). God is bound by his nature to choose justly and righteously, but all history shows that man cannot depend upon his sin-debased judgment when he attempts to specify what or whom God approves or rejects. Here we must be guided wholly by his word, and must also be prayerfully careful not to wrest it. In short, it is safer to say that God chooses absolutely, than to say that God chooses according to my judgment, for human judgment must rarely square with the divine mind. Had the Jew accepted Paul's proposi-

233. How did these choices relate to salvation in Christ?
234. How did God use Pharaoh to show in him His power and to publish abroad His name?
235. How was God's power evidenced in His dealing with Pharaoh?
236. Explain the thought of the hardening of Pharaoh's heart. What part did God have? What part did Pharaoh play?

tion, he might centuries ago have seen the obvious fact that God has chosen the Gentiles and rejected him; but, persisting in his erroneous theory that God's judgment and choice must follow his own petty notions and whims, he is blind to that liberty of God's of which the apostle wrote, and naturally—

"For, Och! mankind are unco weak,
an' little to be trusted;
If self the wavering balance shake,
It's rarely right adjusted!"

Text

9:19-29. Thou wilt say then unto me, Why doth he still find fault? For who withstandeth his will? 20 Nay but, O man, who art thou that repliest against God? Shall the thing formed say to him that formed it, Why didst thou make me thus? 21 Or hath not the potter a right over the clay, from the same lump to make one part a vessel unto honor, and another unto dishonor? 22 What if God, willing to show his wrath, and to make his power known, endured with much longsuffering vessels of wrath fitted unto destruction: 23 and that he might make known the riches of his glory upon vessels of mercy, which he afore prepared unto glory, 24 even us, whom he also called, not from the Jews only, but also from the Gentiles? 25 As he saith also in Hosea,

I will call that my people, which was not my people;
And her beloved, that was not beloved.

26 And it shall be, that in the place where it was said unto them,
Ye are not my people,
There shall they be called sons of the living God.

27 And Isaiah crieth concerning Israel, If the number of the children of Israel be as the sand of the sea, it is the remnant that shall be saved: 28 for the Lord will execute his word upon the earth, finishing it and cutting it short. 29 And, as Isaiah hath said before,

Except the Lord of Sabaoth had left us a seed,
We had become as Sodom, and had been made like unto Gomorrah.

237. What did the Jews accept in the case of Pharaoh that they resented in their own case?
238. Explain verse 18, paying special heed to the notes.

REALIZING ROMANS, 9:19-29

422. Who would express the thought of vs. 19?

423. If God is so powerful, why doesn't he destroy the Jews, or anyone else who opposes him? Is this the thought of vs. 19?

424. One of our greatest needs is to understand, with our hearts, the nature of God. Is this what Paul is saying in vs. 20?

425. How could the clay speak to the potter? Why then is the figure in vs. 20b used?

426. If God "makes us" honorable or dishonorable, are we responsible? Note please in answering this the meaning of "honorable."

427. What period of time and what event is referred to in vs. 22?

428. In the case cited in vs. 22, who was responsible for the condition of the vessels?

429. Does the foreknowledge of God relate to the reason for man's action?—i.e., does man act *because* God knows how he will act? Does God influence the actions of man? If so, in what way?

430. In what sense were Christians (saints in Rome) "afore prepared unto glory"?

431. How does God call out a people for his name? cf. vs. 24.

432. The quotations from the prophets prove two great points. What are the points they prove?

433. We become the people of God by a definite process. What is God's part? What is man's part?

434. Note carefully the words that discuss the beautiful relationship man has to God. cf. vs. 25, 26

435. Isaiah indicated how many Jews would be saved. How can we harmonize this with the thought, "All Israel shall be saved" in 11:25, 26?

436. In this difficult section remember that the Christians in Rome understood this letter. You are no different than they. Define vs. 28

437. What was "the seed" left by the Lord? cf. vs. 29

Paraphrase

9:19-29. But thou will reply to me, Since God is to cast off the Jews, why doth he still find fault? By destroying them, he might easily have put an end to their provocations. For who hath resisted his will?

20 Nay, but, O man, who art thou that arguest to the dishonor of God? Is it reasonable for the thing formed, who hath its being merely by the will and power of its maker, to say to him who made it, why hast thou made me thus?

21 To use the argument whereby God formerly illustrated his sovereignty in the disposal of nations, Jer. xviii. 6. Hath not the potter power over the clay, to make, of the same lump, one vessel fitted to an honorable use, and another to a meaner service?

22 Yet, not to rest the matter on God's sovereignty, if God, willing to show him wrath for the abuse of privileges bestowed, and to make known his power in the punishment of such wickedness, hath upheld, with much long-suffering, the Jews, who, because they are to be destroyed, may be called vessels of wrath fitted for destruction, where is the fault?

23 And what fault is there, if God hath long preserved these vessels of wrath for this other purpose; that he might make known the exceeding greatness of his goodness on the objects of his favor, whom, by his dealings with the Jews, he had before prepared for the honor of becoming his people?

24 Even us whom, instead of the Jews, he hath called his church and people, not only among the Jews, but also among the Gentiles, because we have believed the gospel.

25 This need not surprise the Jews: It is agreeable to what God saith by Hosea, 'I will have mercy on her that had not obtained mercy;' on the ten tribes whom I cast off for their idolatry: 'and I will say to them which were not my people, Thou art my people;' I will call the Gentiles my people.

26 The calling of the Gentiles is foretold by Hosea still more plainly: And it shall come to pass, that in the countries where it was said to the idolatrous Gentiles, Ye are not my people, there they shall be called the sons of the living God; the heirs of immortality, by believing the gospel.

27 Besides, the rejection of the Jews at this time is not more contrary to the promises, than the rejection of the ten tribes who were carried into captivity by the Assyrians, a rejection almost total; for Isaiah lamenteth concerning Israel, that 'though the number of the children of Israel,' who are carried away captives, 'be as the sand of the sea, only a remnant of them shall return.'

28 For, as the same prophet adds, ver. 22. finishing and executing speedily this rejection, according to the righteous threatening of God, certainly the Lord will make their rejection a speedy work upon the land of Israel.

29 And as Isaiah hath said before, (chap. 1:9), Unless the Lord of Hosts had left unto us a very small remnant of our nation, we should have become as Sodom; and been made like to Gomorrah, we should have been utterly destroyed as a nation.

Summary

But if God makes men what he pleases, why does he still find fault with them? He does not do so. He finds no fault with them for being what he makes them, but only for their own voluntary wrong. Again, in these choices, God's creatures should not presume to question him. They must take for granted that he acts justly. He has the absolute right to do what he does, and since he cannot do wrong, he must not be questioned.

But God, though determined to punish evil-doers in the end, has always borne long with them. Surely none can say this is unjust. He may do as he pleases. And that he might show the abundance of glory he has to bestow on those who prove themselves worthy of it, he called his disciples both from among the Jews and the Gentiles. He has thus shown himself perfectly impartial.

God did no injustice in choosing the Jews at first and in rejecting the Gentiles. Neither now does he do any injustice in choosing the Gentiles and rejecting the Jews. He has always intended to accept those who obeyed his Son, whether Jews or Gentiles, and to reject all the rest. This he long ago foretold both by Hosea and Isaiah.

Comment

c. Third Objection Stated and Answered. 9:19-29

(1) Objection Stated. 9:19. Paul is very patient with the prejudiced mind of the Jew. We find the apostle in the next verse inferring that the Jew would certainly place the wrong construction upon what he has just said. He has established the fact that in the Old Testament period God exercised his absolute sovereignty in certain worldly choices. Not one word was said about God's choices concerning eternal life, but from the questions of the Jew, "Why doth he still find fault? For who withstandeth his will?", we can see that the Jew supposed God's selections related to eternity as well as this world. 9:19

(2) The Holy Spirit did not even deem this position worthy of consideration. So repulsive was it when viewed in its true perspective that to offer an answer would have been to entertain a thought that was totally out of harmony with the position of man and the character of God. Indeed, it would have been even as Paul stated. It would present the awful spectacle of a mere creature of dust

239. What false construction was placed upon Paul's words by the Jews?
240. What was evidently the Holy Spirit's estimate of the third objection?
241. What illustration or analogy is used to show the absurdity of the objection?

arguing with the eternal Creator. The case is presented in the words of Isaiah (29:16; 45:9), "Shall the thing formed say to him that formed it, 'Why didst thou make me thus?' " 9:20

This idea of man criticizing God's choices is utterly preposterous. Even if he did foreordain or predetermine every soul by external acts for heaven or hell (which of course we know he didn't) we would have absolutely no right to question his justice. The relationship of man to God is as the potter to the clay: "Or hath not the potter a right over the clay, from the same lump to make one part a vessel unto honor, and another unto dishonor?" 9:21

To ascertain the meaning and extent of the words "honor" and "dishonor," all we have to do is to look back upon those vessels of honor, Isaac, Jacob, Moses, and realize that the honor was purely of this earth and had to do with God's choice of men who would be best suited to carry out God's purpose through his children *in the world.* The honor bestowed upon them by God had nothing to do with their eternal destinies. And those vessels of dishonor, Ishmael, Esau and Pharaoh, were dishonored in a way which is the exact opposite of the way the other three were honored. 9:21

Over against the facts just stated and in addition to them is the following thought: "What if God, willing to show his wrath, and to make his power known, endured with much longsuffering vessels of wrath fitted unto destruction: . . ." Paul now adds this thought: "You could not understand the selection of God in the cases just cited. Yet you agree to the justice in them. If you could not understand that, what will you say to the longsuffering of God with the sin of man? We all know that those who are wicked should be and will be punished, and Jehovah assents to this and is willing that it should be so. But are they who have fitted themselves for destruction, such as Pharaoh, punished immediately, or soon after their rejection of righteousness? We know that God is long suffering with them and withholds his punishment to the intent that they might repent (cf. 2:4-5). This is all true, we know, but *WHY?* Oh, they are speechless before the mercy of God—they have no answer. Well, how then can they be so egotistical as to question any of those decisions which are exclusively Jehovah's?" 9:22

Verse 23 presents a reason for the action described in verse 22. The purpose of God's longsuffering with the wicked is that in thus

242. What is the meaning of the words "honor" and "dishonor" in verse 21?
243. Explain the analogy of verses 21 and 22.
244. Explain how the riches of God's glory are shown in the lives of the saints by his long suffering with sinners.

acting he can manifest the "riches of his glory upon vessels of mercy." How can this be? It is easy to see that if the judgment of God fell immediately upon the wicked, there would be no time for them to repent, and thus would there be torn up some potential wheat along with the tares (Mt. 13:28-30). He withholds his judgment even as he states that he might make known the riches of his glory (referring to the eternal glory in contradistinction to "destruction") upon the vessels of mercy "which he afore prepared unto glory . . ." How was this accomplished? It was surely not done in an arbitrary way. We know this is true from what we have already studied on the subject. Then how? It seems to us that God long ago prepared (before the foundation of the world) a plan whereby man, if he were obedient to God's plan, could inherit heaven, that all those who were called by the gospel and were faithful to the plan of God were thus "afore prepared unto glory." 9:23

Now comes the out-and-out statement of what has formerly only been directly inferred. What has been the purpose in all that has been said in this chapter? Has it not been to demonstrate to the Jews the reasonableness of their rejection in relation to the economy of God? If then the Jew is rejected, who is accepted? The answer is: all those in Christ Jesus. Whom does that include? Here we have the answer: ". . . even us, whom he also called, not from the Jews only, but also from the Gentiles." The statement just quoted is the latter portion of the repudiation of the question in verse 19, but it also contains the conclusion to the whole matter. 9:24

Paul, having established the reasonableness of God's rejection of Israel, now quotes from the prophets to show that they looked forward to this very circumstance. The first quotation is found in Hosea 2:23. It says that the time is coming when those that are not now accounted people, i.e., the Gentiles, will be called and considered as God's people, and those which are not his beloved (the Gentiles again) will be then "beloved." Again another prophet is summoned to speak on behalf of this truth. Hear Isaiah as he speaks: "And it shall be, that in the place where it was said unto them, ye are not my people, there shall they be called sons of the living God." The place referred to simply means among the Gentiles generally. 9:25-26

245. Explain how the vessels of mercy were "afore prepared unto glory."
246. How does verse 24 form a conclusion to all that has been said in this chapter?
247. What do verses 25-26 add to the argument just given?

There are two great facts to be established in this section: (1) that the Gentiles are to become the children of God; (2) that only a remnant of the Jews will be saved or finally become the true children of God. The first point was well established by the whole discussion from 9:1-24. The quotations from the prophets corroborate it. The fact that only a remnant of Israel would be saved must have surely suggested itself to the mind of the thoughtful Jew; but now we find the full proof of this from their own prophet Isaiah. "And Isaiah crieth concerning Israel, If the number of the children of Israel be as the sand of the sea, it is the remnant that shall be saved." This prophecy is self-explanatory if we understand what has just been said. 9:27-28

The final word of Isaiah on the thought of a mere remnant being saved is found in Isaiah 1:9: "Except the Lord of Sabaoth (Lord of Hosts) had left us a seed (speaking prophetically of those Jews who would accept Christ) we (the nation of Israel) had become as Sodom and had been made like unto Gomorrah." That is, in the sight of God, if the small number of Jews that had accepted Christ would have failed to do so, God would have considered the Jews as extinct and condemned as Sodom and Gomorrah. What a need was there then and is there now for the nation of Israel to accept the Messiah! 9:29

Text

9:30-33. What shall we say then? That the Gentiles, who followed not after righteousness, attained to righteousness, even the righteousness which is of faith: 31 but Israel, following after a law of righteousness, did not arrive at that law. 32 Wherefore? Because they sought it not by faith, but as it were by works. They stumbled at the stone of stumbling; 33 even as it is written,

Behold, I lay in Zion a stone of stumbling and a rock of offence:
And he that believeth on him shall not be put to shame.

Realizing Romans, 9:30-33

438. Notice please that verses 30-33 are a conclusion to the section. The conclusion is easily understood. Reasoning from the conclusion, who would you say was responsible for the rejection of Israel?

439. Define the word "righteousness" as here used.

440. It is possible to seek to be righteous "by works" today? How?

441. Why was Jesus such a stone of stumbling to the Jews?

248. What are the two great facts to be established by the ninth chapter? What do verses 27-29 develop?

249. What two thoughts had been presented to the Jew that must surely convince him that God was just in rejecting Israel?

Paraphrase

9:30-33. What then do we infer from these prophecies? Why this: That the Gentiles, who being ignorant of the righteousness necessary to salvation, did not pursue righteousness, have obtained righteousness by embracing the gospel: not that righteousness which consists in a perfect obedience to law, but a righteousness of faith.

31 But the Jews, who endeavored to obtain righteousness by obedience to the law, have not obtained righteousness by obedience to law.

32 For what reason have they not obtained it? Because not by obedience to the law of faith, but verily by obedience to the law of Moses they pursued it; for they stumbled at the stumbling-stone, and fell: they refused to believe on a crucified Messiah, and were broken.

33 This happened according to what was foretold, Behold I place in Zion a stone of stumbling, and a rock of offence: Yet whosoever believeth on this crucified Christ, as a sure foundation of the temple of God, and rests his hope of righteousness on that foundation, shall not make haste out of the presence either of men or of God, as ashamed of believing on him.

Summary

The Gentiles, for some reason, were not seeking justification, yet they found it. Why? Because with glad hearts they received Christ in whom alone it is found. But Israel was seeking justification, and yet they did not find it. Why? Because they sought it not by belief in Christ, but by works of law, a way in which it can never be found.

Comment

3. Conclusion as to Why God Rejected Israel. 9:30-33

The inspired author has now shown that God, in rejecting the Jews and receiving the Gentiles, has not been unjust, but has acted on principles which the Jews themselves approved. Their prophets had spoken of this time; hence it should not surprise them. We find in the three closing verses of chapter nine the conclusion of the topic of the chapter. The conclusion is stated in a rather paradoxical form. Paul says in substance: "It is strange, isn't it, that the Gentiles who were not looking or searching for justification, found it, and you Jews who were diligently seeking for a means of justification failed in your search? Why was this so? It was simply because the Gentiles attained a righteousness of justification by faith, or through Christ;

250. Show in your own words the touching and tragic picture of Israel's rejection as presented in verses 30-33.

on the other hand, you Jewish brethren were seeking to be justified by works, the works of the law." As to what was included in the faith of the Gentiles, enough has already been said to let us know that it was inclusive of obedience to the gospel. In further description of the tragic state of Israel, we can say that they fulfilled the very words of the prophet (Is. 28:16) and stumbled at the stone of stumbling. They were bound and determined to find justification through the law—any other method would be haughtily rejected. Hence when Christ came and offered in fulfillment of God's plan, justification through his blood, they accomplished to the letter the words of Isaiah: "Behold I lay in Zion (amidst Israel) a stone of stumbling and a rock of offence; and he that believeth on him shall not be put to shame." 9:30-33

Rethinking in Outline Form

Objection Stated: "God is arbitrary and unrighteous." 9:14a.

Objection Answered: 9:14b-18.

    a. God forbid! The case of Moses indicates that God's choices are not influenced by man. 14b, 15.

    b. Man's willingness, or lack of it, have no influence on the mercy of God. 16.

    c. The example of Pharaoh; he was raised up to show God's power. 17, 18.

Objection Stated: "If God acts as he does in the cases of Moses and Pharaoh how can man be responsible?" 9:19.

Objection Answered: 9:20-29.

    a. You are the clay and have no right to question. 20.

    b. God, the potter, decides, not the clay. 21.

    c. God is very merciful when dealing with the sinfulness of men. 22.

    d. The purpose of his mercy is to give man an opportunity to decide which he will be, a vessel of mercy or of wrath. 23, 24.

    e. Hosea and Isaiah both support the answer of Paul. 25-29.

3. Conclusion as to why God rejected Israel. 9:30-33.

    The Jews failed to find righteousness because they looked in the wrong place. The Gentiles who were not looking for it found it. 30-33.

Text

10:1-13. Brethren, my heart's desire and my supplication to God
is for them, that they may be saved. 2 For I bear them witness that
they have a zeal for God, but not according to knowledge. 3 For
being ignorant of God's righteousness, and seeking to establish their
own, they did not subject themselves to the righteousness of God.
4 For Christ is the end of the law unto righteousness to every one
that believeth. 5 For Moses writeth that the man that doeth the
righteousness which is of the law shall live thereby. 6 But the righteousness which is of faith saith thus, Say not in thy heart, Who shall
ascend into heaven? (that is, to bring Christ down:) 7 or, who shall
descend into the abyss? (that is, to bring Christ up from the dead.)
8 But what saith it? The word is nigh thee, in thy mouth, and in thy
heart: that is, the word of faith, which we preach: 9 because if thou
shalt confess with thy mouth Jesus as Lord, and shalt believe in thy
heart that God raised him from the dead, thou shalt be saved: 10 for
with the heart man believeth unto righteousness; and with the mouth
confession is made unto salvation. 11 For the scripture saith, Whosoever believeth on him shall not be put to shame. 12 For there is
no distinction between Jew and Greek: for the same Lord is Lord of
all, and is rich unto all that call upon him: 13 for, Whosoever shall
call upon the name of the Lord shall be saved.

REALIZING ROMANS, 10:1-13

442. Is it right to pray for sinners? Does Paul do this in vs. 1?
Explain.
443. Being sincere is not enough. We must have a "plus factor."
What is it?
444. How did the Jews express their zeal for God?
445. In just what manner did the Jews attempt to establish their
own righteousness?
446. "Christ is the end of the law." What law? In what manner
is he "the end"? Show two or three ways.
447. A man could be justified by the law. Verse five so indicates.
Explain how.
448. Why would anyone ask that Christ be brought down from
heaven?
449. What is "the abyss" of vs. 7?
450. The righteousness of faith is as close as our heart and mouth.
Explain.
451. Verse nine contains a very positive unqualified statement. Can
we be saved by faith and confession without repentance or
baptism?

452. Would we be fair to emphasize the fact that faith and confession are "unto" salvation and not "into"? Be very careful here.
453. There is a rich blessing in vs. 11. Please, please, do *not* be superficial in your study of these verses. Give the meaning of this
verse.
454. In what sense is "there no distinction between Jew and Greek"?
455. On the day of Pentecost men called on the Lord and were
saved. (Acts 2:14-41) How shall we understand the words
"call" and saved"?

Paraphrase

10:1-13. Brethren, knowing the punishment which they shall suffer who reject Jesus, my earnest desire and prayer to God for Israel
is, that they may be saved from the sin of unbelief. See chap. xi. 26.

2 For I bear them witness, that they have a great zeal in matters of
religion: (see examples, Acts xxi. 27-31. ch. xxii. 3.) But their zeal
not being directed by knowledge, hath misled them.

3 Wherefore, being ignorant of the righteousness which God appointed at the fall, as the righteousness of sinners; and seeking to
establish their own righteousness, by observing the sacrifices, and
ceremonies, and other duties enjoined in the law of Moses, they have
not submitted to the righteousness of God's appointment by faith:

4 Although the believing on Christ as the Messiah is the end for
which the law was given, that righteousness might be counted to
every Jew who believeth.

5 For Moses thus describeth the righteousness which is by the law,
That the man who doth its statutes shall live by them. Now, that
kind of righteousness being impossible, the law obliges all to have
recourse to Christ for righteousness; ver. 4.

6 But the gospel, which enjoins the righteousness which is by
faith, to show that it is attainable, thus speaketh, Say not in thine
heart, who shall ascend into heaven? that is, to bring down Christ to
take possession of the kingdom, as if that were necessary to one's
believing on him.

7 Or who shall descend into the deep? that is, to bring again
Christ from among the dead, raised to life, as if the crucifixion of
Jesus had proved him an impostor.

8 But what does it say farther? Why this, The matter required of
thee by the gospel is nigh thee, and hath its seat in thy mouth, and in
thy heart: that is, the matter of faith which we preach, as the righteousness appointed by God, is nigh thee; is easily understood and attained.

9 For we preach, that if, notwithstanding the danger accompanying it, thou wilt before the world confess with thy mouth the Lord Jesus, as the seed in whom all nations are blessed, and, as the ground of that confession, wilt sincerely believe that God hath raised him from the dead, thou shalt be saved.

10 For with the heart we believe, so as to attain righteousness, and with the mouth we confess our belief in Christ, so as to have in ourselves a strong assurance of salvation.

11 That all who believe on Christ, and confess him, shall be saved, is certain: for the scripture saith, Whosoever believeth on the precious corner-stone, shall not make haste out of the presence of God or men, as ashamed.

12 Indeed, in the salvation of mankind, there is no distinction of Jew or Gentile; For the same Lord of all is rich in mercy towards all who call upon him. He will save not those only who believe on Jesus, but all in every nation who sincerely worship the true God.

13 For so the prophet Joel hath declared, chap. ii. 32. Whosoever will worship the true God sincerely, shall be saved.

Summary

Paul desires in heart, and prays for the salvation of Israel. He testifies to their zeal, but declares it to be not according to knowledge. Their zeal displayed itself in seeking to establish their own theory of justification, and a rejection of God's. There is no justification except to the believer in Christ. The justification of the law is shown to be impracticable. No insuperable difficulties must be surmounted in order to be justified by belief. On the contrary, its requirements are easy, and lie within reach of all. Belief and confession will secure it. There is no longer any difference between Jew and Greek in receiving God's favor. All may enjoy it on the same conditions.

4. Why Israel Was Rejected. 10:1-21

INTER-CONNECTING REMARKS

The unanswerable logic of the Holy Spirit through Paul has presented in the ninth chapter the fairness of God in rejecting Israel. The discussion of Israel's rejection as developed in the ninth chapter was "God-ward," an explanation of the reasonableness of *Jehovah's* actions in the case. The tenth chapter is likewise a presentation of God's rejection of Israel, but it is "man-ward," a discussion of *Israel's* part in the rejection. What did they have to do with God's decision to reject them? What were their actions in the circumstance? These questions are answered in the tenth chapter.

251. How are the ninth and tenth chapters alike, yet different?

a. They were rejected because they sought justification by another means than that provided by God. 10:1-5

This chapter begins very much as did the ninth. In the ninth chapter we find Paul strongly affirming his love for the Hebrew nation; it is likewise here. In speaking to the brethren at Rome he says: "Brethren, my heart's desire and my supplication to God for them (is) that they may be saved." The longing of his burdened heart and the prayer of his compassionate soul is for the salvation of Israel. One further admirable trait concerning Israel suggests itself, that "they have a zeal for God." Indeed they have, for an enormous amount of energy had been and still was being exerted in Paul's day by the Jews for their God. But alas, their holy ardor was misdirected, for it was not according to knowledge. Not that it was totally devoid of knowledge, but it lacked the greatest of all facts, that is, that Jesus of Nazareth was their Messiah and Savior. This knowledge relating to the Messiah found a consummation in the justification or "righteousness" provided by him. Thus were they "ignorant of God's righteousness." This would have been tragic enough, but they were not only blinded to God's, but what is far worse: "They sought to establish their own (method of righteousness)." Therefore, they would not submit to God's means of justification, since they were seeking through their own method to attain it. It is a law of universal application that as long as man feels self-sufficient he feels no need of help from God. 10:1-3

Christ was the very one sent to bring the law to its grand conclusion. The law pointed ever toward this one who would come to fulfill the law, nailing it to the cross (Col. 2:16-17). There were many things in which "the law was not perfect," so Christ came to "take it out of the way" and to supply a "new covenant" which would be "perfect." The imperfections of the law all had to do with its fundamental lack, which was its inability (because of the weakness of the flesh) to provide justification. Thus Christ came to fill up this lack and provide "righteousness" or justification, "to everyone that believeth." 10:4

252. State in one sentence the content of 10:1-5.
253. Did Paul pray for the salvation of the lost? If so, how did he think his prayer would be answered?
254. What is meant by the statement, "not according to knowledge"?
255. What twofold tragedy was enacted by the Jews in respect to righteouness?
256. How can we say that Christ is the "end of the law"?
257. What was the fundamental lack of the law?

The contrast of the two methods of justification is clearly brought out in verse five. Moses plainly stated the way in which a man could stand just before God through the law. The law demanded absolute obedience, so if one wanted justification by the law he would have to obey it to the letter. "Cursed is everyone that continueth not in all the things that are written in the book of the law to do them." Gal. 3:10, 10:5

If Israel were to escape rejection, they had to be justified by faith. What follows is an explanation of this method of justification.

b. Justification by Faith Explained. 10:6-13

The method of attaining justification by the law has been spoken of. There remains the method of justification by faith. How does it operate? How is justification obtained by this method?

Once again we find the apostle anticipating the thoughts of the Jewish mind on this subject. The method of justification by faith is personified, and is made to speak the mind of the Jewish critics. The one underlying difficulty of the Jew who in this section objected to justification by faith was that he wanted to dictate the terms of his belief; or better stated, he wanted to lay out the points of evidence which would constitute his basis for belief. These points are found in the sixth verse. He is heard to say, "If you will go up into heaven where you say Christ has ascended, and bring him down with you that I might see him, then I will believe." (This is very similar to what the same persons said at the foot of the cross. Matt. 27:39-42) Going to the other extreme, there were those who would better express the unbelief of the Jew by saying, "Go down into the abyss, (the place of departed spirits) and there having found this Christ, bring him up, and then we will believe on him." But all of this is an absurdity, for were it accomplished there would be no faith, but rather knowledge. Knowledge excludes faith, and we are discussing salvation by "faith" and not by "sight." It is not only absurd, but it is unnecessary, for all the evidence necessary to belief has been given. (cp. Jn. 20:30-31) There is no need to go to such great lengths in attaining salvation by faith. One need look no farther than his own mouth—than his own heart. This method of justification by faith is

258. What is described in verse 5? What is implied by this description?
259. What is the main thought of verses 6-13?
260. What was the one underlying difficulty suggested in verse 6?
261. Why was the thought of verses 6 and 7 an absurdity as well as unnecessary?
262. How does verse 8 develop the thought of verses 6 and 7?

attainable now. "How is that?" someone is heard to say. The answer is found in the meaning of the words, "in thy mouth and in thy heart," as they relate to justification. "Because if thou shalt confess with thy mouth Jesus as Lord and shalt believe in thy heart that God raised him from the dead, thou shalt be saved (or justified)." 10:6-9

The Jew wanted to make God's method of justification as difficult and complicated as was the method under the law, hence the suggestions just made. The apostle answers that nothing like this is demanded or at all needful, for what Moses said of "the commandment" (Deut. 30:41) can be applied to justification by faith. Restating what has been said by way of conclusion, we have the tenth verse: "For with the heart man believeth unto righteousness and with the mouth confession is made unto salvation (or justification)." This is a mere reiterating of two parts of the method of God for justification. It is not here to be concluded that these two conditions are all that is required by God for justification, for we find repentance and immersion likewise connected with salvation, remission of sins, justification (which are all synonyms expressing the same condition). Acts 2:38, 22:16; Mk. 16:16; I Pet. 3:21.

Verses eleven through thirteen give to the Jews the substantiation of the Old Testament of the method of justification just described. Verse eleven speaks from the Old Testament scriptures of the necessity of belief (Isa. 28:16). Verse twelve gives the real meaning to the word "whosoever" used by Isaiah in connection with belief. Paul says the word "whosoever" is to be understood in its broadest sense. In those that believe there is to be no distinction, neither in those who call upon the Lord. Then in verse thirteen we have the reference from the prophet Joel to the effect that this confession of Christ was to be enjoined upon all—"Whosoever shall call upon the name of the Lord shall be saved." (Joel 2:32). Why the apostle did not here connect repentance and baptism with salvation as well as faith and confession is probably found in the fact that the subject of a death to sin through repentance and a burial into Christ through baptism have already been discussed. (See comments on the sixth chapter.) 10:11-13

263. What did the Jew want to do with God's method of justification?
264. How is it that repentance and baptism are left out of the obtaining of justification in this place?
265. Give the content of verses 11 through 13.

Text

10:14-21. How then shall they call on him in whom they have not believed? and how shall they believe in him whom they have not heard? and how shall they hear without a preacher? 15 and how shall they preach, except they be sent? even as it is written, How beautiful are the feet of them that bring glad tidings of good things!

16 But they did not all hearken to the glad tidings. For Isaiah saith, Lord, who hath believed our report? 17 So belief cometh of hearing, and hearing by the word of Christ. 18 But I say, Did they not hear? Yea, verily,

Their sound went out into all the earth,
And their words unto the ends of the world.

19 But I say, Did Israel not know? First Moses saith,
I will provoke you to jealousy with that which is no nation,
With a nation void of understanding will I anger you.

20 And Isaiah is very bold, and saith,
I was found of them that sought me not;
I became manifest unto them that asked not of me.

21 But as to Israel he saith, All the day long did I spread out my hands unto a disobedient and gainsaying people.

REALIZING ROMANS, 10:14-21

456. Why is the need for a preacher now introduced into the discussion? Please connect this with the preceding verses.

457. How shall they preach except they be sent? Who is to send them? Answer from the context.

458. For those who sit in darkness and pain, the sound of the footfall of the doctor is indeed welcome. What comparison is made here? What shall we *do* about it?

459. Why did they not hearken to the glad tidings?

460. Why does Paul mention how faith is obtained? cf. vs. 17

461. Does verse 18 suggest that the gospel had been preached "unto the ends of the world"? If not, what does it say?

462. Paul is saying in vs. 19-21 that Israel did know, but what was it they knew?

463. Both Moses and Isaiah spoke of the salvation of the Gentiles; but more, they told of the effect it would have on the Jewish nation. What was that effect?

464. The cause and result of Israel's rejection are clearly seen in vs. 21. What are they?

Paraphrase

10:14-21. But in the passage just now quoted, Joel cannot be supposed to speak of the Gentiles. For how shall they worship the true God, in whom they have not believed? and how shall they believe in him, of whom they have never heard? and how shall they hear of him, without a preacher to declare him?

15 And how shall they preach God to the Gentiles, unless they be sent by him? which ought to have been done long ago, because such preachers would have been well received, as Isaiah insinuates, chap. lii. 7. saying, How beautiful are the feet of him that bringeth good tidings, that publisheth peace, that bringeth good tidings of good!

16 Nevertheless, that the preaching of the true God would have been acceptable to the Gentiles in former times, is not certain; since all of the Jews, to whom the preaching of the Messiah ought to have been acceptable, have not obeyed the good tidings; for Isaiah saith, Lord, who hath believed our report?

17 So then you acknowledge, that belief in the true God cometh from hearing concerning him; and this hearing, by the word or speech concerning God, uttered in some intelligible manner.

18 Be it so. But I ask, Have the Gentiles not heard concerning the true God? Yes, verily, they have all heard. For the Psalmist says, 'The heavens declare the glory of the Lord, etc. Their line is gone out through all the earth, and their words to the end of the world.'

19 But to the salvation of the Gentiles I object, that Israel, God's ancient church, hath not known any thing of that matter. If they are ignorant, it is their own fault. For, first, Moses saith, I will move you to jealousy by those who are not a people of God; by a foolish nation I will enrage you; namely, by granting salvation to the Gentiles.

20 Besides, Isaiah is very bold, in speaking of the calling of the Gentiles, when he saith, (ch. lxv. 1.), 'I am sought of them that ask not for me; I am found of them that sought me not. I said, Behold me, behold me, to a nation that was not called by my name.'

21 But concerning the Israelites he saith, I have spread out my hands all the day long, to a disobedient and rebelling people; I have long earnestly entreated that unbelieving and rebellious people to return: But to no purpose.

Summary

In order to call on the Lord, men must believe in him; in order to believe him, they must hear of him; in order to hear of him, he must be preached. But although all have not obeyed Christ who have heard of him, still the hearing is necessary, since by it belief comes. All Jews in Judea, and many Gentiles, at the time, had either heard of Christ or had the opportunity to do so, for the preachers of the gospel had offered it to them. Israel was ignorant of the fact of its rejection, notwithstanding the fact that both Moses and Isaiah had plainly foretold it.

Comment

The inspired author has just connected salvation with calling upon the name of the Lord, but as facts stood, vast multitudes of Gentiles and Jews had never called upon the name of the Lord. This was true for the simple reason that they did not believe in him. Indeed, this situation prompts the inevitable question: "How could they believe in him of whom they have never heard?" The answer is obvious—they could not; and yet the need can be met by the means God has provided—the preacher. They cannot believe without hearing, and they cannot hear without a preacher. The last question in this series of pointed questions bears the solution to all the needs. If the preacher is sent and he preaches Christ, then they will hear, then they will believe, then they will call upon the Lord, then they will be saved. Isaiah realized the terrible and yet beautiful import of sending forth the messengers of glad tidings. Note the words: ". . . and how shall they preach except they be sent? even as it is written, How beautiful are the feet of them that bring glad tidings of good things!" Indeed, the feet of those that carry the glad tidings of salvation are made beautiful by the news they bear. As it has already been stated, the preaching of the gospel bears in its train all the benefits of Christianity. 10:14-15

It would be well to call to mind at this point the outline and purpose of this chapter. The heading of the chapter is, "Why Israel was Rejected." It could be outlined as follows: (1) Verses 1 and 2 speak of Paul's earnest desire and prayer for the salvation of Israel. (2) Verses 3 and 4 tell us that Israel was rejected because they sought to establish their own method of justification, and in doing this they rejected God's method in Christ. (3) Verses 5-13 describe the two methods of justification: the one through the law, the other

266. What is the meaning of "calling upon the name of the Lord"?
267. What one thought is the answer to the needs spoken of in vs. 14a?
268. How are the feet of the preacher made beautiful?

through the gospel. The insufficiency of the one is shown in contrast to the all-sufficiency of the other. (4) Verses 14-15 offer an explanation and answer to the inquiry, "How shall they call on him in whom they have not believed?" (5) Finally, we have in verses 16-21 an objection respecting the gospel method of justification.

It might seem to some, thought Paul, that since there were so many who had not accepted the message, the fact of their rejection would cast reflection upon the truthfulness of the method. (Behind all of this discussion there was the answer of the apostle to the Jew's attempt to escape their rejection.) Indeed, "All have not hearkened unto the glad tidings." This in itself suggests that some did hearken. The fact that all who heard it did not hearken was spoken of in prophecy by Isaiah. This prophet, looking down the corridors of time, saw that all would not heed the glad tidings. (Isa. 53:1) Even if all have not believed the report, we can learn a lesson from the circumstance. We can learn of the method of obtaining faith. How were persons brought to belief? They were brought to believe by hearing the spoken word. "So belief cometh of hearing and hearing by the word of Christ." This, incidentally, destroys utterly the theory that faith is a gift of God separate from the Word. 10:16-17

In verse 18 Paul takes up the answer to the problem at hand. All did not (and do not now) believe, but is it because they did not hear? No, for they had in truth heard. The fulfillment of the psalmist's words—"Their sound went out into all the earth, And their words unto the ends of the world"—has taken place in the preaching of the gospel; yes, they had heard. v. 18. The reason why Israel was rejected even though they heard can be found in the fact that they failed to understand the word of their own prophets. When the message of the Messiah was preached they failed to see that Jesus was the Messiah described in their scriptures. One of their illustrious leaders had spoken of God's reception of the Gentiles and also of the consequent jealousy of the Jews (Deut. 30:14), but they had utterly failed to understand. Further than this, Isaiah was so bold as to say: ". . . I was found of them that sought me not; I became manifest unto them that asked not of me." vs. 20 (Isa. 65:1). But Israel missed entirely the meaning of these words. The same prophet spoke of God's great love for Israel as well as his tender efforts to

269. Give, in your own words, the outline of chapter 10.
270. What was the objection offered in verse 16?
271. What good lesson is taught in the fact that all did not believe?
272. What was the objection suggested by the fact that all did not believe? How is it answered here?

bring them the truth. Hear him: "But as to Israel he saith, All the day long did I spread out my hands unto a disobedient and gainsaying people." In the same phrase we have the underlying reason for Israel's rejection—disobedience to God's will and contradiction of his word. vs. 21. 10:18-21

Rethinking in Outline Form

4. Why Israel was rejected. 10:1-21.
   a. They were rejected because they sought justification by another means than that provided by God. 10:1-4.
   b. The two methods of justification explained. 5-13.
   c. How they shall call on him. 14, 15.
   d. Objection to the gospel method of justification. 16-21.

   Objection Stated: So few have accepted Jesus as Messiah, so he must not be the Messiah. 16.

   Objection Answered: Isaiah said few would accept. All heard and could believe but they chose not to do so. 17-21.

273. To what extent had the gospel been preached? cf. Col. 1:23.
274. Why was Israel rejected even though they heard? What two prophets are quoted?

Text

11:1-10. I say then, Did God cast off his people? God forbid. For I also am an Israelite, of the seed of Abraham, of the tribe of Benjamin. 2 God did not cast off his people which he foreknew. Or know ye not what the scripture saith of Elijah? how he pleadeth with God against Israel: 3 Lord, they have killed thy prophets, they have digged down thine altars; and I am left alone, and they seek my life. 4 But what saith the answer of God unto him? I have left for myself seven thousand men, who have not bowed the knee to Baal. 5 Even so then at this present time also there is a remnant according to the election of grace. 6 But if it is by grace, it is no more of works: Otherwise grace is no more grace. 7 What then? That which Israel seeketh for, that he obtained not; but the election obtained it, and the rest were hardened: 8 according as it is written, God gave them a spirit of stupor, eyes that they should not see, and ears that they should not hear, unto this very day. 9 And David saith,

Let their table be made a snare, and a trap,
And a stumblingblock, and a recompense unto them:
10 Let their eyes be darkened, that they may not see,
And bow thou down their back always.

Realizing Romans, 11:1-10

465. The question of the first verse is not easy to understand. God has cast off his people. The last chapter demonstrated that. Why, then, does Paul ask the question here? Note Paul's answer.

466. Paul was an Israelite, but was not cast off. What should this teach the Jews?

467. In what sense could we say God has *not* cast off his people?

468. How did the foreknowledge of God enter into his decision not to reject Israel entirely?

469. The attitude of Elijah was the same as someone else's. Who was it?

470. "The remnant according to the election of grace" refers to whom?

471. Who does the voting in this election?

472. The election of those among Israel was on a basis of God's choice and their faith. Explain how this shows the grace of God.

473. Verse seven is most difficult of understanding until it is related to the actual circumstances of the obtaining and rejecting of salvation by the Jews. Refer to an example in the book of Acts and explain.

474. Remember now as you attempt to understand verses 8-10 the example you have just worked out. "The spirit of stupor," "eyes that should not see," etc., are caused by God, but in what manner?

475. As best you can, explain the figure David uses. (vs. 9, 10)

Paraphrase

11:1-10. I ask then, Do you from these prophecies infer that God hath cast off his people for ever? By no means. For even I am one of the ancient people of God, a descendant of Abraham, and sprung of the tribe of Benjamin: Yet I am not cast off; I am still one of God's people, by believing in Christ.

2 God hath at no time cast off the whole of the Jewish nation whom he formerly chose. In the greatest national defections, there were always some who continued faithful to God. Know ye not what the scripture saith was spoken to Elijah, when he complained to God against the Israelites as having all followed idols, saying,

3 Lord, 'The children of Israel have forsaken thy covenant, thrown down thine altars, and slain thy prophets with the sword, and I, even I only, am left, and they seek my life to take it away.' I Kings xix:10.

4 Elijah imagined that the whole nation had been guilty of idolatry. But what saith the answer of God to him? I have left me seven thousand in Israel, all the knees which have not bowed unto Baal; I Kings xix. 18.

5 So then, even at this present time, there is a remnant, who, by believing on Jesus, continue to be the people of God still, according to an election by favor.

6 And if this election to be the church of God is by favor, it cannot have happened on account of works performed, otherwise favor is no more favor: but if it be on account of works meriting it, there is no more favor in it, otherwise work is no more work: it merits nothing.

7 What then is the sum of my discourse? Why this: The honor of continuing to be the people of God, which the Jewish nation earnestly seeketh, that it hath not obtained, having rejected Jesus; but the elected remnant hath obtained that honor, and the rest are blinded.

8 Blindness hath ever been the disease of the Jews, as appears from what is written: 'The Lord hath poured out upon you the spirit of deep sleep.'—'Hear ye indeed, but understand not; see ye indeed, but perceive not;' which stupidity and blindness hath continued with the Jews to this present day.

173

9 And to show the causes and consequences of that spiritual blindness, David saith of Messiah's enemies, 'Let their table become a snare to them, and that which should have been for their welfare, let it becomes a trap,' (Psal. lxix. 22.), and a stumbling-block, and a punishment to them.

10 'Let their eyes be darkened, that they see not, and make their loins continually to shake:' In consequence of their sensuality, their understanding shall be darkened, and as a punishment they shall be made slaves.

Summary

God has not wholly rejected Israel, as the case of Paul itself would prove. To suppose them wholly rejected is to repeat the error of Elijah. That prophet imagined that all God's prophets, except himself, had been killed. But God let him know that seven thousand still remained true to him. In like manner, there is now a large remnant of Israel who have not been rejected. This remnant is a chosen remnant, the choice proceeding from a principle of favor, and not from works or perfect obedience. Had the choice proceeded from perfect obedience, it could not have been from favor, for favor and perfect obedience mutually exclude each other. Israel sought to be retained as God's people, but failed through unbelief. The chosen, however, have been retained because they sought the honor by belief in Christ. The rejected Jews have grown hard in heart and feeling, as well as dull in perception—all of which has happened in accordance with predictions of their prophets.

Comment

5. This Rejection Neither Total Nor Final. 11:1-36
Introductory Remarks.

We come now to the final section in the study of God's rejection of Israel, and also to the closing chapter of the doctrinal portion of the book. The last two chapters have been concerned with but one subject: "the rejection of the Jews." In the eleventh chapter Paul is still discussing their rejection, but he here demonstrates that it was neither total nor final. This thought would help the Jews to realize that God had not rejected them unconditionally, nor was their rejection without hope of restoration.

a. Their Rejection Not Total. 11:1-10

275. What was the underlying reason for Israel's rejection?
276. What particular phase of Israel's rejection is discussed in the eleventh chapter?
277. What subject is discussed in the first ten verses of chapter 11?

(1) Reasons for concluding that their rejection was not total. vs. 1-5

In verse one the question is raised: "I say then, did God cast off his people?" That is, did God cast off his people en masse? Did he cast them from him as a nation? The answer comes immediately in the negative: "God forbid." This thought of total rejection is not to be entertained for a moment. One good reason for repudiating this idea is found in the fact that Paul was an Israelite. Indeed, he was of the seed of Abraham and of the tribe of Benjamin. Was Paul rejected? No, God had not rejected him; he had rather dealt with him in a special way. Jehovah had abundantly shown to Paul that he was in his favor. The conclusion then to Paul's case is that God has not cast off or rejected his people completely, for Paul could not have stood in God's favor if this were true. v. 1

The first part of verse two is the conclusion to the case of Paul. But what is the meaning of the words: "whom he foreknew"? We take the position that Paul is speaking of the nation of Israel, of the special favor they enjoyed, that of all the nations of the history God "knew" or recognized the Jews. In other words, we might say, "God has not rejected his people whom he has known for so long." He will not with one sweep of divine wrath reject the people he has known and loved over all these centuries. v. 2a

An illustration is now given of the true condition of Israel. Was it possible that God had totally forsaken Israel? That was what Elijah thought, for the scriptures tell us how he pleaded with God respecting Israel because they had killed all the prophets, they had "digged down thine altars". Elijah believed Israel to be forsaken of God. The only faithful one left in the nation was Elijah, and his life was in danger. But this complaint was made in ignorance, for the Lord made it known that there were yet seven thousand men who had not bowed the knee to Baal. The application of this illustration is made in verse five: "Even so then at this present time also there is a remnant according to the election of grace." In other words, although a vast segment of Israel was cast off through their rejection of Christ, yet there were those here and there who had accepted him, and together they served to make up "the remnant." This remnant is referred to as being "a remnant according to the election of grace." What is the import of this?

The same subject has appeared before in our study, and there we

278. What is the thought of the question raised in verse 1? How is it answered?
279. What is the meaning of the phrase "whom he foreknew"?
280. What illustration is given to answer the objection? How does it answer it?
281. Who is the remnant and how is it saved "according to the election of grace?

discovered that the election of certain individuals to become participators in God's grace was dependent upon their own choice, not upon the arbitrary election of God. So, then, we can say that this remnant was made up of those Jews who heard of "the grace of God" through Jesus Christ and chose to accept him. Thus they became God's remnant. God chose to elect all those who would choose to accept the grace extended through his son. vs. 2b-5

(2) The Reason for Their Rejection. 11:6-10

The words, "election of grace," suggest the thought that is developed in verses 6 through 10. Israel was rejected because they rejected the grace of God. Paul deems the thought of "election by grace" worthy of an extended explanation since this was the reason for the rejection of Israel. Notice his comments upon this subject.

(a) Acceptance by God is by grace; it cannot be by works, for works exclude grace, just as grace excludes works. vs. 6

(b) This acceptance Israel sought but did not find; the elect alone obtained acceptance. vs. 7a.

(c) All but the elect (those who chose the grace of God through Christ) "were hardened," even as it was prophesied: "God gave them a spirit of stupor, eyes that they should not see and ears that they should not hear unto this very day." David also spoke about this condition when he said: "Let their table be made a snare, and a trap, and a stumbling block, and a recompense unto them: and bow thou down their back always." vs. 7b-10

How were the rest hardened? One look at the occasion of hardening will answer this question. The statement is made that the elect obtained acceptance. How did they obtain it? By accepting Christ. And what happened to those who heard but did not accept? The answer in the words of the apostle was simply, "they were hardened." How did it come about? Through their own rejection, choosing rather to obey Satan and his suggestions than the grace of God.

But how can the words of the prophets be understood? "God gave them a spirit of stupor, eyes that they should not see, and ears that they should not hear." If we will keep before us the circumstances of this action, we will encounter little difficulty in understanding them. Let us remember that Paul was speaking of the Jewish rejection of the gospel and Jesus as the Messiah.

282. Why is the thought of "election by grace" discussed here?
283. Give two points in the discussion of salvation by grace.
284. How were "the rest hardened"?
285. How can it be said that "God gave them a spirit of stupor"?

When we consider the refusal of the Jews to accept the plain evidence before them, we can understand that the spirit of stupor was brought about by their own stubbornness, and not by an arbitrary act on the part of Jehovah. The spirit of stupor was the result of a continual refusal to heed the truth. As in the case of Pharaoh, God provided in his love the means of convincing man of the truth at hand, but man perverted these provisions and the result was even as Isaiah and David prophesied.

It has ever been the nature of God to give man abundant opportunity to do his will, but when man rejects this opportunity, then God cannot and will not project himself into the realm of man's free choice. Man is then left to receive the recompense of his wrong choice. David's descriptive words in verses 9 and 10 tell of the dire results of rejecting Christ. These words have had and are now having their fulfillment in the lives of the Jews who have rejected their Messiah.

Text

11:11-24. I say then, Did they stumble that they might fall? God forbid: but by their fall salvation is come unto the Gentiles, to provoke them to jealousy. 12 Now if their fall is the riches of the world, and their loss the riches of the Gentiles; how much more their fulness? 13 But I speak to you that are Gentiles. Inasmuch then as I am an apostle of Gentiles, I glorify my ministry; 14 if by any means I may provoke to jealousy them that are of my flesh, and may save some of them. 15 For if the casting away of them is the reconciling of the world, what shall the receiving of them be, but life from the dead? 16 And if the firstfruit is holy, so is the lump: and if the root is holy, so are the branches. 17 But if some of the branches were broken off, and thou, being a wild olive, was grafted in among them, and didst become partaker with them of the root of the fatness of the olive tree; 18 glory not over the branches: but if thou gloriest, it is not thou that bearest the root, but the root thee. 19 Thou wilt say then, Branches were broken off, that I might be grafted in. 20 Well; by their unbelief they were broken off, and thou standest by thy faith. Be not high-minded, but fear: 21 for if God spared not the natural branches, neither will he spare thee. 22 Behold then the goodness and severity of God: toward them that fell, severity; but toward thee, God's goodness, if thou continue in his goodness: otherwise thou also shalt be cut off. 23 And they also, if they continue not in their unbelief, shall be grafted in: for God is able to graft them in again. 24 For if thou wast cut out of that which is by nature a wild

286. Are there other cases of hardening besides the one referred to here?
287. Explain verses 9 and 10.

olive tree, and wast grafted contrary to nature into a good olive tree; how much more shall these, which are the natural branches, be grafted into their own olive tree?

Realizing Romans, 11:11-24

476. Paul says Israel did not stumble in order to fall. Explain.
477. Explain how the rejection of the gospel by the Jews opened a door to the Gentiles. Use a scriptural example.
478. Is God here spoken of as being responsible for producing jealousy? Explain.
479. "The riches of the world"—Explain "riches" and "world."
480. Are "the riches of the Gentiles" and "the riches of the world" the same thing?
481. Please do not grow discouraged in the midst of this difficult section. Remember, there is always more of each section that you do understand than that which you do not. Emphasize that which you *do* know. Attempt an explanation of "the fullness" of the Jews.
482. Paul's ministry to the Gentiles was glorified in what act?
483. If a Jew was "provoked to jealousy," just what would his attitude be toward his own nation? toward the Gentiles?
484. Does Paul suggest in vs. 15 that one day there shall be a great turning to Christ among the Jews?
485. Who or what is "the first fruit" and "the lump"?
486. The root and branches are the same in thought as the first fruit and the lump. Do you agree?
487. It is not at all difficult to determine who "the branches" are of vs. 17. The problem is, who or what is "the olive tree"? What is your explanation?
488. How could the Gentiles "glory over" the Jews? How could they overcome glorying?
489. The power of faith is here seen. What is it?
490. In what sense did God "not spare" the Jews?
491. God's severity is surely tempered with mercy. Explain.
492. The grafting-in process is accomplished by both man and God. Explain each one's part.
493. It would be easier for a Jew to become a Christian than for a Gentile. Explain.

Paraphrase

11:11-24. By applying these prophecies to the Jews, you represent them as in a state of utter rejection. I ask, therefore, Have they stumbled so as to fall for ever? By no means; but through their fall salvation is given to the Gentiles, to excite the Jews to emulation, that by believing they may obtain the same privilege.

12 Now, if the destruction of the Jewish church be the enriching both of the Jews and Gentiles, by making room for the gospel church, and if the stripping of the Jews of their privileges be the occasion of conferring these privileges on the Gentiles, how much more will their filling the church be followed with great advantages to the Gentiles?

13 Now the rejection of the Jews, and the happiness of the Gentiles in their restoration, I make known to you Gentiles; and in as much as I am the apostle of the Gentiles, by proving these great secrets from the Jewish scriptures, I do honor to my ministry;

14 If by any means I may excite to emulation those of my nation, and may save some of them, by persuading them to enter into the church.

15 This I desire also for the sake of the Gentiles: Because, if the casting away of the Jews be the occasion of reconciling the Gentiles, what must the resumption of them be, but life from the dead? It will occasion a revival of religion, after a great decay.

16 Their conversion will be pleasing to God: For if the first Jewish believers have been accepted of God, the whole nation will be so through their faith.

17 Now, if many of Abraham's children were cast out of the covenant for their unbelief, and thou who art a Gentile, art, on thy believing the gospel, ingrafted instead of them, and, though unfit for such a favor, art become a joint partaker with the believing Jews of all the privileges of God's covenant and church;

18 Do not speak contemptuously of the broken off branches, as thinking thyself more excellent and more in favor with God than they: For if thou dost, know that thou bearest not the root, but the root thee.

19 Thou wilt say, however, the natural branches were broken off, that we Gentiles might be admitted into the covenant and church of God.

20 True; By unbelief they were broken off, and thou by faith standeth in their place. Do not think highly of thyself, as more favored of God than they. But be afraid, lest through pride thou also be broken off.

21 For if God spared not the natural members of his covenant, but cut them off for their unbelief, perhaps he will as little spare thee, if thou behavest unsuitably to thy privileges.

22 Admire then both the goodness and severity of God: towards the Jews, who are cast out of his covenant, severity; but towards the

Gentiles, whom God hath admitted into his covenant, goodness; if thou continuest in the state wherein his goodness hath placed thee, by improving thy advantages, otherwise thou also shalt be cut off.

23 And even the Jews, when they abide not in unbelief, shall be brought again into the church of God: for God is able and willing to unite them again to his church, on their believing the gospel.

24 For if thou wert separated from thine idolatrous countrymen, and, contrary to thy nature, which was full of ignorance and wickedness, wert made a member of the covenant with Abraham, how much rather shall the Jews, who are the natural members of that covenant, be restored again to their own honors and privileges, by believing the gospel, which is the accomplishment of the ancient revelations made to themselves?

Summary

The Jews stumbled at Christ. Did they stumble merely that they might fall? Certainly not. Rather, they stumbled that thereby they might contribute to the salvation of the Gentiles. If now their fall proves advantageous to the Gentiles, their reception back into the divine favor will prove still more so. This implies that they may be again received. And why not? The first converts from them were accepted. Surely then all will be received when they become converted. The Jews were rejected because of unbelief. Let them then but believe, and they will be accepted. And you, Gentiles, stand by belief. Do not grow proud and over-confident. For if God spared not the Jews when they did wrong, neither will he spare you. Towards the Jews, God has been severe in cutting them off; towards you he has been kind. Be careful now to deserve a continuance of his kindness. If not, you too will be rejected as the Jews have been.

Comment

b. Their Rejection Not Final. 11:11-24

This section opens with a question, the meaning of which is not immediately apparent. The fall of the nation of Israel prompts the one last inquiry: "Did they stumble that they might fall?" The Israelites had as a whole stumbled over Christ. What Paul is asking here is: "Was it the intention of God to place this stumbling block in their path with the express purpose of causing them to be eternally lost?" In other words: "Was their stumbling of such a nature as to cause them to be forever without hope?" "Nay," replies the apostle. Then follow in close succession two reasons for denying this thought. (1) It was not God's purpose that in the stumbling of the

288. Give in your own words the meaning of the question in 11:11.

Jews they be without hope, but rather that in this way he might give opportunity to the Gentiles to be saved. It is wonderful to observe from time to time as we read the Word, the way the Father makes use of Satan's efforts and apparent victories to finally bring glory to his eternal name. If the Jews must reject Christ, then God will make out of it, not a means of bringing his vengeance upon his people, but rather of offering salvation directly to the Gentiles instead of through the Jews as he originally planned. (2) They did not stumble and fall in such a way as to be eternally lost, however. One day when they opened their blinded eyes to the purpose of God among the Gentiles, and were caused to think how God would so work among the Gentiles who were in times past "no people," they would see that he would certainly work among those who had been his people, providing of course they accepted Jesus as Messiah, the source of God's blessing among the Gentiles. v. 11.

Verse 12a develops the thought suggested in 11b. In verse 11 Paul has said that through the fall of Israel salvation was given to the Gentiles. Now in 12a he describes this salvation as: the "riches of the world" and "riches of the Gentiles." These riches were given because of, or through the "loss" or "fall" of Israel. How so? A clear case of this very thought is found in Acts 13:44-48. The Jews of Antioch of Pisidia were offered the riches of the gospel of Christ, but they refused it; they stumbled over it. Then it was that Paul said, "Lo, we turn to the Gentiles . . . And as the Gentiles heard this, they were glad and glorified God; and as many as were ordained to eternal life believed." Thus did the fall of the Jews become the riches of the Gentiles. Thus did the stumbling of the Jew become the riches of the world. It was necessary first that the gospel be carried to the Jews. If they had received it, they would have carried it to the Gentile world; but since they refused even the message, it was given to the Gentiles directly through the apostles. vs. 12a.

In verse 12b we have the positive side of this two-sided truth. The thought is this: although some Gentiles were blessed with the riches of the gospel as a result of the fall of the Jews, how much more will they (the Gentiles) be blessed in "the fullness" of the Jews. We take this thought of fullness to mean the turning of the Jews to Christ, that when the Jews finally do turn to Christ in great numbers, then the Gentile world will be blessed even more in the

289. What is the twofold answer to this question? Show the great wisdom of God in it all.
290. What is meant by "provoke them to jealousy"?
291. What is the meaning of the phrase, "the riches of the world"?
292. Give an example of the "fall and loss" of the Jews and the meaning of "their fullness". Explain in your own words.

riches of salvation than they were when the nation first rejected Christ. The Jews will one day be the evangels of the cross and cause such a stir among the world as it has never known. Now this might appear to be a rather fanciful interpretation if we did not have Paul's own explanation of this very matter in the 15th verse. In this verse he explains verse 12b. Verses 13 and 14 are parenthetical in thought and contain a personal word of admonition to the Gentile readers to give heed to what Paul is saying. As he says, he was an apostle to the Gentiles, and in saying the things that he has just said and is about to say he glorifies (the purpose of) his ministry. He further says in this interposed thought that he is only saying these things that he might arouse in his brethren, the Jews, a godly jealousy so that they will desire and accept salvation in Christ. Now back to the thought broken by these words: Paul has just said that the Gentiles were blessed richly by the loss of the Jews, but he says this first blessing will not in anywise compare with the great blessing to be received when they finally lift the veil from their eyes and accept Christ. Now he states in verse 15 the same thought in other words: "For if the casting away of them is the reconciling of the world (referring of course to the reconciliation that is to be found for the whole world in Christ) what shall the receiving of them be but life from the dead." Here we see that they who were once cast away will one day be received. How were they "cast away"? By their own willful rejection. How will they be received? In the same manner: by their own choice. And Paul says that this will be to the Gentile world like a resurrection. The power of God throughout the world will be so strong at this time that it will be as if God had caused a resurrection to occur over the land. In this case a resurrection of righteousness will occur in the conversion of the Gentiles. In verse 16 we have two similes which present pictures of the coming of the Jews to Christ. The first one is in the form of the familiar "first fruits" offering. It doubtless has reference to the example of Numbers 25:20. The harvest was gathered and the flour ground; then a general mass of dough was formed which must be consecrated before it was used. A portion of it was taken and baked into a small cake. This was offered to the Lord. In this way the Jews were saying that all belonged to God even as did the representative small portion. Who in this analogy would represent the first portion? Before answering remember that the apostle is discussing

293. Compare verses 12 and 15.
294. What relationship do verses 13-14 have to verses 12 and 15?
295. What is meant by "life from the dead"? cf. Rev. 20:5-6.
296. What is the purpose of the two metaphors in verse 16?

the general turning of the Jews to Jesus as the Messiah. Therefore, I believe that the first portion, or "first fruits" were those few Jews in Paul's day who had accepted Christ. Because they had, they testified that all could if they would. And then looking back to the thought that the rejection of Israel was not final, we can see in this a picture of God's estimation of Israel. He looks upon them as "holy," not in the sense that they were saved, but his heart went out to them for all that they had been to him, and for what they could be to him if they would but accept his Son. Israel is not without hope; they will one day return, and even now God looks upon them as objects of his love. vs. 16. As to the meaning of the second picture, we quote from Moses E. Lard, page 360: "The same sentiment is reiterated, with the imagery changed. The root corresponds to the first Jewish converts, the branches to the rejected nation. Assuming the root of a tree to be holy, we naturally infer holiness of its branches. Such is the argument. The word "holy" has here the same meaning as in the preceding clause. If God has accepted the root, or first converts from the Jews, he will accept the whole nation when converted. Such is the import of the passage. It is a short, striking metaphor, with a perfectly clear meaning." Who were the branches in the last metaphor? Yes, the Jews. In verse 17 we have the statement that some of these branches were "broken off." This plainly speaks of the rejection of Christ among Israel. By that rejection they were "broken off." We do not maintain that these metaphor in verses 16 and 17 are connected in any other sense. There is no need to carry the application of these simple pictures any farther than the apostle does. He simple states that some of the branches were "broken off"; he does not allude to the tree. He places no emphasis upon the tree; why should we? The thought is rejection, and it is plainly stated—let us leave it there. vs. 17a.

Now appears once again the same comparison and thought of the Jew's rejection that has been dealt with throughout the discussion. The reception of the Gentiles is stated in these words: "And you, being a wild olive, have been grafted in among them." There were some branches who were not broken off; these of course were the Christian Jews. It was among these branches that the Gentiles were grafted in. The whole thought, of course, has reference to the salvation of the Gentiles as forming part of the church with the Christian Jews. vs. 17b.

297. Explain the first metaphor. Who is the first fruit? Who is the lump?
298. Explain the second simile. Who is the root? Who are the branches?
299. Who was broken off and who was grafted in? What is the tree?

In the midst of this imagery there is the practical note and admonition of the 18th verse. It is well to realize the blessing of partaking of the wonderful benefits of the gospel as described in "partaking of the root and fatness of the olive tree." But then we must not become high-minded or proud and speak against the Jews, for, "Remember," says the apostle, "that salvation came of the Jews." We do not mock the branches, but keep in mind that we owe a great deal to those branches, for without them we would have no Saviour, no revelation, no salvation. The Jews are like the root of the tree, and we are like the ingrafted branches of this tree. vs. 18.

A rather veiled objection is now raised by the imaginary Gentile. "Were not the branches broken off that I might be grafted in?" In a sense this might be true, for even as we have said, the Gentiles were given opportunity to hear the gospel through the refusal of the Jews. But on the other hand, it was not to be supposed by the Gentiles that God loved them or preferred them above the Jews, and because of this he cast out the Jew that he might receive the Gentiles. No, the Jews were broken off only because of their unbelief. And further consideration of the matter will show us that we only stand in God's favor because of our trusting reliance on Christ. Now if we begin to trust in ourselves and our position, we will have fallen into the same snare as the Jews. Considering this, "be not high-minded but fear: for if God spared not the natural branches (when they looked to self-effort) neither will he spare thee (if you act in the same manner)." vs. 21.

As a conclusion to this thought of acceptance and rejection, we have verse 22. In all that has been said, it is easy to see the immutable decisions of the Creator. We behold his goodness and severity. God must, and always does, maintain justice. Those who willfully refuse he must sever; but, on the other hand, his goodness is always accessible. The Gentiles were the recipients of God's goodness, which was summed up in the salvation they enjoyed. However, the Gentiles must also remember that a continuance in faith is as important as is the initial decision. The thought of continuing in God's goodness as here used refers to the steadfastness on the part of man in the provisions God has made for his life and hope, rather than trusting in his own wisdom or good works. So it was that Paul admonished the Gentiles to behold the overall picture and realize that a trusting, humble reliance upon God through Christ was the

300. What is the admonition of verse 18?
301. What is the objection of verse 21? How is it answered?
302. How can we see in this circumstance the justice of God? What warning is given?

only thing that could keep them from being cut off as was the Jew. vs. 22.

Now once again back to the thought of this whole section: The nation of Israel was not without hope, for if they would but cease in their course of unbelief they would be grafted in. There was only one barrier—their unbelief. God was ready and God was able to graft them in, even as he did the Gentiles. vs. 23. Yes, indeed, he can graft them in. In some respects their acceptance by the Almighty would be more natural than his receiving of the Gentiles. A further point of comparison is made in the olive tree simile to emphasize this thought. The usual grafting process has been reversed in the case of the Gentiles. No one acquainted with the laws of grafting would graft a portion of a wild tree into the root of a tame tree, but this God has, in his mercy and wisdom, performed The wild branch of the Gentiles was grafted into the root of the Christian Jews. The plan of God was that the Messiah was predetermined to come to the world through the Jewish nation. Everything about him appeared in shadow and type in the scriptures of the nation of Israel. It should have been that Jesus would be welcomed as the crowning glory of Israel's heritage. The church should have been accepted as the wonderful new creation of the Messiah. Yes, the church was meant to be the Jews' "own olive tree," but they stumbled over the "suffering servant" and missed his glorious kingdom. But then, one day when they will finally open their eyes, how they will then understand it all, how then will the dark things be made plain and the great pattern of God all fit together! This we take to be the import of the thought of the grafting in of the Jews "into their own olive tree." vs. 24.

Text

11:25-32. For I would not, brethren, have you ignorant of this mystery, lest ye be wise in your own conceits, that a hardening in part hath befallen Israel, until the fullness of the Gentiles be come in; 26 and so all Israel shall be saved: even as it is written,

> There shall come out of Zion the Deliverer;
> He shall turn away ungodliness from Jacob:
> 27 And this is my covenant unto them,
> When I shall take away their sins.

28 As touching the gospel, they are enemies for your sake: but as touching the election, they are beloved for the fathers' sake. 29 For the gifts and the calling of God are not repented of. 30 For as ye in time past were disobedient to God, but now have obtained mercy

303. Explain the two "grafting in" processes.

by their disobedience, 31 even so have these also now been disobedient, that by the mercy shown to you they also may now obtain mercy. 32 For God hath shut up all unto disobedience, that he might have mercy upon all.

Realizing Romans, 11:25-32

494. How would ignorance of the "hardening of Israel" be a temptation to the Gentiles?
495. What is "the fullness of the Gentiles"? Remember what you said about the "fullness" of the Jews?
496. When the fullness of the Gentiles is reached, then the Jews in great numbers will turn to Christ. Is that the thought of this passage?
497. Do you know the significance of the name "Zion"? This is the key word in this passage. Explain.
498. The nation of Israel was both an enemy and beloved. Explain.
499. What "gifts" do we have from God in connection with this subject? What calling of God do we have?
500. The disobedience of man and the mercy of God provided salvation, *but* man must do something about it—both Jews and Gentiles. Explain the responsibility of both Jews and Gentiles in the light of God's mercy.
501. In what sense is God responsible for our disobedience? Before you answer, read vs. 32 again.

Paraphrase

11:25-32. For, brethren, that ye may not have an high conceit of yourselves, on account of your being made the people of God in place of the Jews, I must show you this secret, that the blindness of the Jews in part, will continue only till the generality of the Gentiles come into the Christian church. For that illustrious event will render the evidences of the gospel irresistible.

26 And so, laying aside their prejudices, all Israel, by believing the gospel, shall enjoy the means of salvation, according as it is foretold, Isa. lix. 20. The redeemer shall come to Zion, and to them that turn from transgression in Jacob.

27 For this is my covenant with them, when I shall take away their sins of unbelief. 'My spirit that is upon thee, O Messiah, and my word which I have put in thy mouth, shall not depart out of thy mouth, nor out of the mouth of thy seed, saith the Lord, from henceforth and for ever.'

28 With respect to the gospel indeed, they are, through their unbelief, enemies to God on your account; your reception into the

church. But with respect to their original election to be the people of God, they are still beloved of God, on account of the promise to their fathers, that he would be a God to them in their generations.

29 For God's free gift, and his calling Abraham's posterity by Isaac his people, are unalterable on the part of God, who, if they repent, will receive them again.

30 Besides, as ye Gentiles also in times past have disobeyed God by your idolatry, yet now have obtained the mercy of being admitted into God's covenant and church, through the disobedience of the Jews to the gospel;

31 Even so the Jews also have now disobeyed the gospel on your being admitted into Gods' covenant, yet so as by your receiving that great favor, the gospel being continued in the world, they also shall obtain the mercy of being at length admitted into God's covenant.

32 For God hath shut up together all under sentence of death for their disobedience, that, in admitting them into his covenant and church, he might make them sensible (aware) that he bestows a free gift upon all.

Summary

Hardness in part has come upon Israel until the full sum of the Gentiles come into the church. By that time the hardness of Israel will give way, they will then become believers, and so a great many of them will be saved. You Gentiles should know this mystery to keep you from becoming puffed up with self-importance. The rejected Jews are still beloved on their Father's account, and you Gentiles have now to preach the gospel to them, and so convert them to Christ. They are thus at last to realize the divine mercy through you. Their fall has proved a blessing to you, and your conversion is to prove a blessing to them.

Comment

c. Mercy to All; The Ultimate Purpose of God. 11:25-32

In verse 25 we have a bold statement of fact that has before only been given in analogy. Lest the brethren in Rome (a great share of whom were Gentiles) distort the aim of this figurative language into a conclusion concerning their own self-importance, Paul says, "For I would not, brethren, have you ignorant of this mystery, lest ye be wise in your own conceits, that a hardening in part has befallen Israel, until the fullness of the Gentiles be come in." The thought of "hardening in part" refers back to the thought that their rejection was not entire, but only "in part." The time element spoken of here points once again to the fact that their rejection is not final, only until "the fullness of the Gentiles be come in." But what can the meaning of "the fullness of the Gentiles" be? We have had a reference to the "fullness" of the Jews (cf. vs. 12b). In this case we found the term "fullness" to be descriptive of the turning of the Jews to Christ, and in great numbers. Since then, the same subject is here being discussed, the turning of men to Christ, we could likewise say the fullness of the Gentiles refers to the extensive acceptance of Christ among these peoples. But there is one contrast in this comparison, for the fullness of the Gentiles is said to "come in." What is the thought here? This would seem to mean that there are a certain number of persons in that multitude, and when that number has been reached then will come to pass the fulfillment of the promise. We do not mean that no further Gentiles will be saved; indeed, we have already said that the fullness of the Jews would mean "life from the dead" among the Gentiles. The thought is that a change will take place as to who will carry God's good news. 11:25

The apostle emphatically affirms that when the fullness of the Gentiles has been reached, "All Israel will be saved." Along with the salvation of Israel, Paul promises that the words of Isaiah, the prophet, will find their fulfillment. How is it that all Israel shall be saved? How is it they were lost? This is not difficult to answer. They were lost because they turned from Christ; they then will be saved when they turn to Christ. Notice please that the turning of the Jews to Christ is tied up inseparably with the fullness of the Gentiles. This would give us some light on the reason for the turning of the nation of Israel to their Messiah. It would seem that there will be something in the bringing in of the fullness of the Gentiles that will cause all Israel to be saved. This could be nothing short of the faithful preaching of the gospel by the Gentiles to the Jews. When the Gentiles have accomplished this in the way and manner that God wants it done, then will come to pass the fullness of the Gentiles and the salvation of Israel. That it could take place in any other way seems inconsistent with God's means for man's salvation. To state that "all" Israel will be saved does not necessitate the salvation of each individual in the nation, but only as the word "all" is used in other instances which speak of a large portion as "all." The "Deliverer" who was to come out of Zion could be none other than Christ. Zion in this instance would refer to Israel and the results will be that ungodliness will be taken from Jacob. Since the Jews

304. What temptation was possible on the part of the Gentiles at Rome as they read this chapter?
305. How did Paul combat this temptation?
306. What is the meaning of "the fullness of the Gentiles"? How can it be said to "come in"?

are descendants of Jacob, this would refer to them. When the day comes that Israel accepts the salvation provided in Christ, then will they be able to look back upon these words of Isaiah and behold their fulfillment. The covenant made by God with Israel concerning this was probably made with Abraham and now finds its fulfillment in Christ. vs. 26-27

Still speaking of Israel, the inspired writer speaks of their relationship to the gospel. When Jehovah views Israel in the light of the gospel he must say, "They are my enemies." It is not that God has refused them, but rather that they have refused him. But as has been considered before, God used this as a means of saving the Gentiles. When viewing Israel in relationship to his eternal purposes or "election," he says, "They are beloved." Why were they beloved and in what sense? As to why they are beloved, we have the answer given: "For the fathers' sake." Who are the fathers here spoken of? Notice that it does not refer to the heavenly Father, but rather to "the fathers." This we take to mean the fathers of the Hebrew nation, namely, Abraham, Isaac, Jacob, Joseph, etc. Because of the promises made to these great men of God, he yet loves Israel. The 29th verse serves to explain his consideration of Israel for the fathers' sake. He is saying in essence that many among the Jews will one day turn to Christ, for he so purposed it when he promised to these men of old that he would be their God and they his children. These are called "gifts and calling." God is not sorry that he thus made these promises, for although it might now appear as a mystery, it will one day be made plain, even as he purposed. 11:28-29

In conclusion to this whole matter of the salvation of the Jews and Gentiles, we have the statement of verses 30-32. Let us read verse 32 first and then see how it finds its explanation and fulfillment in verses 30-31. Notice: "For God hath shut up all unto disobedience, that he might have mercy upon all." Consider first the disobedience of the Gentiles. This was described in the first chapter of this book, but was purely introductory and had nothing to do with mercy. Now we notice the disobedience of the Jew. This was so for a twofold purpose: not only that Gentiles might obtain mercy through Christ, but that we might bring the gospel to the Jewish people and thus cause them to enter into God's mercy. This only more firmly established the thought we before expressed, which

307. How will the "fullness of the Gentiles" save "all Israel"? What is meant by the term "all Israel"?

308. Who is the "Deliverer out of Zion"?

309. Explain in your own words verse 28.

is that the turning of the Jews to Christ is dependent upon the preaching of the gospel by the Gentiles. So then, we can indeed see that God shut up all unto disobedience, (in the case of the Gentiles, before Christ; in the case of the Jews, after Christ) "that he might have mercy upon all." Of the fulfillment of this we have just written. 11:30-32

Text

11:33-36. O the depth of the riches both of the wisdom and the knowledge of God! how unsearchable are his judgments, and his ways past tracing out! 34 For who hath known the mind of the Lord? or who hath been his counselor? 35 or who hath first given to him, and it shall be recompensed unto him again? 36 For of him, and through him, and unto him, are all things. To him be the glory for ever. Amen.

REALIZING ROMANS, 11:33-36

502. What would prompt the doxology in vs. 33-36?
503. Show the difference between "knowledge and wisdom" as here used. cf. vs. 33a.
504. Since we cannot know the mind of the Lord, what should be our attitude toward his will?
505. We are so much in debt to God. Explain how this is true, and the response we should make to the debt.
506. Concerning God, we are "of him," "through him," "unto him." This calls forth a response on our part which is "to him." Explain each.

Paraphrase

11:33-36. In surveying the divine dispensations, instead of finding fault, We ought to cry out, O the greatness, both of the wisdom of God in contriving and ordering these dispensations, and of the knowledge of God in foreseeing the effects which they would produce! How unsearchable are his determinations, and his ways past finding out!

34 For what man or angel hath comprehended all the reasons of God's determinations, so as to be able to judge of his ways? Or who hath given him advice, respecting either the planning or the managing of the affairs of the universe?

310. What is meant by the "gifts and calling" of God?
311. Show how all were shut up unto disobedience that all might obtain mercy.

35 Or has any one laid an obligation on God, by first conferring a favor on him? Let him show the obligation, and he shall have full recompense.

36 For from him all things proceed, and by him all things are governed, and to his glory are all things both made and governed. To him alone be ascribed the glory of the creation, preservation, and government of the universe, for ever. Amen.

Summary

Great is the depth of God's resources, and wisdom, and knowledge in working out the redemption of the world. We cannot know beforehand what his decisions are, nor how he moves in effecting his ends. No one has ever been privy to his counsels, nor any appointed to aid him. All things originate in him, and all things are for his honor and glory.

Comment

d. Conclusion: 11:33-36

We can think of no better words to express the thought of this conclusion than the paraphrasing of these verses as given by W. Sanday on p. 333 in the International Critical Commentary. 11:33 "When we contemplate a scheme like this spread out before us in vast panorama, how forcibly does it bring home to us the inexhaustible profundity of that Divine mind by which it was planned! The decisions which issue from that mind and the methods by which it works are alike inscrutable to man. 34 Into the secrets of the Almighty none can penetrate. No counsellor stands at His ear to whisper words of suggestion. 35 Nothing in Him is derived from without so as to be claimed back again by its owner. 36 He is the source of all things. Through Him all things flow. He is the final cause to which all things tend. Praised forever be His name! Amen."

Text

12:1,2. I beseech you therefore, brethren, by the mercies of God, to present your bodies a living sacrifice, holy, acceptable to God, which is your spiritual service. 2 And be not fashioned according to this world: but be ye transformed by the renewing of your mind, that ye may prove what is the good and acceptable and perfect will of God.

PART THREE
The Practical, The Hortatory, and Conclusion. 12:1—16:27
Our Duties to God and Man. 12:1—15:13

Realizing Romans, 12:1-2

507. "Beseech" is a strong word. Would we be disobedient if we fail to obey what is taught in these verses?

508. How have chapters one through eleven formed a background for the conclusion here stated?

Rethinking in Outline Form

5. This rejection neither total nor final. 11:1-36.
   a. Their rejection not total. 11:1-10.
     (1) Reasons for concluding it was not total. 1-5.
       (a) Paul was an Israelite, but he was not rejected. 1, 2a.
       (b) Conditions then were like those in the days of Elijah. 2b-5.
     (2) Reasons for their rejection. 11:6-10.
       (a) Acceptance is by grace. 6.
       (b) The elect found it—not Israel. 7a.
       (c) The rest were hardened. 7b-10.
   b. Their rejection not final. 11:11-24.
     (1) Their fall was an advantage to the Gentiles. 11.
     (2) Their fall was a blessing to the Gentiles but it does not compare to the blessing their fullness will be to the Gentiles. 12.
     (3) The Jews will one day turn to Christ. This will be like life from the dead. One day God will graft in the branches that are now broken off. The rejection of the Jews should be a warning to the Gentiles. 12-24.
   c. Mercy to all the ultimate purpose of God. 11:25-32.
     (1) The hardening of Israel will last only until the fullness of the Gentiles comes in. 25, 26.
     (2) God is able to show mercy to all. 27-32.
   d. Conclusion. 11:33-36.
     We can cry out in amazement at the great wisdom and love of God. 33-36.

Realizing Romans, 12:1-2

509. Upon the basis of God's mercies, not his condemnation, we are called upon to make a living sacrifice. Explain this.

510. Our bodies are to be "a living sacrifice." Explain in your own words how this relates to your body.

511. If our bodies are not so presented to God, are they acceptable to him?

512. It would help you in your understanding of the inspired text if you would read it from several translations. In doing this you would find a new meaning for the word "spiritual" in vs. 1b. What is the meaning of the word?

513. Is the fashion of the world always wrong? How can we tell just what is fashionable with the Lord and with the world?

514. Isn't it wonderful to know we can be transformed? Not just changed or improved, but transformed!! Honestly now, do you believe this is possible? Transformed into what?

515. "The renewing of the mind": If we never had "new" minds to begin with, how could they be "renewed"? How often should this process be practiced? How often is it practiced with you?

516. Here is experimental religion in its purest form. We can come to prove to ourselves, to others, and most of all to God that which is good, acceptable, and perfect in life. We are here saying that we believe the practice of God's will in our lives will produce the greatest amount of real happiness for man. Do you agree? Tell why.

Paraphrase

12:1-2. Since the Jewish church, with its sacrifices, is removed, and the Christian church is erected in its place, I beseech you, brethren, by the mercies of God, that ye present to him your bodies, wherein sin formerly ruled, a living sacrifice, holy and acceptable to God, by consecrating its members to his service, which is your reasonable worship.

2 And be not fashioned like to the men of this world, by adopting their corrupt principles, their carnal temper, their rotten speech, and their vicious practices, but be changed from what ye were, by having your understanding enlightened, that ye may approve what is that good, and acceptable, and perfect will of God, which is made known in the gospel.

Summary

We are continually to present our bodies a living, holy sacrifice to God. This is made our reasonable service by all the facts and teachings in the foregoing part of this letter. Our minds are to be changed by being renewed. This change is necessary in order to understand God's will correctly.

1. Full consecration to God. 12:1, 2

Comment

Whereas we cannot comprehend many aspects of the nature of

God, there is one quality of God which we can understand, and which calls for a response on our part. We can understand the mercies of God. A review of the history of his dealings with both Jew and Gentile will show "he hath not dealt with us after our sins nor rewarded us according to our iniquities." The goodness of God should indeed lead us to repentance, to "a change of mind." We are not abused at all, but marvelously blessed. In the heart of Paul so strong was this concept of God's goodness that he used a very strong word in calling for our response to God's mercies. He said, "I *beseech* you." It is as if he were saying, "Come here apart with me, and let me impress upon you face to face the inescapable responsibility each of us have as Christians in response to mercies to us." In the chapters to follow, Paul is to call upon believers to do many things, both for God and man, but now there is but one injunction which was inclusive of all others: "Present your bodies a living sacrifice, holy, acceptable to God." When this is done, all other expressions of devotion and service will issue forth. Note, please, that the body does not present itself. "We" must offer it up to God. By God's grace and in response to his mercy, we *do* have control over this body of flesh; we *can* make it an offering to God, or Paul would never have called for it. Other Christians have done it; they are now doing it. Can we do less?

When we thus present our bodies to God, he will deem them holy and acceptable. Not that we by such a surrender become sinless or infallible, but he who looks on the heart so counts us holy and acceptable on the basis of his grace and our offering. Such action and devotion on our part is but the natural, sensible response of the heart and life to God. Anything short of this reflects upon our willingness to follow out the divine plan of God in dealing with man through Christ.

In verse two are the details of the living sacrifice. If our bodies are to be laid upon the altar of devotion to God, it will be because the volitional, responsible part of man has been renewed, not once but day by day, for that is how often this sacrifice is to be made. Perhaps a morning and an evening oblation would be in order. How shall we dress? How shall we talk? How shall we think? If we see and follow only those things and persons which are near, we shall be like them, corrupt, full of lust. But it is wondrously possible to

312. We can know one quality of God. What is it? How do we discover this quality?
313. Why should the goodness of God lead us to repentance?
314. Is it unreasonable to expect such a complete commitment of fallible man?
315. When we fail to present our bodies to God we fail our own selves also. How is this true?

set a "new fashion" by following Christ, who is the "fashion designer" of the Christian. To be in "fashion" with Christ calls for time, thought, energy on our part. All of this means we must set our minds on the things that are above, and not once, but continually, to have that divine power work in us both to will and to do his good pleasure. When our minds are renewed, so is our life. Our bodies then become "instruments of righteousness."

What are we trying to prove? Better yet, *to whom* are we trying to prove it? We are proving the good, acceptable, and perfect will of God, or that God's will is good, acceptable and perfect. When once we have made this surrender, we will know it ourselves. It will be good, acceptable and perfect to us—life indeed! It will likewise appear so to other Christians, some who need such demonstration. Above all, it will prove to Satan that God's way is the best way, *good, well-pleasing, and perfect.* We feel the emphasis is upon proving it to ourselves, but the other aspects of the thought are also true.

Text

12:3-16. For I say, through the grace that was given me, to every man that is among you, not to think of himself more highly than he ought to think; but so to think as to think soberly, according as God hath dealt to each man a measure of faith. 4 For even as we have many members in one body, and all the members have not the same office: 5 so we, who are many, are one body in Christ, and severally members one of another. 6 And having gifts differing according to the grace that was given to us, whether prophecy, let us prophesy according to the proportion of our faith; 7 or ministry, let us give ourselves to our ministry; or he that teacheth, to his teaching; 8 or he that exhorteth, to his exhorting: he that giveth, let him do it with liberality; he that ruleth, with diligence; he that showeth mercy, with cheerfulness.

9 Let love be without hypocrisy. Abhor that which is evil; cleave to that which is good. 10 In love of the brethren be tenderly affectioned one to another; in honor preferring one another; 11 in diligence not slothful; fervent in spirit; serving the Lord; 12 rejoicing in hope; patient in tribulation; continuing stedfastly in prayer; 13 communicating to the necessities of the saints; given to hospitality. 14 Bless them that persecute you; bless, and curse not. 15 Rejoice with them that rejoice; weep with them that weep. 16 Be of the same mind one toward another. Set not your mind on high things, but

316. What is the responsible part of man?
317. How can we be "in fashion" with Christ?
318. The Christian is trying to prove something. What is it?

condescend to things that are lowly. Be not wise in your own conceits.

REALIZING ROMANS, 12:3-16

517. What is "the grace" of vs. 3?

518. We are not to think of ourselves "highly," but rather "soberly." Explain.

519. God has granted to each man "a measure of faith." I thought faith came by hearing, and hearing of the Word of God. (Cf. Rom. 10:17) In what sense are both of these ideas correct?

520. There are persons, some of them in the dark, who are prejudiced against God for making them the way they are. This is tragically wrong. Explain why.

521. We all have some God-given office to hold in his body. Is this the thought of verses 4 and 5?

522. We are not only members of the body of Christ, the church, but of one another. Explain this thought.

523. Prophecy is a gift. How could "the ministry" be a gift? Are these natural or supernatural gifts?

524. It would seem from vs. 8 that exhorting was a separate function or office in the Roman church. Should it be so today?

525. How could "giving" be a gift of God? Are we not all to give?

526. Is showing mercy a gift? Some of these gifts are present in the church today. Designate which ones.

527. What are some of the masks worn by those who are insincere in love?

528. What a wonderful quality is hate when directed toward evil. Explain the word "abhor" in vs. 9.

529. We are "to be glued" to that which is good. In a very practical way show how this is done.

530. If we fulfilled the injunction of vs. 10, would we be accused of emotionalism? Explain why.

531. In an everyday example, show how we could "in honor" prefer one another.

532. Isn't vs. 11a a contradiction? How could a person be "diligent" and "slothful" at the same time?

533. What "spirit" is meant in vs. 11?

534. The sense of service for the Lord escapes us many times; as a result, we begin to serve ourselves or one another. What is the outcome?

535. What "plus factor" must be present in our hearts if we practice the blessed trinity of vs. 12? Cf. Rom. 8:28.

536. Please remember as you read vs. 13 that you are not the recipient but the giver. Do the saints of today have needs we can

meet? How would you define "hospitality"? How are we to consider these words: as suggestions, or ideals, or commands?

537. Just how can we practice blessing those that persecute us? Give an example.

538. Many times we are too busy to have a sincere interest in the happiness or sorrow of others. When we fail to do this, who do we fail? Can we be like Christ without this interest?

539. Is Paul suggesting a loss of individuality in vs. 16? What is he saying?

Paraphrase

12:3-16. Also, by the apostolical authority which is given to me, I command every one among you, without exception, not to have an higher opinion of himself, nor a lower opinion of others, than he ought to have, but to think of both justly, so as always to behave wisely in his own station, without aspiring after offices in the church which he is not fit for; and to employ himself in the duties of his station and office, according as to each God has distributed his measure of spiritual gifts.

4 These gifts are necessarily different, both in their nature and dignity, (ver. 6.) For, as in one body we have many members, but all these members have not the same office in the body;

5 So we, the many disciples of Christ, are but one body, or religious society, under the government of Christ; consequently we are all members of one another, receiving edification and comfort from each other.

6 Having then spiritual gifts, differing according to the offices assigned us in the church; if our gift be prophecy, let us prophesy only according to the extent of our inspiration, without adding to or taking from the revelations made to us, or meddling with subjects not revealed to us:

7 Or if our gifts fit us for the stated ministry of the word, let us be diligent in preaching, not disheartened by dangers: or if one's gifts fit him for teaching the ignorant, let him be diligent in teaching such:

8 Or if they fit him for exhorting, let him employ himself in exhortation. He whose gifts fit him for distributing the church's alms, let him do it with honesty, disinterestedness, and impartiality: he whose gifts fit him for presiding, let him do with assiduity and prudence: he whose gifts qualify him for taking care of the sick, the afflicted, the imprisoned, and of widows and orphans, let him perform these services with cheerfulness.

9 Let your professions of love be real: abhor every evil action: adhere closely to a virtuous course of life.

10 In love to one another as brethren in Christ, show that kindness

of affection which near relations bear to one another. In every honorable action, go before, and leading on one another.

11 In caring for each other, be not slothful. In spirit be fervent, when ye serve the Lord in the ordinary duties of religion, or in spreading the gospel.

12 Rejoice in hope of eternal life. Be patient in affliction. And as the best consolation in trouble, continue earnest in prayer, although your prayers be not immediately answered.

13 Communicate your riches, for relieving the necessities of the brethren. Practise hospitality to strangers, especially those driven from their homes by persecution.

14 Bless them who persecute you: bless them by praying God to bless them, but never curse them.

15 Rejoice with them who are in prosperity, and grieve with them who are in adversity: these things are acceptable both to God and man.

16 Be of the same hospitable, forgiving, sympathizing disposition towards one another, as towards strangers and persecutors. Do not aspire after the grandeur of this life; nor affect the company of those who are in high stations: rather associate with men who are weaned from the world. And be not puffed up with an opinion of your own wisdom, lest it make you despise instruction.

Summary

We should not be high-minded because we are gifted, but we must be right-minded, that we may place a proper estimate upon everything, especially upon gifts, our own as well as those of others. If we have a gift, we must exercise it, neither being proud of it, nor looking down upon others as inferiors because they have a less shining gift. Whatever we are best qualified to do, that we must do, and nothing else. This alone gives success.

Our love must be unfeigned, for otherwise it is hypocrisy. It is not enough that we simply oppose evil; we must abhor it. We must cling to what is good at every cost. Our love for the brotherhood must be very tender, while in the matter of showing esteem, we must be examples to one another. In serving the Lord, we must be full of zeal, and fervent in spirit. In affliction, we must be patient, constant in prayer, and full of hope. We are to share each other's wants, lovingly caring for strangers in our homes. We must bless even our persecutors, and never curse them. We are not to pattern after proud ways and high life, but evince a preference for lowly ways and meek life.

Comment

2. Duties to those within the church. 12:3-16

Paul was inspired, and his utterances came by divine inspiration, but he was not so blessed of God because he deserved it. He had such a ministry through the unmerited favor of God. We should heed his words as the words of God, and all the more so when we see reflected in the life of the inspired spokesman the very truths he seeks to impart. The church at Rome was graced with a number of spiritual gifts. There were men in the congregation who had the gift of prophecy (vs. 6); evidently some had the gift of supernatural wisdom or knowledge (vs. 7; cf. I Cor. 12:8.) Others were ministering (vs. 7a) and still others exhorting (vs. 7b). They were ministering and exhorting only by God's power and wisdom. There was a strong temptation to misuse these gifts, particularly in the area of pride. Let us put ourselves in their place. If we were blessed with the gift of prophecy, would we not consider such a power the greatest blessing of our lives? Would it not be a strong temptation to convince every other member of the church that what we had received from God was indeed high and holy? Find ten men and women with this same idea, and there will be confusion and collision!

What is here said of spiritual gifts is also applicable to the ordinary places of service in the church today.

A clear "renewed" mind will reveal reality. Sober judgment will be made and sound decisions formed. In the exercise of the supernatural gifts, faith on the part of the one gifted had to be exercised. For example: Peter and John could not heal the lame man at the beautiful gate without faith (Acts 3:1-10), but it was not the faith of the lame man but of Peter and John (cf. Acts 3:16). "The measure of faith" had reference to the power exercised by those possessing the gifts. The expression, "according as God hath dealt to each man a measure of faith," would seem to refer to the gift itself. It does so only in the sense that sometimes the result is put for the cause. The result was the exercise of the gift; the cause was the faith of the gifted. The faith, too, was a "gift" of God.

In verses 4 and 5, the human body as compared to the spiritual one is discussed. This passage is not the first time Paul uses such a comparison, nor the last one. (cf. I Cor. 12:12-27) There is perfect unity through diversity in the human body. The hidden, though inevitable, conclusion is that such is only true because there is a unified

319. Paul's words are all the more meaningful to us because of his life. Why?
320. Why was instruction concerning the proper use of spiritual gifts necessary?
321. Why are we admonished to think "soberly"?

response to the one head. In the spiritual body, the church, Christ is the head (Eph. 1:22, 23). There should be that perfect willingness on the part of each one to count the other better than himself and as necessary as himself—no one indispensable and yet all doing what none other can do. When we realize that our proper relationship to the head depends upon our proper relationship to every other member of the body, we will work together without highmindedness.

Note, please, the attitudes to be adopted by those who exercise their gifts, as in vs. 6-8. The gifts differ, but not the source. The expressions differ, but not the purpose. Each is to be used to its fullest extent, but with no attempt to control the use of another of God's gifted ones. There are seven areas of services here mentioned. In four of them we can see a need for special supernatural gifts: in prophecy, in ministry, in teaching and in exhorting, but not in the remaining three. We conclude, therefore, that the admonition is both specific and general. To those who are divinely blessed, as well as to those who serve without such needed aid, "do it with all that in you is" without thought of comparison with others. "He that giveth" evidently refers to those who have of this world's means and yet love the Lord. They are to give with liberality, perhaps realizing how rare such a person is and how needed is the gift. The rulers are doubtless the elders of the churches. Idleness or indifference will not produce an elder who rules well. A real word of emphasis needs to be sounded on "he that showeth mercy," or perhaps better translated, "he that showeth pity." It is easy enough to show pity or mercy to someone who is ill or shut-in the first time or the second or third visit, but how is our cheerfulness after the 100th call on the same unfortunate one? It should be the same as the attitude we expect from God when we ask him to attend to our needs (and many times the same ones) the 100th time.

In verses 9-13 are a list of attributes to be found in the life of a genuine Christian. Let us not love in word, but in deed and in truth. If we pretend in our love, it is only a pretense to man; God is not deceived. In our relationship to one another, our motives and purposes should be transparent.

It is not enough to pronounce a definition of evil; we must have an aggressive opposition to it. Within our inmost beings we must

322. What is the meaning of the expression "measure of faith"?
323. Why does Paul use the figure referring to the human body?
324. In what sense are we all essential yet not indispensable?
325. Both to those with supernatural aid and to those without what was the word of admonition?

hate sin. It is fully as necessary to speak out against evil as it is to speak up for righteousness. This marks a very vital aspect of our relationship to Christ and God. If our emotions are not involved in our religion, we worship in vain. Intellectual assent to right and wrong will never accomplish God's will in our lives. There must be within us an emotional response to God's will, or we simply do not love the Lord.

We are "to be glued to what is good." We are to adhere with all our hearts to the good. How many Christians are truly "lovers of good"? Too many are *grey* instead of *white* in their conception of good and evil. As a result, there is no conviction in either direction. We can be sure they are in the power of Satan.

In our love for each of God's family, we should have no mere polite acceptance of one another. Must we always find some attribute of loveliness in someone before we can love them? If our Lord had so waited, we would all be lost. Let us love one another with a true feeling of the family relationship for Jesus' sake.

"In honor preferring one another" could also be translated, "setting an example for one another." Let us challenge (provoke) one another to love and good works. "If he can do it for Christ, so can I," is the thought here.

In the care of the needs of one another do not be negligent. What a reproach this is to the average church! We do not even know the needs of one another, physically or spiritually; if we do, many times we do nothing about it. "It's the job of the preacher," or, "Let the elders take care of that," is often heard. Here it is enjoined upon all.

In zeal be "boiling over." Someone defined zeal as "communicated feeling." We love the Lord and one another, but our love is of no help to others or to our Lord until it is communicated.

"Serving the Lord": never for an instant should we lose the sense of serving him, as a slave to a worthy Master.

Here is a trinity of triumph for every Christian: (1) the hope of heaven; (2) the providence of God; (3) steadfast prayer. These qualities must become a veritable part of us. The factual knowledge that, on the basis of the death of Christ, we have the hope of glory is not at all enough. There must be the eagerness of a pilgrim going home, the joy of a true child at a family reunion. We can and will be patient with complete abandon in any and all tribulation. "All

326. Who are those who rule?
327. Why is it difficult to show mercy with cheerfulness?
328. How do our emotions become a vital part of our religion?
329. What is the meaning of "in honor preferring one another"?

things work together for good to them who love God and are called according to his purpose." All our hope and trust must be undergirded with constant, fervent prayer.

When one suffers, all suffer. We come to the aid of one another as a loving brother or sister. When a brother in the flesh is seriously ill, how concerned we become. What of the ills of the spirit and the flesh of our brothers in the Lord?

Moses E. Lard translates the next phrase, "keeping on in love for strangers." This was an Old Testament practice. It should indeed be the practice of each and every one as a Christian. Perhaps this could have reference to Christians who are strangers, but it should not stop there.

Continuing the list of those wonderful qualities of a true child of God: "Bless the persecutors, bless and curse not." This was the admonition and practice of our Lord. Oh, that we might practice it today with those who misunderstand us and despitefully use us! A genuine feeling of good will toward those who are unfriendly to us is the only Christian attitude.

Verse fifteen contains a real barometer of our spirituality, showing how we can sympathetically share the joys and the sorrows of others when we have the mind of Christ. He bore our sorrows and carried our griefs. How this is needed today!

"Let there be no distinction of persons" is the admonition of verse 16b. There are natural preferences that develop among brethren. The Christian, and especially any leader of God's flock, cannot allow such personality traits to cause him to show a distinction to the extent of slighting one and honoring another.

"Condescend" is a meaningful and strong word: "Be *carried away*" by (or "condescend to) the things that are lowly. Not only "things" but people are involved in this. It should be our desire to be hidden as much as possible by the work we do. No task or person should be too small or menial in the service of Christ.

"Be not wise in your own eyes." This is not an admonition concerning wisdom alone. Paul here says we should manifest our wisdom or sound judgment before God and men rather than before the mirror. The estimate we hold of our wisdom should be one of true humility, seen in the light of our mistakes and lack of knowledge.

330. Is Paul suggesting that all are responsible for the needs of others?
331. Define "zeal."
332. How can we bless our persecutors?
333. Give the "trinity of triumph" for the Christian.

Text

12:17-21. Render to no man evil for evil. Take thought for things honorable in the sight of all men. 18 If it be possible, as much as in you lieth, be at peace with all men. 19 Avenge not yourselves, beloved, but give place unto the wrath of God: for it is written, Vengeance belongeth unto me; I will recompense, saith the Lord. 20 But if thine enemy hunger, feed him; if he thirst, give him to drink: for in so doing thou shalt heap coals of fire upon his head. 21 Be not overcome of evil, but overcome evil with good.

REALIZING ROMANS, 12:17-21

540. How do the two thoughts of vs. 17 relate to each other?
541. Is Paul suggesting in vs. 18 that after we have tried to maintain peace and found it impossible that we are at liberty to fight?
542. Human vengeance is destructive in two ways. Name them.
543. It is difficult to believe that finally justice will prevail, and yet the Scriptures plainly teach it. When will we see it?
544. We know from vs. 20 that the "coals of fire" are good deeds. In what manner do they become "coals of fire"? Who is being burned?
545. Is it always possible to overcome evil with good? If not, are we less obligated?

Paraphrase

12:17-21. Unto no one return evil for the evil he hath done you. Premeditate how to make your actions beautiful in the sight of all men; of your enemies as well as of others.

18 What relates to you is, live in peace with all men, whether friends or foes, if it can be done consistently with piety and truth.

19 Beloved, do not avenge yourselves of your persecutors, but give place to the wrath of God, whose prerogative it is to punish. For it is written, Deut. xxxii. 35. Vengeance belongs to me, I will repay, saith the Lord. See also Lev. xix. 18.

20 Therefore, if thy persecutor hunger, instead of avenging thyself by suffering him to perish, give him meat; and if he thirst, give him drink: for by so doing thou wilt soften him, and make him lay down the enmity which he bears to thee.

21 Be not overcome of evil, so as to be made evil yourselves, but overcome the evil dispositions of your persecutors, by doing them all the good ye can.

334. How can we tell whether we have the mind of Christ?
335. The Christian should be "carried away" with something. What is it?
336. What is the meaning of being "wise in our own eyes"?

Summary

Injuries, we must not retaliate, and we are to be thoughtful to do what, in every one's estimation, is right. As Christians we must strive for peace.

We must never attempt to avenge ourselves, but leave that wholly to the Lord. On the contrary, if our enemy be hungry, we must feed him; if thirsty, we must give him drink. We must be God-like in dealing with him. We must not allow his evil to conquer us; rather we must conquer his evil by our good.

Comment

3. The Christian's duties toward those without the church. 12:11-21.

This is a fine sentiment, "Render to no man evil for evil," but who does it? The desire to get even with those who do evil to us is not the Christian attitude. Rather, let us make it a rule of life that we shall not retaliate. If such a conviction is developed ahead of time, we shall be able to so respond when someone does evil to us.

In contrast to the "eye for an eye" attitude is that in vs. 17b. We are to take thought beforehand so as to conduct ourselves in such a manner that all men, Christian and non-Christian, will come to appreciate our concern for them, and will see the consistency of our profession. A Christian will never go out of his way to offend anyone. On the other hand, he will make a conscious effort to bring happiness to all.

Verse eighteen seems to be an amendment of vs. 17. It will not always be possible to avoid conflict. Others will force evil upon the child of God. Never let it be said that any blame is due the Christian. We can be at peace with others, even though others are not with us.

What is the distinction between verse nineteen and verse seventeen? It would seem that verse nineteen is stronger, in the sense that some not only retaliate with an eye for an eye and a tooth for a tooth, but they actually become the judges, meting out what God alone has wisdom or power to do. If we believe God is concerned about our lives, we will allow him to act as judge in matters that hurt us. The Lord's anger is always pure—ours never. Besides these considerations is the bald fact that God has stated the case in plain words, "Punishment is mine, I will repay it."

337. How shall we ever be able to fulfill the admonition "render to no man evil for evil"?

338. We should plan ahead of time to so conduct ourselves that our actions will show something to all. What is it?

Someone is certainly going to say that the thought of verse twenty has gone too far. This is true from a human standpoint. We would never think of treating our enemies as here described. But we are partakers of the divine nature. God does daily feed and care for those who are his enemies. Can we refuse to do it?

The "coals of fire" of verse 20b probably refers to the burning of the conscience of the one so treated. When we return good for evil we are making an attempt to stir up his conscience to a recognition of his own guilt and our innocence. In this condition he is a candidate for the truth.

Who will win in this great contest of right and wrong? Either we give place to wrath and are overcome, or we overcome the wrath of others by returning good for evil. We must overcome the desire to give evil for evil within our own heart before we can hope to conquer evil in the heart of anyone else.

Looking back over the twenty-one verses of chapter twelve, we can now see in all its practical reality what it means to be transformed by the renewing of our minds.

Rethinking in Outline Form
Part Three
The Practical, The Hortatory, and Conclusion. 12:1—16:27.
A. Our duties to God and Man. 12:1—15:13.
  1. Full consecration to God. 12:1-2.
  2. Duties to Those Within the Church. 12:3-16.
      a. Paul speaking as an apostle. v. 3a cf. Rom. 1:5; 15:15.
      b. Addressed to all. v. 3b.
      c. How to think. v. 3c. cf. I Cor. 8:2; 10:12; Gal. 6:3.
      d. Many members yet all in one body. Each part has its function vs. 4-8.
      e. Love to be true. v. 9a cf. II Cor. 6:6; I Tim. 1:5.
      f. Abhor evil, cleave to good. v. 9b.
      g. Tender love for the brethren. v. 10a. cf. I Thess. 4:9; Heb. 13:1; Jn. 13:34-35.
      h. In honor preferring one another. v. 10b cf. Phil. 2:3.
      i. In diligence not slothful. v. 11a.
      j. Fervent in spirit. v. 11b.
      k. Serving the Lord. v. 11c cf. Matt. 6:24.
      l. Rejoicing in hope. v. 12a cf. 5:2.

339. In what way does verse eighteen amend verse seventeen?
340. Explain the difference between verse seventeen and verse nineteen.
341. In what very practical way could we say we have fulfilled verse twenty?
342. What are "the coals of fire"? Why are they so called?

m. Patient in tribulation. v. 12b cf. 5:3-5.

n. Continuing steadfastly in prayer. v. 12c cf. I Thess. 5:17.

o. Communicating to the necessities of the saints. v. 13a.

p. Given to hospitality. v. 13b.

q. Bless them that persecute you. v. 14 cf. Matt. 5:44; Lu. 6:28; I Cor. 4:12.

r. Share joys and sorrows. v. 15.

s. Be of the same mind one toward another. v. 16a cf. 15:5; II Cor. 13:1.

t. Keep the mind on lowly things. v. 16b.

u. Be not wise in your own conceits. v. 16c cf. 11:25; Prov. 3:7.

3. The Christian's Duties to Those Without The Church. vs. 17-21.

a. Render to no man evil for evil. v. 17a.

b. Take thought for things honorable in the sight of all men. v. 17b cf. II Cor. 8:21.

c. Be at peace with all men. v. 18 cf. Mk. 9:50; Rom. 14:19.

d. Leave vengeance to the Lord. v. 19 cf. Deut. 32:35.

e. How to treat your enemy. v. 20 cf. Prov. 25:21-22; II Kgs. 6:21-23.

f. How to overcome evil. v. 21.

Text

13:1-7. Let every soul be in subjection to the higher powers: for there is no power but of God; and the powers that be are ordained of God. 2 Therefore he that resisteth the power, withstandeth the ordinance of God: and they that withstand shall receive to themselves judgment. 3 For rulers are not a terror to the good work, but to the evil. And wouldest thou have no fear of the power? do that which is good, and thou shalt have praise from the same: 4 for he is a minister of God to thee for good. But if thou do that which is evil, be afraid; for he beareth not the sword in vain: for he is a minister of God, an avenger for wrath to him that doeth evil. 5 Wherefore ye must needs be in subjection, not only because of the wrath, but also for conscience' sake. 6 For this cause ye pay tribute also; for they are ministers of God's service, attending continually upon this very thing. 7 Render to all their dues: tribute to whom tribute is due; custom to whom custom; fear to whom fear; honor to whom honor.

Realizing Romans, 13:1-7

546. Are we not a bit hasty in referring to "the higher powers" as the government? Why not think of the higher powers as the power of God instead of man?

547. God is not the author of confusion, war, etc. Is God the one behind all types of government? Explain vs. 1.
548. Remember that Paul was writing under the Roman government. Is he saying that disobedience to Roman law was disobedience to God?
549. God has placed rulers as a means of "terror to evil." Explain.
550. We should respect "the powers that be." Why?
551. The policeman is a minister of God. In what way?
552. There are two reasons for obeying the laws. Give them. Does this apply to driving over the speed limit?
553. Suppose we are charged an exhorbitant amount of tax. Should we pay it?
554. In what other area of living could we apply the principle of verses 1-7?

Paraphrase

13:1-7. Let every man, whatever his office in the church or his spiritual gifts are, be subject to the established government. For there is no power of government but from God; and the governing powers in all countries are subordinate to, and useful for carrying on God's benevolent government of the world.

2 Wherefore, he who opposeth government, by disobeying its wholesome laws, or by attempting the lives of the governors, or by obstructing the due execution of their office, resisteth the ordinance of God: and they who do so shall be punished

3 For rulers are appointed not to terrify those of the citizens who do good works, but who do evil. Wouldst thou then live happily in any country, without being afraid of the magistrates and the laws, carefully do the good actions which they enjoin, and thou shalt have protection and favor from the same.

4 For the ruler, according to the true design of his office, is a servant of God, appointed to make thee and the rest happy, by maintaining all in their just possessions. But if thou do evil, if thou are rebellious, impious, injurious, or addicted to any vice inconsistent with the peace of society, be afraid of the magistrate, because the power of punishing is not committed to him by God and the people in vain: for he is a servant of God, appointed to avenge the community by punishing evil doers.

5 For these reasons, it is necessary for you to be obedient to the laws and rulers of the countries where ye live, not only from the fear of punishment, but also from a principle of conscience.

6 From the same principle, pay ye taxes also to the magistrates, because they are public ministers, appointed by God to attend con-

tinually to the affairs of government, and to the distribution of justice, that the people may live in peace.

7 Render, therefore, to all, without fraud, what is due by law. To whom tax is due, tax: to whom custom for merchandise is due, custom: to whom fear is due, as having the execution of the laws in their hands, fear: to whom outward respect is due on account of their office or rank, outward respect.

Summary

All civil governments derive their origin and authority from God, and when doing right, have his sanction. He therefore requires his children to be obedient to them; where they fail, they resist not merely the government but him. Civil officers, too, are designed to be for good to God's children, and not a source of fear. Neither, therefore, must they be resisted. Consequently, there are two reasons why we should obey the constituted authorities of the State: first, that we may avoid being punished, and, second, that we may not violate our conscience. Moreover, for these same reasons we pay tax, customs, etc. Besides, whenever it may be necessary, we must go farther and even honor those in authority. By all these acts we shall please God and promote our own happiness.

Comment

Duties to the Civil Government. 13:1-7

Law and order are principles which come from God. The condition of a people governed by law and the resulting order originated in the mind of God. Here is a general principle which must be heeded without question, as long as the authorities do not demand of us anything inconsistent with our Christian profession. There is no authority but from God. God is the original source of all power—not that he ordains power to do wrong, but he does originate the power of authority, and sets it into operation through civil government.

To the Jew it would be no light thing to ask him to submit to the government of Rome as being ordained of God. Paul goes farther—not only is government ordained of God, but whoever resists, resists God. It would not always be easy or convenient, but the true Christian has no choice if he is to obey God.

The Christian has no need to fear the rulers of a land whose laws

343. Must we always be in subjection to the higher powers?
344. What divine reason is given for submitting to the government?
345. We need never fear the appearance of a policeman. Why?
346. Give the twofold obligation of the Christian to the government.

do not conflict with the Word of God, and no terror need rise in the heart of that child of God when he sees a policeman. The Christian is in subjection to God's more perfect revelation through Christ; such makes him the very finest of the State's citizens. To be free from the fear of government interference, we of the free world do that which is good. We as Christians will be honored by God because of our exemplary conduct.

Those in power are to be obeyed because they are God's servants and are so serving to do us good. There are always some so-called "free spirits" who want to throw off all restraining influences and live by their own rules; even among Christians this is true. To such, the words of Paul have particular force, "an avenger for anger upon him who does evil."

The Christian has a twofold obligation to the government—not only because he naturally fears the just anger of those in power, but for a much higher motive: his conscience has been educated by the Word of God, and upon such a basis he obeys.

An application of the above truths could be: pay your taxes. When we fail to comply with those who collect taxes, we are disobeying God. This is a very pointed, up-to-date application in light of much loose thinking and acting on such matters today.

Verse seven is a generalization and conclusion of all that has been said in the previous verse (1-6):

Pay dues on exports and imports, and all other legal dues.

Pay your taxes; they are your legal, as well as divine obligation.

Pay proper respect to authorities.

Pay with honest commendation those who serve well in public office.

Text

13:8-10. Owe no man anything, save to love one another: for he that loveth his neighbor hath fulfilled the law. 9 For this, thou shalt not commit adultery, Thou shalt not kill, Thou shalt not steal, Thou shalt not covet, and if there be any other commandment, it is summed up in this word, namely, Thou shalt love thy neighbor as thyself. 10 Love worketh no ill to his neighbor: love therefore is the fulfillment of the law.

Realizing Romans, 13:8-10

555. Does verse eight cancel all credit buying?

556. We all have a great debt. What is it?

557. If we truly loved our neighbor, would there be any need for law? Explain.

558. Was there some particular purpose in using part of the ten commandments as examples of law?

559. Show how the purpose of law is fulfilled in love.

Paraphrase

13:8-10. Pay all your debts, and owe no man any thing, unless mutual love; because that debt can never be fully discharged. He who loveth another, hath fulfilled the law respecting his neighbor.

9 For the precepts, Thou shalt not commit adultery, thou shalt not kill, thou shalt not steal, thou shalt not bear false witness, thou shalt not covet; and if there be an other commandment prescribed in the word of God, or dictated by right reason, which hath others for its object, it is summed up in this precept, namely, thou shalt love thy neighbor as thyself: love him as a part of thyself, on account of his usefulness in promoting thy happiness.

10 For love restraineth a man from doing evil to his neighbor, and leadeth him to do his neighbor every good office in his power; wherefore love is the fulfilling of the law respecting one's neighbor.

Summary

Christians must pay to all whatever is due them, whether tax, customs, or honor. The only exception is that we must be always owing one another a debt of love, which we are to be constantly paying, yet never able to pay in full. We are never to feel that we have finally discharged the debt. The reason is that he who loves another is sure to keep the whole law towards him. We will not only never injure him whom we love, but will do him whatever good we can.

Comment

Duties of love to all men. 13:8-10

We must produce a good report from Christians and non-Christians. Here are personal obligations that must be paid. "Owe no man anything," would be a good motto to hang on the wall of the preacher's study, or on the wall of the elder's home. But we *do* have a debt—an obligation of love. Perhaps one is inseparately linked to the other. We cannot love one another if we fail to pay what we owe. We need not worry about moral regulations when we love in deed and in truth. We shall find, to our joy (and that of our neighbor), that we have gone far beyond whatever regulations man has set up for right or wrong.

347. In what sense are we to "owe no man anything"?
348. Show how the debt of love relates to debts of money.
349. In what way should we go beyond the law man has set up?

The Ten Commandments are all summed up in one word—"love." How could we commit adultery, kill, steal or covet if we love our neighbor?

Text

13:11-14. And this, knowing the season, that already it is time for you to awake out of sleep: for now is salvation nearer to us than when we first believed. 12 The night is far spent, and the day is at hand: let us therefore cast off the works of darkness, and let us put on the armor of light. 13 Let us walk becomingly, as in the day; not in revelling and drunkenness, not in chambering and wantonness, not in strife and jealousy. 14 But put ye on the Lord Jesus Christ, and make not provision for the flesh, to fulfil the lusts thereof.

Realizing Romans, 13:11-14

560. We can indeed know "the times and the seasons" in one particular. What is it?

561. In what sense is salvation nearer today than when we first believed?

562. The eternal morning is about to dawn. Cast off "the works of darkness." Would the Christians in Rome be involved in such things? Why does Paul give the command?

563. What a glorious expression: "Armor of light." Explain its appropriateness.

564. If you are looking for prohibitions against many of the popular sins of our day, you will find them in vs. 13. The incentive for laying such aside is there. What is it?

565. Do a little research on the meaning of "chambering and wantonness."

566. Please notice that the sins of strife and jealousy are also "works of darkness." What are the indications of strife and jealousy?

567. Is it possible to "make *no* provision for the flesh"? The word "put ye on" is a theatrical word referring to "getting into character." How does it apply to us?

Paraphrase

13:11-14. This also I command: Form a better judgment of the present season, that it is already the hour for us to awake out of that sleep into which the sensual practices of heathenism have cast us; for now the doctrine of salvation, the gospel, is better understood by us than when we first believed.

12 The night of heathenish ignorance is drawing to a conclusion, and the day of gospel light is about to shine with meridian splendor in all countries. Let us, therefore, who know this, put off the works

of darkness which we used to perform in honor of idols, and let us put on the armor proper for the day of the gospel.

13 Let us walk about decently habited (dressed) as becometh those who walk in the day, not employing ourselves, like the idolatrous Gentiles, in revellings and in drinking to excess; not in lying with harlots, and in lasciviousness, whether in action, discourse, or dress; nor in quarrelling about riches, or honors, or opinions, and in envying the prosperity of others.

14 But be ye clothed with the dispositions of the Lord Jesus Christ; his piety, temperance, purity, charity; in short, his whole character; and, like him, make no provision for gratifying the lusts of the flesh.

Summary

It is now time for us to awake from the sleep of the old unregenerate night through which we have been passing, and to do our whole duty in everything. The reason is that the day of salvation will soon be upon us, and for it we must be ready. All our former evil deeds must be utterly abandoned, and the new life in Christ fully assumed. Henceforth we must live for the Savior, not for the flesh.

Comment

The Fact of Salvation Before Us Helps to Enforce These Duties.
13:11-14.

We all need an incentive to prompt us to obey. God has surely supplied such. If the eyes of our understanding were enlightened, we should see how near we live to eternity. We can patiently endure hardship and tribulation when we see Heaven just ahead. Each day brings us one day closer to our eternal home. Could it be that some of the saints in Rome were sleepy? The night of life is nearly over; the morning of eternity is already streaking the eastern sky. Wake up! Dress up! Go to work! (We are all working on a night shift.)

We are preparing for another time and place of work, in the Father's house. To enter here we must have on "the armor of light." We cannot have on the panoply of God's soldier, and the clothes of darkness at the same time. To quote Moses E. Lard on vs. 13a:

"The *komos* was a sort of carousal in which a number of persons participated, and which commonly ended by the whole party parading the streets with music, songs, and dancing. It was simply a noisy drunken frolic. The *komoi* were very common among the idolatrous Gentiles, particularly among the devotees of Bacchus." (Romans, pp. 408, 40a)

How could it be said that some Christians were involved in such sins as prostitution and lewdness? In Rome such was the rule among the populace. Many of "the saints" in the Roman church had once walked in these things. The strong desire to yet practice them was with many. Paul bluntly states that such things cannot be practiced if we are to walk in the light of the eternal day.

The marvelous solution to the whole problem of returning to the old life is found in vs. 14. The expression, "put ye on," can have reference to the theater. Actors and actresses "put on" the character they attempt to portray. It is sometimes called "getting into the character." The true actor literally "becomes" another person. We are not play-acting—this is real—but we are to "become" the living representation of the Lord Jesus. How shall we do this if we do not know "the script"? We have a copy of it—the New Testament—in which is found the eyewitness account of our Lord by Matthew, Mark, Luke and John. Many actors and actresses memorize as much script copy as is in the New Testament to portray one of the prostitutes or drunkards spoken of in vs. 13. We can become another man, another woman, by the transformation of our minds. Christ is then formed within us. "It is no longer I that live—"

Rethinking in Outline Form

4. Duties to the Civil Government. 13:1-7 cf. Tit. 3:1; I Pet. 2:13-17; Matt. 22:17-21; I Tim. 2:1-2.
    a. Law and order ordained of God. v. 1.
    b. Law and order a terror to the evil, but a blessing to good. v. 3-4.
    c. To be in subjection because of wrath and conscience. v. 5.
    d. Tribute, dues, custom, fear, honor. vs. 6-7.
5. Duties of Love to All Men. vs. 8-10.
    a. Owe no man anything. v. 8a.
       This no doubt refers back to the taxes and dues of the preceding verses.
    b. Love your neighbor and you fulfill the law. vs. 8b-10.
6. The Fact of Salvation Before Us Helps to Enforce These Duties. 13:11-14.
    a. Eternal salvation nearer each day. v. 11 cf. Jas. 5:8; I Pet. 4:7; II Pet. 3:8-11; Eph. 5:14; I Thess. 5:1-11.
    b. Cast off darkness and put on armor of light. v. 12 cf. Eph. 5:11; 6:11-17.

350. What wonderful incentive for obedience has God given us?
351. In what sense are we all "working on a night shift"?
352. What is the preparation necessary for working in the Father's house?
353. Explain the meaning of the expression "put ye on the Lord Jesus Christ."

c. To walk becomingly. v. 13 cf. I Thess. 4:12; Gal. 5:21; Eph. 5:18; I Pet. 4:3; II Tim. 2:14, 23-24; I Tim. 6:3-5.

d. To put on the Lord Jesus Christ. v. 14 cf. Gal. 3:27; Eph. 4:24; Col. 3:9-10; Gal. 5:16-24; I Pet. 2:11.

Text

14:1-12. But him that is weak in faith receive ye, yet not for decision of scruples. 2 One man hath faith to eat all things: but he that is weak eateth herbs. 3 Let not him that eateth set at nought him that eateth not; and let not him that eateth not judge him that eateth: for God hath received him. 4 Who art thou that judgest the servant of another? to his own lord he standeth or falleth. Yea, he shall be made to stand; for the Lord hath power to make him stand. 5 One man esteemeth one day above another: another esteemeth every day alike. Let each man be fully assured in his own mind. 6 He that regardeth the day, regardeth it unto the Lord: and he that eateth, eateth unto the Lord, for he giveth God thanks; and he that eateth not, unto the Lord he eateth not, and giveth God thanks. 7 For none of us liveth to himself, and none dieth to himself. 8 For whether we live, we live unto the Lord; or whether we die, we die unto the Lord: whether we live therefore, or die, we are the Lord's. 9 For to this end Christ died and lived again, that he might be Lord of both the dead and the living. 10 But thou, why dost thou judge thy brother? or thou again, why dost thou set at nought thy brother? for we shall all stand before the judgment-seat of God.

11 For it is written, As I live, saith the Lord, to me every knee shall bow,

And every tongue shall confess to God.

12 So then each one of us shall give account of himself to God.

Realizing Romans, 14:1-12

568. What is the meaning of the word "receive" in 14:1?

569. How would one be received for "decision of scruples"?

570. Someone must be right in this matter of eating. Who is it?

571. Is strength or weakness in faith dependent upon knowledge? In what way?

572. There is one mutual responsibility. What is it?

573. How could God receive someone who was not correct in his views?

574. Is Paul teaching "irresistible grace" in vs. 4? Please explain the phrase, "for the Lord hath power to make him stand."

575. Could we apply the principle here stated to Christian baptism or the Lord's Supper? Why?

576. Should we esteem the Lord's day as above all other days? How will the instruction here given apply if we do esteem Sunday?
577. Why is it so important that we be fully assured in our own mind?
578. Why should we feel the Lord has any interest in eating or days?
579. How deeply grateful we should be to our Heavenly Father. In everything we should give thanks. How can we do this if there is a difference of opinion as to right or wrong?
580. It is easy to see how none of us lives unto himself. How is it that "none dieth unto himself"?
581. We belong to the Lord Jesus by right of purchase. It then becomes no matter of choice with us. How must we settle all questions?
582. Christ is Lord of the dead according to vs. 9. How is this so?
583. Should we delay our judgment on all matters in favor of the final judgment of God? Explain.
584. Are Christians going to stand before the judgment seat of God? If so, for what purpose?
585. Does gossiping about the ignorance or frailties of our brethren constitute judging? Will we be judged for such action?

Paraphrase

14:1-12. The Jewish Christian who is weak in the faith concerning meats and days, receive ye into your company, but not in order to passionate disputations concerning his opinions.

2 The Gentile Christian, indeed, believeth that he may eat every kind of meat; but the Jewish Christian, who is weak in the faith, eats vegetables only in heathen countries, because he cannot find meats which he thinketh clean.

3 Since both act from conscience, let not the Gentile who eateth every kind of meat, despise the Jew who eateth not certain kinds; and let not the Jew who eateth not certain kinds, condemn the Gentile who eateth all kinds: for God, by the spiritual gifts bestowed on the Gentile, declareth that he hath accepted him.

4 Who art thou that condemnest another's household servant? He is accountable to his own master, and not to thee; so that by his own master's sentence he must be acquitted or condemned: and he shall be acquitted; for God hath power to acquit him at the judgment, and will do it, if he hath acted conscientiously.

5 With respect to days, the Jewish Christians, indeed, thinketh one day more holy than another; the new moons, for example, and sabbaths: but the Gentile Christian, better informed, thinketh every

day alike holy, because the law of Moses is not the law of Christ's kingdom. Let every one direct himself according to his own conviction.

6 He who observeth the Jewish holy days, observeth them in obedience to Christ, who he thinks hath commanded them: He who doth not observe these days in obedience to Christ, he doth not observe them, knowing that Christ hath abolished them. He who eateth all kinds of meat indiscriminately, eateth them in obedience to Christ, who has permitted them to be eaten; for he giveth God thanks for them, in the persuasion that they are permitted; and he who eateth not every kind, in obedience to Christ he eatest them not, and showeth his persuasion that they are not permitted, by giving God thanks for the food he is allowed to eat.

7 In thus declaring their subjection to Christ, both of them act properly: for none of us liveth by his own will, and none of us is allowed to die by his own will.

8 But whether we live by the will of Christ: or whether we die, we die by the will of Christ. Whether we live therefore or die, we are Christ's subjects; and should not, in religious matters, be guided either by our own will or by the will of others, but by his.

9 To this implicit obedience from all he hath the completest title: for to this end Christ both died and rose, and liveth again in heaven, that he might rule and judge both the dead and the living.

10 But thou Jew, why dost thou condemn thy Gentile brother, because he neglecteth the distinction of meats and days? Or thou Gentile also, why dost thou despise thy Jewish brother as a weak bigot, because he observeth these distinctions? In such matters we should not judge one another; for we shall all be placed before the judgment-seat of Christ, to be judged by him.

11 This was declared to the Jews long ago; 'For it is written, I have sworn myself, saith the Lord, the word is gone out of my mouth,' and also, 'That unto me every knee shall bow, and every tongue shall swear.'

12 Well, then, every one of us shall give an account concerning himself to God, whose indulgence to the sincere will make many ashamed of their harsh judgments.

354. How does the discussion of the weak and strong relate to the renewing of the mind?
355. Why not attempt to instruct the weak brother?
356. What is meant by saying some matters are matters of "indifference"?
357. Explain the phrase "for the Lord hath power to make him stand" (vs. 4b).

Summary

A brother who is weak in belief, and consequently narrow in his views, we are nevertheless cordially to accept, but in receiving him, we must let alone those thoughts of his which arise out of his weakness. Their correctness or incorrectness is not a question for our decision. And where one brother regards certain days as sacred, while another holds all days to be alike, the rule is to let each be fully satisfied in his own mind, and act accordingly. In this case, the strong who esteems every day alike, is not to despise the weak; nor is the weak, who thinks one day better than another, to judge the strong. The same rule applies also in the case of meats thought to be clean or unclean. In matters of indifference, each man is a law to himself. Accordingly, in such cases we must leave each to act out his own sense of right. And as to judging one another in such matters, we must wholly abstain from it. We are accountable to God only, and he will judge us.

Comment

Forbearance in Matters of Opinion for Those Who are Weak in the Faith. 14:1-15:13.

1. The weak in the faith should not be harshly judged. 14:1-12.
    Once again we could say: if we are to be transformed by the renewing of our minds, here is a guide to our thinking. The Christian brother who feels a thing to be wrong and a sin for him to engage in, let him be. Do not argue with him about it. Receive him into your fellowship as a Christian brother. In particular, the reference Paul has in mind has to do with eating. There were those persons who did not have a complete knowledge of God's will on this subject. They felt it would be wrong for them to eat meat. "When you talk with him," says Paul, "please do not invite him to your table at which you serve meat. On the other hand, the weak brother ought not to feel he has a superior type of righteousness and attempt to instruct you in the ways of the vegetarian." In all of this conversation between the two brothers, there is much more than mere discussion. The action of judgment also enters in when one says, "I am right and you are wrong; *therefore* you are condemned." There are many matters of indifference, matters not wrong within themselves. Since each saint is responsible for a knowledge of "the faith," (Jude 3) and each member of the body is answerable to the head, who are we to judge our brother? To use the figure of Paul: "This man does not work for you; he is employed by another, even the Lord. To whom then is he answerable? To his own master. If the Lord is pleased with him, who are you to be displeased? You may be dis-

pleased, but this must never enter into the area of judgment. It is not necessary for either of you to understand or "see" how each can stand in the day of judgment. God is able to make each do so by his own divine power and wisdom."

Now, as to "special" days—are we at liberty to insert the word "special" as related to "days"? I think not. We can infer that here is a discussion of the desire of certain Jewish Christians to put a special emphasis upon the seventh day and certain other days in the Jewish calendar. I do not believe that Paul's teachings uphold the observance of "special" days. When the Jewish law was abolished was not all responsibility toward holding one day above another also abolished? Is it not what we do on Sunday that is sacred rather than the day itself? At least there were some in the Roman church who felt every day was just alike. All days are the gifts of God. The observance of the Lord's Supper on the first day of the week does not make the day (all twenty-four hours) holy; at least we have no word of scripture to say so. This will not at all be the opinion of some who read this. Very well—one regards "all days alike" because he feels it pleases the Lord, and one regards some days as "special" for the same reason. Let each mutually agree not to set the other at nought. There are two very important considerations for each Christian. However one regards the matters of indifference, let it be *his* opinion and not just the mouthing of someone else's reasoning. One must be "fully" assured in his *own* heart. The second is equally important. Whatever one does, do it unto the Lord. Let him thank God with sincerity for vegetables if he will not eat meat, thank God with sincerity if he observes Sunday (the day) as sacred. The opposite must also be true.

The great, eternal reason behind such conduct is found in verse seven. We are responsible to and for others. In our living we influence others—we are not living an exclusive life—we are constantly associated with others and in the presence of God. We should be careful so to live in eating and drinking and observing as to never put a stumbling block in our brother's path. There is one act which we shall all perform: we must all die; but even dying can be an example to others. Indeed it shall be—for good or bad. We can read into this verse that we are responsible for the eternal destiny of the souls of our brothers and sisters. They will come up to

358. Is Sunday a special day? In what respect?
359. What is the meaning of the expression—"Let each one be fully assured in his own heart."?
360. What is the great, eternal reason behind our need for full assurance of faith?

death in about the same way you do. Will this be adequate? Are you ready to die? If you are not, and others are following you, are you not also responsible to and for them? Let us live in such a manner in all things that our life will a be true example of the preparation for death.

Verse eight is the foundation on which this whole discussion (vs. 1-7) rests. We live for the honor of Christ and we die for the honor of Christ; i.e., in such a manner as to bring him honor. This we do because we belong to him. Being the living property of another, we essentially have no will in the matter. Most especially is this true when we consider the circumstances of our purchase.

What a wonderful Lord we serve. He not only rules as king here, but also over those in eternity. We indeed belong to him for he "ever lives." We are owned and ruled by him in heaven as well as on earth.

There is a question for the weak and the strong in vs. 10. Paul asks the weak, "Why do you judge your brother?" He asks the strong, "Why do you despise your brother?" Paul also has an answer: "We all shall appear before the judgment seat of God." This being true, why should we enter into the prerogatives of God? Since every inequality will be balanced, every question answered, why attempt it ourselves? Indeed, we sin when we do. The prophet Isaiah speaks of God's lordship. It shall be enough to account for our sins on judgment day. Our brother rests in the hands of an all-wise God.

Text

14:13-23. Let us not therefore judge one another any more: but judge ye this rather, that no man put a stumblingblock in his brother's way, or an occasion of falling. 14 I know, and am persuaded in the Lord Jesus, that nothing is unclean of itself: same that to him who accounteth anything to be unclean, to him it is unclean. 15 For if because of meat thy brother is grieved, thou walkest no longer in love. Destroy not with thy meat him for whom Christ died. 16 Let not then your good be evil spoken of: 17 for the kingdom of God is not eating and drinking, but righteousness and peace and joy in the Holy Spirit. 18 For he that herein serveth Christ is well-pleasing to God, and approved of men. 19 So then let us follow after things which make for peace, and things whereby we may edify one another. 20 Overthrow not for meat's sake the work of God. All things

361. We have no will in certain matters—what are they?
362. In what way is Christ the "Lord of the dead"?
363. We shall all appear before the judgment seat of Christ. We should not therefore judge one another. Show how the two thoughts are related.

indeed are clean; howbeit it is evil for that man who eateth with offence. 21 It is good not to eat flesh, nor to drink wine, nor to do anything whereby thy brother stumbleth. 22 The faith which thou hast, have thou to thyself before God. Happy is he that judgeth not himself in that which he approveth. 23 But he that doubteth is condemned if he eat, because he eateth not of faith; and whatsoever is not of faith is sin.

Realizing Romans, 14:13-23

586. It would seem some brothers will stumble over anything. Are we to remove all objections for all brothers? Explain.

587. Why not ask the "weak brother" to study and become strong?

588. Verse fourteen contains a principle for all of us to learn and apply. Be careful how it is applied. Be more careful that it is applied. Is any meat "unclean" today?

589. We could and should forego many things because of those who are weak. How does this relate to tobacco or the theater or TV? Are any weak ones destroyed by these things?

590. What is "the good" in vs. 16?

591. Is the church the kingdom of God? We are not to spend our time and energies on matters of eating and drinking. On what should we expend our time and energies? What is "joy in the Holy Spirit"?

592. Who are "the men" of vs. 18?

593. Verse nineteen should be made into an attractive plaque and sold in stores frequented by preachers and Sunday School teachers. Mention one practical application of this verse to everyday living.

594. Who is involved in vs. 20b? i.e., who is eating with offence?

595. The stumbling in vs. 21 has reference to the loss of the soul, not the "loss of face." Do you agree?

596. On matters of indifference we are to keep quiet. Sometimes when we speak we do so to our own hurt. Explain how with special reference to vs. 22b.

597. If faith cometh by hearing, (Rom. 10:17) and we are in chapter fourteen dealing with matters of indifference, how could the principle of vs. 23 be applied?

Paraphrase

14:13-23. Let us therefore no more judge one another bigots or profane persons, because our opinions and practices are different: but ye Gentile Christians, pass this sentence rather on yourselves, that ye will not do any thing which may endanger your brother's virtue, or occasion him to sin.

14 I know by the light of reason, and am persuaded by revelation from the Lord Jesus, that there is no kind of meat unclean naturally. Nevertheless, to him who believeth certain kinds to be unclean, to that man they are unclean; and he will sin if he eat them, either to indulge his own taste or to gain the favor of others.

15 Wherefore, if thy brother, who thinketh certain meats unclean, is made to sin through thy eating such meat, whether it be by hating thee as a profane person, or by following thy example contrary to his conscience, or by apostatizing to Judaism, thou no longer actest according to the love thou owest to thy brother. Do not become the occasion of destroying him with thy meat, for whom Christ died.

16 Let not then the good liberty which belongeth to you be evil spoken of, as an indulgence of appetite to the prejudice of others.

17 Ye need not use your liberty always; for the religion of Christ does not consist, either in abstaining from or in using meat and drink, but in a righteous and peaceable behaviour, and in joy in the Holy Ghost.

18 And the brother who, by righteousness, peace, and joy in the Holy Ghost, serves Christ his Lord, (vs. 9), is acceptable to God, and will be approved of men.

19 Well, then, let us pursue the things which promote peace, and the things which advance that mutual edification which we ought to reap from one another's example.

20 Do not for the sake of the pleasure of eating this or that kind of meat, destroy your brother's virtue, which is the work of God. All kinds of meats, indeed, are clean under the gospel; yet that meat is bad to the man who eateth it, not from a persuasion of its lawfulness, but through the influence of example.

21 It is commendable neither to eat flesh of any kind, nor to drink wine, or to do any thing, however innocent, whereby thy brother is brought into danger of sinning, or is made to sin, or is weakened in his attachment to the gospel.

22 I own thou hast a just persuasion concerning the lawfulness of all kinds of meat. Hold that persuasion fast, so far as respects thine own conduct in the presence of God; but do not use thy liberty, so as to lead others to sin. Happy is he who doth not subject himself to punishment, by doing what he approveth as lawful.

23 For he who seeth a difference in meats, is liable to punishment, if through thy example he eat what he thinks unclean; because he eateth not from a persuasion that it is lawful, but to please others. This is wrong; for whatever is done without a conviction of its lawfulness, is really a sin, though it be lawful in itself.

Summary

Instead of judging one another in questions respecting days and meats, let each decide, rather, that he will be very careful not to place a stumbling-block or occasion of falling in the way of his brother. This is the proper kind of judging for Christians. But in the matter of meats, and in all similar cases, if eating it grieves a brother, an effect which he may be unable to prevent, we are to abstain from it in deference to his feelings. Should we not do so, we may either drive him from the church, or induce him to follow an example which he is in danger of following too far, and so ruin him. In order to avoid these results, we must abstain from eating meat, where any one is hurt by it. We must not do anything that will imperil the salvation of a brother. The strong belief which enables us to do so many things that the weak cannot do, we must keep to ourselves. We are not at liberty to use it, when by so doing we injure others.

Comment

2. The Liberty of the Gospel Should not Be Used to the Injury of Others. 14:13-23.

Speaking of judgment, we have no need to judge one another. Indeed, to do so is wrong. If we wish to exercise our powers of evaluation, let us do it in this regard—that we place no stumbling block in our brother's way. This is addressed particularly to the strong. The weak brother might actually lose his soul over this matter. Let us be careful in what we consider indifferent—it is not so to him. If someone persuades him to eat meat, he could in his present frame of mind be sinning. He might feel he should go farther, since he sinned in eating meat, and become an idolater. It is not likely he would go back to idol worship, but neither would he remain with the church. He could not continue to associate with such, and would withdraw himself from fellowship.

In verses 14 and 15 is a most marvelous principle—a principle which, if exercised, would solve so very many of today's problems. Paul presents it by stating, "No meat is unclean." Paul knew this, since he knew the mind of Christ. But all men do not have this knowledge—to those who do not, the meat is unclean. One's attitude toward it changes it for him. Let us not force a man to violate his conscience even on a matter of indifference. When we wilfully act in opposition to our own sense of right and wrong, we break down our walls of defense against Satan. More than this, if we continue to insist in

364. We are to judge one another—but in what regard?
365. How could the weak brother lose his soul over eating meat?

this matter of food, we no longer act out of love. Our consideration for the weak brother is woefully lacking.

Let it be noticed please that the eating of meat by the stronger brother was no sin, and the weak brother was not to look upon it as such *for the stronger brother*. On the other hand, since it offends the weak brother, the one who is strong will refrain from eating in the presence of the weak. Since Christ died for both, neither should judge the other. It is possible even to cause the loss of the soul. If Christ loved him so much as to come all the way from heaven to die for him, we can show a little consideration in these matters.

"I see nothing wrong in that." "The practice of such doesn't hurt me." Such expressions are often heard. When self alone is involved, such might be true, but we do not live unto ourselves—others are watching. What appears permissible to us may be offensive to them and cause criticism for the whole body. What then is good to us becomes a point of offense. What shall we do? Give up that which we thought "good" for the sake of the cause of Christ. Someone else wants to know just how far one should go in applying this rule. The answer is—just as far as is necessary to avoid criticism of the cause of Christ.

Some persons, of course, who raise such an objection do not want to apply the rule at all. They raise such a question as a subterfuge behind which they can hide.

The important matters in the church, or the kingdom of God, are not meats and days, eating or not eating, but righteousness, peace and joy in the Holy Spirit. We should give the greatest attention to whether we are right by divine law, not by human opinion, to a settled peace in our own heart and the promotion of peace in the church as a whole—blessed indeed are the peacemakers—and to the joy which the Holy Spirit himself alone can give. . . . joy, that delicate regard for the feelings of one another which, under the strengthening presence in all of the Holy Spirit, shall give joy and not grief."

The Christian who thus serves Christ is acceptable to God (whether some brethren ever accept him or not) and approved by all men who stand on the sidelines to observe the Christian race. Such was the position of the Jerusalem church when they said (and meant) that "nought they possessed was their own. They were one heart and one soul." In this they found unity among themselves and

366. Even if eating meat is not a sin, thinking it is a sin will make it wrong. Why?
367. The strong is not to eat meat in the presence of the weak. Why?
368. How far can we go in applying the rule of being careful for the weak?
369. State the important matters in the Kingdom of God.

"favor with all the people." Let's make it the aim of our lives to pursue the ways and words of peace, not contention. We are here to help, not hinder one another. In verses 19 and 20 is a description of a house being built and pulled down, the house of God. We are either engaged constructively or destructively in our work on God's home, the church. "For the sake of food pull not down the work of God."

It is good to know that all food is clean (from the distinctions of the law) but even then it can become very evil to us when we, through our eating, cause our brother to stumble or apostasize.

Verse 21 sums up in one sentence the whole point of the section. It is not a matter of right or wrong, but rather of love and concern for our brother. Does it injure him? Abstain from it.

Remain quiet about your superior knowledge of meats and days; it is a matter of indifference or opinion; not of faith. Hold it to yourself. If you do not, (speaking to the strong brother) you will condemn yourself by the very thing in which you condemn others. God will judge the man who causes the weak to fall.

Verse 23 states the principle from which all service to God must spring. What we do must be done because we believe he approves of it. When we act in doubt or even against what we feel is right, we are destroying the basis of obedience—faith in God. This we must never do, nor lead others to do so.

Rethinking in Outline Form

7. Forbearance in Matters of Opinion for Those Who are Weak in the Faith. 14:1—15:13.
   a. The weak in the faith should not be harshly judged. vs. 1-12
      (1) To receive the weak brother. v. 1.
      (2) Not to judge in matters of food. vs. 2-4.
      (3) Not to judge (that is condemn) one who esteems certain days. v. 5.
      (4) Everything one does is to be done as unto the Lord. vs. 6-9.
      (5) There is to be no judging of others for all alike will stand before God. vs. 10-12.
   b. The liberty of the gospel should not be used to the injury of others. 14:13-23.
      (1) Not to put a stumbling block in our brother's way. v. 13 cf. I Cor. 8:7-13.

370. How shall the Holy Spirit produce joy in our lives?
371. Who is acceptable with God and "the people"?
372. We are all workmen of one type or another in the house of God. Explain.
373. How do some condemn themselves in their judgment of others?

(2) All food is clean. v. 14 cf. Lev. 11; I Tim. 4:3-5.
But to him that accounts it unclean, to him it is unclean.

(3) If we, through our actions or words, cause our brother
to stumble in this matter then we had better take note
that we are in sin. vs. 15-16.

(4) The essential character of the kingdom. vs. 17-19.

(5) Do not overthrow the work of God for a non-essential.
That is, in your manner of observance. v. 20.

(6) Do nothing that would cause others to stumble. v. 21.

(7) Be careful that you do not judge yourself in the way
you seek to bind that opinion upon another. v. 22.

(8) To act without conviction is a principle condemned
by God. This principle of action is condemned in verse
23.

Text

15:1-12. Now we that are strong ought to bear the infirmities of
the weak, and not to please ourselves. 2 Let each one of us please
his neighbor for that which is good, unto edifying. 3 For Christ also
pleased not himself; but, as it is written, The reproaches of them that
reproached thee fell upon me. 4 For whatsoever things were written
aforetime were written for our learning, that through patience and
through comfort of the scriptures we might have hope. 5 Now the
God of patience and of comfort grant you to be of the same mind
one with another according to Christ Jesus: 6 that with one accord
ye may with one mouth glorify the God and Father of our Lord Jesus Christ. 7 Wherefore receive ye one another, even as Christ also
received you, to the glory of God. 8 For I say that Christ hath been
made a minister of the circumcision for the truth of God, that he
might confirm the promises given unto the fathers, 9 and that the
Gentiles might glorify God for his mercy; as it is written,
Therefore will I give praise unto thee among the Gentiles,
And sing unto thy name.

10 And again he saith, Rejoice, ye Gentiles, with his people.

11 And again, Praise the Lord, all ye Gentiles; And let all the peoples praise him.

12 And again, Isaiah saith, There shall be the root of Jesse, And
he that ariseth to rule over the Gentiles; On him shall the Gentiles
hope.

374. Chapter fifteen discusses the obligations of one brother. Who is it?

375. Why should the strong "give in"? In what manner should the strong bear
the infirmities of the weak?

Realizing Romans, 15:1-13

598. Why would it be displeasing to anyone to bear the infirmities of the weak?

599. What is the nature of the weakness here described?

600. Should we make some definite effort to please our neighbor, or should this happen in the so-called ordinary way of life?

601. In what sense did Christ not please himself?

602. Who is the "thee" of vs. 3b? What is the meaning of such an expression?

603. Show the connection of vs. 3 and 4.

604. Should not the holy scriptures be a source of comfort to us every day? Why is this *not* true in our life?

605. Our God is one of patience and comfort. How can we find this to be true personally?

606. How was Paul's prayer of verses 5 and 6 to be answered?

607. We are to glorify God with our mouth. If you were to attempt to fulfill such an admonition right now, how would you do it?

608. Verse seven presents a principle whereby all hesitation in receiving one another should be removed. Why?

609. What "truth of God" is referred to in vs. 8? What are the promises? Name two.

610. Who is singing in vs. 9? Why?

611. Why this array of references to the Gentiles? cf. verses 10, 11, 12.

Paraphrase

15:1-12. We then, who are well instructed in the Christian doctrine, ought so to behave towards the ignorant, that their errors may hurt them as little as possible; and should not please ourselves only in what we do.

2 Wherefore, let every one of us please his neighbor in things innocent, to the promoting of his virtue and peace, for the sake of edifying the body of Christ.

3 For even Christ pleased not himself: his own pleasure was not the object of his actions, but the glory of God and the good of others; as it is written, The reproaches of them who reproached thee, have fallen on me: the punishment due to the wicked, who by their speeches and actions dishonored God, was laid to me.

4 But whatever things were before written in the scriptures, were written for our instruction, that through our recollecting the patience wherewith holy men have borne reproaches and sufferings for the glory of God, and the consolation which they received, all

recorded in the scriptures, we might have hope of attaining the like patience and consolation in the like circumstances.

5 Now may God, the author of the patience and consolation of the saints, grant you to have the very same disposition towards one another always, according to the will and example of Christ Jesus;

6 That, joining together in religious worship, unanimously with one voice ye may praise the God and Father of our Lord Jesus Christ, for his love to man.

7 Wherefore hold communion [have fellowship] with one another, notwithstanding ye differ in opinion about meats and days, even as Christ also hath received us all into his church, to the glory of God.

8 To Christ's receiving the Gentiles, it is no objection that he never preached to them: for I affirm, that Jesus Christ became a minister of the circumcision, on account of establishing the truth of God, in order that, by converting the Jews, and sending them to preach to the Gentiles, he might accomplish the promises made to the fathers concerning the blessing of the nations;

9 And that the Gentiles might praise God on account of the mercy showed them, as it is written, 'Thou hast made me the head of the heathen; therefore I will glorify thee, O Lord, among the heathen: My disciples will glorify thee for making me the head of the heathen; and sing unto thy name, on account of their being saved by me.'

10 And again, Moses, fortelling the subjection of the Gentiles to God, saith, 'Rejoice ye Gentiles with his people.'

11 And again, 'O praise the Lord, all ye nations; praise him, all ye people.' Praise the Lord, because ye enjoy the privileges of the gospel along with the Jews, whereby his 'merciful kindness is great towards us.'

12 And again, Isaiah saith, (chap. xi. 10). 'In that day there shall be the root of Jesse, which shall stand for an ensign of the people; and to it the Gentiles shall seek for protection, government, and salvation. 'And his rest shall be glorious.'

Summary

The strong are under obligation to bear with the weak, even though it subjects them to inconvenience. This was the course pursued by Christ, and he is our example. As the Savior has accepted us, notwithstanding our imperfections, so must we accept one another regardless of differences on immaterial questions, such as eating

376. How shall we determine when we are indulgent and not helpful?
377. Give the meaning of the expression "Even Christ pleased not himself."
378. Explain how the Old Testament scriptures are a source of help in our helping the weak.

meat and the like. The whole section is devoted to unity of feeling, forbearance, and harmony in action. Every form of alienation among the children of God is wrong, and therefore to be studiously guarded against.

Comment

3. Exhortations to Mutual Helpfulness. 15:1-13

Chapter fifteen continues the thought of fourteen. We are to further understand the proper relationship of the strong to the weak. Particularly is this a discussion of how the strong are to act toward the weak. Those who have no scruples about meats and days should patiently bear with those who do. Since the conscience of the strong would not be violated by observance or lack of observance of these matters, it is altogether reasonable to call on the strong to acquiesce in the matter. Let the strong behave as God does with them—bear (not begrudgingly) with the imperfections of the weak. If the strong in faith were to assert himself and rebuke the weak, it would be on a matter of opinion, and would only please the strong—not God, nor the weak. None of us must act with the thought of self-indulgence.

Our efforts as those who are strong are to be only for the purpose of help. When our neighbor (weak or strong) asks for assistance in doing anything contrary to the will of God, he should be rebuked, not helped. A great deal of wisdom is necessary in determining when we are helpful and not indulgent. If we have a sincere desire to see our fellow Christian advance in wisdom and grace, we shall find ways of helping such a growth.

The attitude of Christ toward others is here given as an example for the action of the weak. Was it always easy for our Lord to bear with the ignorance and misunderstanding of his followers? It would have been easier to please himself—and his pleasure was always right —but this he did not do. If he who had such a divine prerogative did not take it, who are we to insist upon pleasing ourselves? The prophecy of Psa. 69 finds a fulfillment in the attitude of Christ toward the weak. The reproaches of men fell upon Christ. If Christ was willing to bear so much to help all, can we not manifest something of the same love toward one another?

Paul makes an explanation of the purpose of using this reference from the Psalms. He says: "The Old Testament scriptures were written for our instruction—particularly in the area of helping the weak." The scriptures are a great source of patience and comfort. When we do what is right, we retain our hope.

Verse five seems to have the element of a prayer. It is Paul's deepest desire that the God who can produce patience and comfort should so work in their lives as to cause them to be of the same mind, according to the example of Christ.

The true purpose of receiving one another is seen in vs. 6: That we might present to the world one choir of praise to God. This God is the father of our Lord Jesus Christ.

Now, the conclusion: Let us accept one another in the same way we were accepted by God in Christ. If God is willing to overlook all our imperfections, why should we hesitate, especially when we know it brings glory to God. God will be honored even by the unbelieving when they see his power and love in the lives of his followers.

Verse seven begins a new thought, yet one which is associated with the preceding. Christ came to reconcile both Jew and Gentile in one body, and this he did. The application is—if he came to do this, are we not frustrating his purpose if we divide among ourselves? The details of this argument are: Christ was born of the Jewish race in order to save them. He came in fulfillment of promises made by God to the fathers. Not one promise failed—not one word proved untrue. The end result was the salvation of all the world.

We are yet developing the thought of mutual helpfulness. Verses 9-12 contain a series of Old Testament prophecies which show in their promise and fulfillment the unity of Jews and Gentiles. Note: In 9b David is in the midst of the Gentiles confessing the name of God and singing with the Gentiles. In Deut. 32:43 are the words of 10a. Moses is here called to support the thought. In this example the Gentiles are represented as rejoicing among the Jews. Once again in Psa. 117:1 the acceptance of the Gentiles is stated. The joy they have in this acceptance is described. The inference is obvious: "Christ has accepted all; do you then accept one another."

The final word on the subject is given by Isaiah. The "root out of Jesse" was to be exalted at God's right hand for the purpose of ruling the world. All in the world who accept his rule shall find salvation. This is for both Jew and Gentile. The point still carries of mutual acceptance of one another.

Text

15:14-33. And I myself also am persuaded of you, my brethren, that ye yourselves are full of goodness, filled with all knowledge, able also to admonish one another. 15 But I write the more boldly

379. What new thought is introduced by verse seven?
380. Why the use of the Old Testament prophesies in verses 9-12?
381. How does the thought of Christ ruling the world relate to mutual helpfulness?

unto you in some measure, as putting you again in remembrance, because of the grace that was given me of God, 16 that I should be a minister of Christ Jesus unto the Gentiles, ministering the gospel of God, that the offering up of the Gentiles might be made acceptable, being sanctified by the Holy Spirit. 17 I have therefore my glorying in Christ Jesus in things pertaining to God. 18 For I will not dare to speak of any things save those which Christ wrought through me, for the obedience of the Gentiles, by word and deed, 19 in the power of signs and wonders, in the power of the Holy Spirit; so that from Jerusalem, and around about even unto Illyricum, I have fully preached the gospel of Christ; 20 yea, making it my aim so to preach the gospel, not where Christ was already named, that I might not build upon another man's foundation; 21 but, as it is written,

> They shall see, to whom no tidings of him came,
> And they who have not heard shall understand.

22 Wherefore also I was hindered these many times from coming to you: 23 but now, having no more any place in these regions, and having these many years a longing to come unto you, 24 whensoever I go unto Spain (for I hope to see you in my journey, and to be brought on my way thitherward by you, if first in some measure I shall have been satisfied with your company)—25 but now, I say, I go unto Jerusalem, ministering unto the saints. 26 For it hath been the good pleasure of Macedonia and Achaia to make a certain contribution for the poor among the saints that are at Jerusalem. 27 Yea, it hath been their good pleasure; and their debtors they are. For if the Gentiles have been made partakers of their spiritual things, they owe it to them also to minister unto them in carnal things. 28 When therefore I have accomplished this, and have sealed to them this fruit, I will go on by you unto Spain. 29 And I know that, when I come unto you, I shall come in the fulness of the blessing of Christ.

30 Now I beseech you, brethren, by our Lord Jesus Christ, and by the love of the Spirit, that ye strive together with me in your prayers to God for me; 31 that I may be delivered from them that are disobedient in Judea, and that my ministration which I have for Jerusalem may be acceptable to the saints; 32 that I may come unto you in joy through the will of God, and together with you find rest. 33 Now the God of peace be with you all. Amen.

REALIZING ROMANS, 15:14-33

612. Paul gives a very generous compliment in vs. 14. If they were full of both goodness and knowledge, why did he write them as he did?

613. Does the phrase "able to admonish one another" suggest the "order of service" in the Roman church? Are we doing today what they did then in this matter of admonishing one another?

614. Paul wrote to the saints in Rome to stir up their memory. What would they be able to remember that would help them? He gives his authority for so writing. What was it?

615. Paul seems to look upon himself as both a minister and priest in vs. 16. Show how. What is the meaning of "sanctified by the Holy Spirit"?

616. Is the word "boasting" a good synonym for "glorying" in vs. 17?

617. Paul had spoken of many other things even to these brethren. How are we to understand vs. 18?

618. What distinction is there between "the power of signs and wonders" and "the power of the Holy Spirit"? cf. vs. 19.

619. Locate Illyricum on the map and marvel with me at the accomplishments of the Apostle. Is Paul here speaking of his own personal preaching or the preaching he directed?

620. Why would Paul be reticent to "build upon another man's foundation"?

621. Verse twenty-one has marvelous application today. There are 120 countries and only 28 of them have gospel preaching. Why is it we do not answer the call of those who have never heard?

622. Why was Paul hindered from coming to the saints in Rome?

623. From where was this epistle written? What is meant by saying "having no more place in these regions"?

624. Paul planned an evangelistic tour of Spain. Did he go?

625. What were the saints in Rome going to do for Paul on his journey to Spain?

626. At the time of the writing Paul was on his way to Jerusalem with an offering. Read the references in his other letters regarding this offering. Why was it taken? How long did it take to obtain it? Who carried it? From whom was it taken?

627. Paul felt Gentiles had a debt to pay to the Jews. What was it?

628. In what sense is money "carnal"?

629. "Sealed to them this fruit"—what a picturesque phrase. What does it mean?

630. Wasn't Paul a little presumptuous to assume help from the brethren in Rome?

631. What is "the fullness of the blessing of Christ"?

632. Is the "love of the Spirit" in vs. 30 the Spirit's love or our love for the Spirit?

633. Note and number the three requests of Paul's prayer.

634. What effect would prayers have on the disobedient in Judea?
635. Give the meaning of the word "strive" in vs. 30. Are we to "strive" in our prayers? Do you do it?
636. There is in vs. 31 a most wonderful picture of unselfishness. Paul requests earnest prayer on behalf of the reception of an offering. Show the unselfishness in it.
637. Paul came to Rome, but not to rest. What were the circumstances of his coming?
638. In all the doxologies and benedictions there is a request. Just how would it be fulfilled? If it were, how would we know it?

Paraphrase

15:14-33. However, my brethren, though I have given both instruction and reproof, I have not a mean [low] opinion either of your knowledge or virtue. For even I myself am persuaded concerning you, that, in general, ye are full of good dispositions; and that, being filled with all knowledge of the Christian doctrine, ye are able also to instruct one another.

15 But, notwithstanding my good opinion of you, I have written the more boldly to you, brethren, partly as calling things to your remembrance, which I am qualified to do through the grace of apostleship given me of God. (Rom. i. 5. xii. 6.).

16 In order to my being a public minister of Jesus Christ among the Gentiles, ministering to them as a priest the knowledge of the gospel of God, that by their believing it, there might be an offering of the Gentiles most acceptable to God, being cleansed from their former impurities by the influences of the Holy Ghost accompanying my preaching.

17 I have therefore cause of boasting, through Christ Jesus, with respect to my success in things pertaining to God; my success in presenting the Gentiles an acceptable offering to God.

18 Now, though I might justly claim praise on account of the success of my disciples, yet I will not, in this boasting, dare to speak any thing of what Christ hath not wrought, but of what he hath wrought by me personally, in order to make the Gentiles obedient to the gospel, both in profession and practice, (see Rom. i. 5. xv. 26.)

19 By the power of miracles, performed by me on the sick and maimed, and what is still greater, by the power of the gifts of the Spirit of God, communicated by me to the Gentiles; so that, beginning at Jerusalem, and going through the countries round about as far as Illyricum, I have fully and successfully preached the gospel of Christ.

20 And it became me thus diligently to preach the gospel, not where Christ was acknowledged, that I might not build on another man's foundation: that would have been to perform the office of a subordinate teacher, which is far more easy than that of an apostle.

21 But I have preached to the most ignorant nations, so that, as it is written, they shall know the Saviour, to whom nothing hath been told concerning him by their instructors; and they who have not heard the method of salvation explained, shall understand it fully.

22 For which reason also, that I resolved to preach the gospel to those who had never heard it, I have been oftentimes hindered from coming to you.

23 But now, having no more opportunity in these parts to preach to persons who have not heard the gospel, and having for many years entertained a strong desire to come to you who are in Rome,

24 Whensoever I go towards Spain, I will come to you: For in my journey to that country, where, by preaching the gospel, I expect to turn the idolatrous inhabitants from Satan to God, I hope to see you at leisure, and to be accompanied a part of my way thitherward by some of you, after I shall first be made happy for a while with your company.

25 But at present I go to Jerusalem with the money I have collected for the brethren in Judea.

26 For the churches in the provinces of Macedonia and Achaia have been pleased to make a liberal contribution for the relief of the poor of the brethren who are in Jerusalem in great distress.

27 They have been pleased, verily, to make this contribution: and they have done well; because they are under great obligations to the Jewish Christians. For if the Gentiles have received of their spiritual things, if they have received from them the knowledge of the gospel, they ought certainly to minister to them of their worldly goods in their present need.

28 Wherefore, having finished this business, by delivering the money at Jerusalem, and having secured to the Jewish saints the fruit of the love which the Gentiles bear to them, I will go from Judea by you into Spain.

29 And from my experience of God's working by me, I know that when I come, I shall come empowered to bestow on you abundantly the gifts of the Spirit, (Rom. i. 11.), which are the peculiar blessing of the gospel of Christ.

382. How can God fill us with hope and joy?
383. What is the relationship to the joy of the Holy Spirit in our being at peace with one another?

30 Now I beseech you, brethren, by all that the Lord Jesus Christ hath done for you, and by the love which the Spirit hath showed to you, in giving you his manifold gifts, that ye strive together with me, by earnestly praying for me to God;

31 That I may be delivered from the disobedient in Judea, and that my service, in making the collections, which I am performing to the saints in Jerusalem, may be acceptable to them, and contribute to remove the prejudices which they entertain against the Gentile Christians for not obeying the law:

32 That in joy, on account of the reconciliation of the Jewish to the Gentile brethren, I may come to you by the will of God, and may with you be refreshed by the happiness following that reconciliation.

33 Now, may God, the author of peace, and who I hope will produce peace between the Jews and Gentiles, be with you all: and to show my sincerity in this wish, I say Amen.

Summary

The Apostle prays that the God of hope may fill the disciples in Rome with all peace and joy in believing what he has written. Although he has spoken plainly to them, and signified his disapprobation of certain things among them, still he is far from thinking meanly of them. On the contrary, he is persuaded that they are full of knowledge, and altogether able to teach and admonish one another. His bold manner in places is assumed in virtue of his apostolic office. The great object of his labors is that he may be enabled at last to present the Gentiles as a glorious and acceptable offering to God. He mentions the vast extent of his labors, and assigns the reason for wishing to preach where Christ had never been named.

The Apostle's multiplied labors in different countries had often hindered him from executing a purpose long since formed of one day visiting Rome. But now being without a place in those regions to preach the gospel where it had not before been preached, he decides to make the visit soon. But, first, he must go into Judea to carry a contribution from Greece and Macedonia to the poor brethren in Jerusalem. This service performed however, he proposes next a journey to Spain, and decides to see Rome on his way. He very ardently desires to be delivered, while in Judea, from the unbelieving Jews there, and that his alms may be acceptable to the poor disciples for whom they were intended.

384. Why have we said verse fourteen is "a delicate piece of diplomacy"?
385. Why the sharp application in parts of the letter?
386. In what sense did Paul consider himself a priest?
387. How could Paul boast and still be humble?

Comment

II. Conclusion. 15:13—16:27

1. Personal Matters. 15:13-33

Paul is to now speak of some of the results of applying the principles discussed in earlier verses. The great God who is the source and foundation of our hope of heaven can fill us with joy and peace if we believe what has been said about getting along with one another. Only when we are thus full of peace and joy can the Holy Spirit produce in us with power the abounding hope of glory. The importance of being at peace with one another is surely here pointed out.

Verse 14 is indeed "a delicate piece of diplomacy." Paul says that he has the greatest confidence in their goodness and knowledge. He suggests that he is not writing to them because he feels they are stubborn and ignorant. On the contrary, most of them were ready to receive his instructions and well able to carry them out. It is not to be thought that all the saints in Rome were "filled with goodness" or "filled with knowledge," but this was true of many of them. Paul wants to compliment them, and by so doing, to encourage those who lacked, to measure up.

"Parts of this letter are very sharp in application to personal life," says Paul. "This is true so that you saints in Rome might recall to mind the truths you learned when you became Christians, and some of those since that time." Paul says he has done this because of his apostolic office. God has constrained him so to write. Most especially is this true because he was called to minister to the Gentiles. The Roman church had many Gentiles. Paul came to them and to all nations, performing his sacred function in administering the good news of God that Christ Jesus came into the world to save sinners. Paul looks upon himself in analogy, as one standing before the altar of God as a priest offering the Gentiles who have believed up to God. This sacrifice or offering will be acceptable because it is pure and holy, pure because the Holy Spirit has made it pure. It is here stated that we as Christians are kept pure by the Holy Spirit so that one day we will be accepted by God. What a wonderful, encouraging thought!

Because many Gentiles had been presented to God by Paul, he was enabled to "boast in Christ"—which is something far different from boasting in himself—in matters relating to God. Paul rejoices in God's wonderful accomplishments through him.

388. In what sense was the gospel "fully preached"? Did every person hear?

389. Why was Paul hindered in coming to those in Rome? What caused the hindrance?

390. What did Paul expect from those at Rome?

Verse 18 indicates that Paul will mention only those things in which he was personally concerned. "It would be difficult to evaluate the work of another, but what Christ has done in and through me I can most certainly tell." This seems to be the meaning here.

Now follows in three short phrases the summation of all of Paul's work. What did God through Christ accomplish by Paul? Here it is: (1) Many, many wonderful acts by the power of the Spirit; (2) much inspired teaching and preaching by word and deed; (3) the words and deeds fully confirmed in those who heard and received, by signs and wonders. All of this was to one glorious end, "the obedience of the Gentiles."

In carrying out the commission given to him, Paul says that, considering Jerusalem as a geographical center, he has "fully preached the gospel of Christ" even as far as Illyricum. When Paul was in Ephesus "all Asia" heard the word. Paul so labored himself and so encouraged others that the message was spread throughout the whole district in which he preached. Surely he "labored more abundantly than them all."

It was a matter of personal honor with the apostle to work in virgin territory. There might be several reasons advanced for so doing, but the one Paul gave was that he "might not build on another man's foundation." This has real advantages, as any preacher of experience will agree.

Paul saw in this type of preaching a fulfillment of prophecy from Isaiah. To those who have never heard, to those who do not see—to these shall I bring divine understanding and sight. What a grand objective for every preacher.

For the very reason just cited, that he had found so many places where Christ had not been preached, Paul was often hindered in his desire to visit the church at Rome. At the writing of the epistle the situation had changed. In all of the area around the great city of Corinth he had fully preached the gospel. One cannot but wonder just what is entailed in "fully preaching" to the thousands who lived near Corinth. How was it done and who did it?

Paul is not planning a visit to Rome just to see the saints there, but to be helped by them on his way to evangelize Spain. Did Paul fulfill his wish to see Rome? We know he did, but under far different circumstances than he first planned. Did he preach in Spain? We do not know.

391. For whom was the offering taken? How many participated? How long was it in gathering?
392. The love of Christ was surely perfected in Paul. What indicates this?
393. Name the three requests in the prayer of Paul.

It is both encouraging and different to read of Paul's attitude toward the support of the gospel by those in Rome. Paul had never seen them, and yet he assumes in all confidence they will offer him financial and material assistance when he sees them on his way to Spain. Paul expected to be equipped by the brethren in Rome. While there, Paul also expected to rejoice with them in their mutual faith. In this he could not be fully satisfied, for time would not permit.

The time and place of the writing of the epistle are indicated in vs. 25, 26. By referring to the Acts account and other references, we conclude that Corinth and the third missionary journey were the place and time.

The saints of Judea and Jerusalem were very much in need of food and clothing. This need was met, upon the insistence of Paul. It was more than a year in gathering, and seven men were used to carry it. It was taken from a wider area than just Macedonia and Achaia, reaching even to Galatia.

Paul lays down a principle in vs. 27 that would find application in his relationship with many of the Gentile Christians in Rome. The Gentiles of Macedonia (in the churches of Thessalonica, Philippi, Berea) felt a debt must be paid to those in Jerusalem. The offering was a payment in material means for the spiritual blessings of the gospel. The gospel came from the Jews: we are their debtors.

Verse 28 is very much like vs. 24. The addition in vs. 28 is the route he is to take on his way to Rome, and the reason for it.

When Paul arrived in Rome he would come with the "whole council of God." To the holy in Rome he would impart the marvelous blessings of the gospel. There would be signs and wonders to confirm the word, but the spiritual benefit would be in the teaching and preaching.

Verses 30, 31 give an insight into Paul's feelings regarding his visit and gift to the poor in Jerusalem. He says in thought, "It is my most earnest desire that you battle with me in prayers that I might be protected from the merciless hands of certain who hate me in Judea." In addition to this, he says, "Allow the love of Christ and the love of the Holy Spirit to prompt you to join with me in the most earnest of petitions that none in the Jerusalem church will refuse the money I bring for them." How the love of Christ had been perfected in Paul can here be seen. He prayed for those who hated him, for those who misunderstood him, and not in a perfunctory manner but with all his heart and called upon Gentiles to do likewise.

394. What seems to suggest that Phoebe was the one who delivered the letter to Rome?
395. Was Phoebe a "deaconess"?

We might add vs. 32 to the prayer request, for it is a part of it. The whole request has three parts: (1) To be delivered from evil men; (2) the offering to be acceptable; (3) to arrive in Rome with joy and refreshment. The first part was not answered. The second was. The third was modified. Thus does God grant an answer that is better than our requests. He knows what is best, and we are satisfied to rest in this confidence.

Verse 33 contains a most beautiful and meaningful benediction. What more could anyone ask or wish than to have the assurance that God was with him always?

Text

16:1-16. I commend unto you Phoebe our sister, who is a servant of the church that is at Cenchreae: 2 that ye receive her in the Lord, worthily of the saints, and that ye assist her in whatsoever matter she may have need of you: for she herself also hath been a helper of many, and of mine own self.

3 Salute Prisca and Aquila my fellow-workers in Christ Jesus, 4 who for my life laid down their own necks; unto whom not only I give thanks, but also all the churches of the Gentiles: 5 and salute the church that is in their house. Salute Epaenetus my beloved, who is the firstfruits of Asia unto Christ. 6 Salute Mary, who bestowed much labor on you. 7 Salute Andronicus and Junias, my kinsmen, and my fellow-prisoners, who are of note among the apostles, who also have been in Christ before me. 8 Salute Ampliatus my beloved in the Lord. 9 Salute Urbanus our fellow-worker in Christ, and Stachys my beloved. 10 Salute Apelles the approved in Christ. Salute them that are of the household of Aristobulus. 11 Salute Herodion my kinsman. Salute them of the household of Narcissus, that are in the Lord. 12 Salute Tryphaena and Tryphosa, who labor in the Lord. Salute Persis the beloved, who labored much in the Lord. 13 Salute Rufus the chosen in the Lord, and his mother and mine. 14 Salute Asyncritus, Phlegon, Hermes, Patrobas, Hermas, and the brethren that are with them. 15 Salute Philologus and Julia, Nereus and his sister, and Olympas, and all the saints that are with them. 16 Salute one another with a holy kiss. All the churches of Christ salute you.

Rethinking in Outline Form

c. Exhortations to Mutual Helpfulness. 15:1-13.
   (1) The strong to help the weak. v. 1 cf. 14:1; Gal. 6:2.
   (2) To please others. vs. 2-3.
       This is to be limited by pleasing them only in the

things that are good and lead to edifying. This is exemplified by Christ. cf. 14:19; II Cor. 8:9; Psa. 69:9.

(3) Things written aforetime are for our learning. vs. 4 cf. II Tim. 3:16; I Cor. 10:6-13.

(4) To be of the same mind one toward another. vs. 5-7.

    (a) To be of the same mind. v. 5. This condition is from God and according to Christ.

    (b) With one mouth we are to glorify God. vs. 6.

    (c) To receive one another even as Christ received us. v. 7.

(5) Christ made a minister of the circumcision that the Gentiles through the confirmation of the promises given unto the fathers, might glorify God. vs. 8-12.

    Verse 10 is found in Deut. 32:43. verse 11 in Psa. 117:1. verse 12 in Isa. 11:10.

B. Conclusion. 15:14—16:27.

1. Personal Matters. 15:14-33.

  a. Paul's confidence in the Roman brethren. v. 14.

  b. Reason for writing so boldly. vs. 15-16.

  c. His labors as an apostle. 15:17-21.

    (1) His glorying all in Christ. vs. 17-19a.

    (2) He had fulfilled his mission of preaching the gospel. v. 19b.

    (3) He endeavored to preach in new fields. vs. 20-21.

  d. His purpose to visit them on his way to Spain. vs. 22-29.

    (1) Had been hindered by the many new fields opening to preach the gospel. v. 22.

    (2) Now looking toward new frontiers in Spain. vs. 23-24.

    (3) His going to Jerusalem with an offering for the poor. v. 25-27.

      (a) The comparative references that explain this offering are as follows: Acts 24:17; 19:21; I Cor. 16:1-2; II Cor. 8:1-2; II Cor. 9:2.

      (b) The word "contribution" in verse 26 is the same as "fellowship" in Acts 2:42.

      (c) The Gentiles of Macedonia and Achaia owed the Jews material support since it was through them they received spiritual life. v. 27.

    (4) To visit the Romans as soon as he was finished. vs. 28-29. His plans were changed. He was taken prisoner to Rome.

    e. Requests for prayers for himself. vs. 30-33.
       (1) The nature of the request. v. 30.
       (2) That he might be delivered from disobedient ones. v. 31a.
       (3) That his ministration will be acceptable. v. 31b.
       (4) That he might come unto them in Rome with joy. v. 32.

REALIZING ROMANS, 16:1-16

639. Was Phoebe a deaconess?

640. If she wasn't an official servant, why does Paul so speak of her as in vs. 1? Locate Cenchreae.

641. Give the meaning of the expression "worthily of the saints."

642. In what possible manner would Phoebe need the saints in Rome?

643. What work can women do in the church? What assistance do you imagine Phoebe was to many and to Paul?

644. Paul has high words of praise for Prisca and Aquila. At what possible time and place did they risk their lives for Paul?

645. Give three facts about these two as found in other references.

646. Name three churches of the Gentiles that could have been involved in the thankfulness.

647. Did the whole church in Rome meet in the house of Prisca and Aquila?

648. What quality of character does the mentioning of all these names suggest?

649. Someone had been in jail with Paul; they had become very well known and respected by the apostles. Who were they?

650. There was one in Rome to whom Paul sent greetings who had proven himself by suffering. Who was it?

651. How many women and men are mentioned? Count them.

652. Did Paul have relatives among these in Rome? Who were they?

653. Why call the kiss of greeting a "holy kiss"?

654. Is the church ever referred to as "the church of Christ"? Be careful: is it "church," or "churches"?

Paraphrase

16:1-16. I recommend to you who are in Rome, Phoebe our sister in the faith, who is a deaconess of the church which is in Cenchreae.

2 And I desire that ye may show her the respect due to a faithful servant of Christ, as becometh his disciples to do to a person of her excellent character, and assist her in whatever business she may have

need of your good offices. For indeed she hath been a helper of many, and of myself also.

3 In my name wish health to Priscilla and Aquila her husband, my assistants in preaching the gospel at Corinth.

4 These excellent persons to save my life exposed themselves to death; to whom therefore, not I only am thankful, but even all the churches of the Gentiles, who consider themselves as indebted to them, for preserving the life of their apostle and spiritual father.

5 Likewise, with health to the members of the church which is in their house. Salute Epaenetus, whom I dearly love because he is the first person I converted in the province of Achaia.

6 Salute Mary, who underwent great fatigue in spreading the gospel along with us.

7 Salute Andronicus and Junias my kinsmen, and formerly prisoners with me for the sake of Christ, who are in high estimation among the apostles on account of their talents and virtues, and who were in the church of Christ before me.

8 Salute Amplias, whom I dearly love on account of his sincere attachment to Christ.

9 Salute Urbanus, who assisted me in preaching Christ; and Stachys, whom I sincerely love on account of the goodness of his disposition.

10 Salute Apelles, who, by sustaining many persecutions, hath approved himself a firm Christian. Salute the brethren who are of the family of Aristobulus.

11 Salute in my name, Herodion my kinsman. Salute those members of the family of Narcissus who are converted to Christianity.

12 Salute Tryphaena and Tryphosa, women who employ themselves in maintaining the cause of Christ at Rome. Salute Persis, the beloved of all who know her, and who hath laboured much in promoting the cause of Christ.

13 Salute Rufus, who is a most excellent Christian; and do the same to her who is his mother, and, because of her affection to me, my mother also.

14 In my name salute Asyncritus, Phlegon, Hermas, Patrobas, Hermes, and the brethren in their families.

15 In my name salute Philologus and Julia, Nereus and his sister, and Olympas, and all the Christians who are in their families.

16 To show that Christian affection which ye bear to each other, salute one another with a chaste kiss. The churches of Christ at Corinth and Cenchreae, and in all the province of Achaia, salute you.

Summary

Phoebe, a deaconess of the church in Cenchreae, is commended to the disciples, while they, on their part, are requested to receive her as the holy should receive the holy, and to aid her in whatever business she might need them. After this, various brethren, several of them Paul's kinsmen, and also various sisters, are most honorably mentioned, and the brotherhood requested to greet them. Usually, as each person is named, some distinguishing trait or circumstance is named with him, showing how closely the Apostle studied characters, and how generously he awarded praise. The section sheds much light upon the religious life and social habits of life in the first century.

Comment

2. *Commendations, Warnings, Salutations and Benedictions.* 16:1-27.

A Commendation and Salutations. 16:1-16

The fact that Phoebe alone is commended by Paul to the brethren in Rome suggests the thought that she was by herself, and possibly the one who delivered the letter to the church at Rome. Was Phoebe a servant of the church at Cenchreae in the official sense? It makes little difference since she served the church. We really cannot know. She performed her service with "the Apostle's sanction." Whether such women are officially appointed or not, we need more of them. The poor, the sick and the untaught in the community need them. Cenchreae was the seaport of Corinth. Paul visited here on his second missionary journey.

Here is a high recommendation for Phoebe. "Receive her as a Christian; help her in whatever way she may need you, for she has been a helper of many and of my own self." We have no way of knowing what "the business" was in Rome. Evidently Phoebe came for that very purpose. What a splendid epithet, "a helper of many." Did Phoebe have money of her own to enable her to do this? Was she a widow, since no husband is mentioned? These are conjectures of the commentators. The nature of the assistance given to Paul is also a conjecture.

Since Paul is writing this letter from Corinth, the names of Prisca and Aquila are very much in place since Corinth was where Paul met them. Even when first mentioned, we learn they had once lived in Rome. They are now again in the imperial city. From the nature of the greeting, we could suggest they were at Rome to labor for

396. What high recommendation did Paul give to Phoebe?
397. Give three facts about Prisca and Aquila.
398. Who was Epaenetus?
399. Mary of verse six is an example for women today. How?

Christ. Paul worked with them as a tentmaker and they worked with him in preaching and teaching Christ. Prisca and Aquila had the high honor of offering their life for that of Paul. Just where and when we are not told. Paul was in danger many times and in many places. It could have been at Ephesus or even Corinth. The churches in the region around Corinth and Ephesus join in the gratitude expressed to these two. Could it be that the churches of the Gentiles heard of how Paul's life was spared?

In the home of Prisca and Aquila a group of Christians met to worship. To this assembled group Paul wanted greetings sent. Would not this be the answer to the problem of moving into a community where there is no church? Start one in your home.

Verse five mentions one held in high esteem by Paul. One of the first to accept Christ in Asia was at Ephesus, or Philedelphia, or Laodecia. We know not, but Epaenetus was first in conversion and one of the first in memory.

What is the work of the women in the kingdom of God? There is much to be done. In verse six we find a Mary who found much to do for the saints in Rome. Did she do it at Rome, or was it done for them at some other place? Both are possibilities. The point is, she labored much and so should the women of today.

In Andronicus and Junias we might have a suggestion as to how the church began in Rome. It could have been as Lard suggests, and several others, these two men were among "the strangers of Rome" in Acts 2:10. This would account for them being in Christ before Paul and of becoming of note among the apostles. What they did to receive this distinction most assuredly related to service for Christ. Just when these two were imprisoned with Paul, we do not know, but Paul remembers them with him in one of the several prisons where he was held. These two men seem to be blood relatives of Paul.

What a great man was Paul! He need not mention all these persons in his letter, but he does. He has a sincere word of commendation for each one. "He was great in intellect, ardent in feeling, and tender in affection as a woman." Why did Paul especially love Ampliatus? Could it be because he was one of his converts?

Verse nine introduces two interesting persons. When had Urbanus labored with Paul? It must have been for an extended period of time

400. Is there any hint in these verses as to how the church started in Rome? If so what?
401. How is the greatness of Paul seen in the mention of the names of so many in his greetings?
402. Who was Apelles?
403. Which one was Paul's relative?

to give him this title. We wonder what close association Paul had with Stachys to give him such a tender greeting.

It is good to know someone who has come through many tribulations with robes pure and white. Such a "tried" disciple and friend was Apelles. The family of a man named Aristobulus comes to mind. The family was in Rome. Where was Aristobulus? We simply do not know. Any answer is only conjecture.

In verse eleven it would seem one of Paul's relatives had not distinguished himself, for no descriptive word is given. Yet Paul does want to send him greetings. The house of Narcissus was one of great repute in the days of Paul. Not all in the house were in the Lord. The ones who were Christians were the object of the greeting.

Verse twelve indicates Tryphaena and Tryphosa were engaged in working for the Lord as the letter was being written. What was the work of these two women? There were many Apollos's to be taught. There was much in the area of special service for the church, even as there is today. Persis is yet another woman who worked for Christ. How can we think Paul felt that women had no place in the church when so many are here mentioned as fellow laborers?

Verse thirteen suggests two different expressions concerning Rufus, "chosen in the Lord," and the mother of Rufus, "his mother and mine." How shall we interpret these expressions? "Chosen in the Lord" refers to the character of the man, not to "elected" in the sense used by some. Rufus was regarded by Paul as an outstanding person, endowed with abilities, and in this sense chosen. As to the mother of Rufus, we believe the expression is used in a figurative manner. "—his mother literally, mine by courtesy." Such a relationship exists today with certain elderly women whom we call "mother" in respect.

There is a great deal of traditional material available regarding each of the names in this chapter. Since it is only tradition we do not deem it worthy of mention. In verse fourteen are five brothers and certain others, probably their families and other relatives. Of them, we know nothing more than they were worthy of a greeting.

Verse fifteen gives another list of worthy persons unknown to us. The mention of "all the holy brethren with them" might suggest a church in the section of Rome where they live. The same would be true of verse fourteen. It could be that such men were elders in the churches.

404. Was Rufus "elected" by God? Explain.
405. There seems to be a suggestion of several congregations in these verses—how so?
406. Give the meaning of the expression "holy kiss."
407. How is the name "churches of Christ" here used?

The greeting of the early Christians is enjoined in verse sixteen. The custom of so greeting one another existed when Paul wrote. He says make the greeting "holy" or pure. It is easy to see how it could be otherwise. We do not use this mode of greeting; therefore it is not applicable to us. Paul does not create a form of greeting for Christians; he rather shows how to use the one then existing.

The churches in Achaia, and they were no doubt numerous, are here designated "churches of Christ." What they are called in plural form we assume they could be called singly. Perhaps some heard of Paul's letter to Rome and came to send their greetings on behalf of the "churches of Christ." Surely this is a very worthy name, but no more so than any other scriptural designation.

Rethinking in Outline Form

2. Commendations, Warnings, Salutations and Benedictions. 16:1-27.
   a. Commendation. vs. 1-2.
   b. Salutations. vs. 3-16.
      (1) Prisca and Aquila. vs. 3-5a cf. Acts 18:2; I Cor. 16:19; II Tim. 4:19.
      (2) The many salutations. vs. 5b-15.
      (3) Salute one another with a holy kiss. v. 16a.
      (4) The greeting of the churches of Christ in Corinth and in other places to those of Rome. v. 16.
   c. Warnings to those who cause divisions. v. 17-20.
      (1) Mark those who cause the divisions. v. 17a.
           Probably the Judaizing teachers who wanted to impose the law upon the Gentiles.
      (2) They are bringing a contrary doctrine. v. 17b.
      (3) To turn away from them. v. 17c.
      (4) Who they serve. v. 18a.
      (5) The method of their deception. v. 18b.
      (6) What they do. v. 18c.
      (7) Paul rejoices in the Roman's obedience and wants the troublemakers put down. v. 19.
      (8) God to give the victory. v. 20.
   d. Salutations of Paul's companions. vs. 21-24.
      (1) Timothy with Paul at this time. cf. Acts 20:4.
      (2) Lucius. cf. Acts 13:1.

408. Account for the introduction of the subject of division at this place.
409. Who in particular are to be noticed here?
410. Why do some want to have a following of their own?
411. What should we do with our opinions?

  (3) Sopister. cf. Acts 20:4.
  (4) Tertius. The scribe unknown.
  (5) Gaius. cf. I Cor. 1:14.
  (6) Erastus. cf. Acts 19:22; II Tim. 4:20.
  (7) Quartus. Unknown.
 e. Closing Doxology. vs. 25-27.
  (1) Commended to God. v. 25 cf. Eph. 3:20; Jude 24.
  (2) That God would establish them in truth which in times
      past was a mystery but now has been revealed through
      the message Paul brought; namely, the salvation of the
      Gentiles. vs. 26-27.

Text

16:17-27. Now I beseech you, brethren, mark them that are causing the divisions and occasions of stumbling, contrary to the doctrine which ye learned: and turn away from them. 18 For they that
are such serve not our Lord Christ, but their own belly; and by their
smooth and fair speech they beguile the hearts of the innocent.
19 For your obedience is come abroad unto all men. I rejoice therefore over you: but I would have you wise unto that which is good,
and simple unto that which is evil. 20 And the God of peace shall
bruise Satan under your feet shortly.

   The grace of our Lord Jesus Christ be with you.

   21 Timothy my fellow-worker saluteth you; and Lucius and
Jason and Sosipater, my kinsmen. 22 I Tertius, who write the epistle,
salute you in the Lord. 23 Gaius my host, and of the whole church,
saluteth you. Erastus the treasurer of the city saluteth you, and Quartus the brother.

   25 Now to him that is able to establish you according to my gospel and the preaching of Jesus Christ, according to the revelation
of the mystery which hath been kept in silence through times eternal, 26 but now is manifested, and by the scriptures of the prophets,
according to the commandment of the eternal God, is made known
unto all the nations unto obedience of faith: 27 to the only wise
God, through Jesus Christ, to whom be the glory forever. Amen.

REALIZING ROMANS, 16:17-27

655. How can we account for the abrupt change of subject?
656. Could the persons mentioned in verses 17, 18 refer to those who
     caused stumbling because of days and meat?
657. How would such persons be "marked"?
658. What is meant by "turn away from them"? Is this practiced
     today?

659. Did Paul know of such persons?

660. How could false doctrine relate to the stomach?

661. In what sense were certain persons "innocent"?

662. Paul was confident the Roman brethren would follow his word. Why was he so confident?

663. How could it be possible to be "simple unto that which is evil" when Paul was discussing it at such length?

664. What a marvelous word of encouragement is found in vs. 20. How could Paul be so confident of this victory? How is Satan here pictured?

665. What is the meaning of the term "grace" as used in vs. 20b?

666. Some of the names in this chapter we have noticed before in Paul's letters. Does this mean that here we meet them again? Which ones?

667. Paul didn't write the letter himself. How was it written?

668. Gaius must have had a spacious house. Why do we so conclude?

669. The gospel reached a few notable ones. Erastus is an example. Why were there not more?

670. The eternal God is able not only to save us from our sins but to keep us from our sins. How?

671. What is the mystery now manifested?

672. Is this benediction applicable to us? Specify in what ways.

Paraphrase

16:17-27. Now I beseech you, brethren, mark them who set up separate assemblies for worship, and who occasion the weak to fall by false doctrine, or by enjoining things indifferent as necessary, contrary to the doctrine which ye have learned from me in this epistle, and avoid them.

18 For such teachers, whatever they may pretend, do not serve our Lord Jesus Christ, but their own lusts; and by plausible discourse and hypocritical wishes of happiness, they draw away the affections of the innocent, who have no suspicion of their wickedness.

19 Now your obedience, in turning from idols to the true God, is reported through the whole empire: I therefore rejoice on your account. Nevertheless, I wish you to be wise with respect to good, so as to discern and practice it habitually, and to be pure with respect to evil, by avoiding all false doctrines and wicked actions.

20 And God, who is the author of peace, will produce peace among you by bruising Satan under your feet soon: I mean the unbelieving Jews and Judaizing teachers, who make divisions among you. The favor of our Lord Jesus Christ be with you. Amen.

21 Timothy, my assistant in the ministry, and Lucius, and Jason, and Sosipater, my kinsmen, who are at present with me, salute you.

22 Tertius, who wrote this letter from the apostle's autograph, am permitted by him to salute you as the disciples of Christ.

23 Caius, with whom I lodge, and who shows hospitality to all the members of the church here, wishes you health. So doth Erastus, the chamberlain of Corinth, and Quartus, one of your own church, who at present is with me.

24 Loving you affectionately, I give you my apostolical benediction a second time. (See vs. 20.) The favor of our Lord Jesus Christ be with you all. Amen.

25 Now to him who is able to establish you in the belief, that by faith and not by the law the Gentiles shall be saved, according to my gospel and the preaching concerning Jesus Christ by all the apostles, according to the revelation of the mystery to them, which though contained in the covenant with Abraham, was kept secret in the time of the Mosaic dispensation,

26 (But is now fully published to the world, by the preaching of the gospel; and, according to the commandment of the eternal and unchangeable God, contained in the prophetic writings of the Jews, is made known to all the Gentiles, in order to produce in them the obedience of faith),

27 To the wise God alone, who possesses all perfection in and of himself, through the illumination of Jesus Christ, I say with understanding, to him be the glory of the salvation of the world ascribed for ever. And for the truth of all that I have written, I appeal to God, by saying Amen to the whole.

Summary

In this section, the subject of divisions or factions is strangely isolated, and made to receive special notice. The brotherhood are commanded to watch such as cause divisions and occasion stumblings, and to turn away from them. Such persons are severely characterized as not serving Christ, but their own stomachs.

After this digression, the Apostle returns to the subject of personal greetings. These ended, he closes his great letter with a most wonderful outburst of praise—wonderful, because of its comprehension, complexity, and strength.

412. When we teach as a doctrine of God our own conclusions we merit what from God and the elders?
413. What should be done with those who cause divisions? Who is to do it?
414. The defeat of Satan in Rome was only temporary. Why say this?
415. Name three who were with Paul when he wrote.

Comments

b. Warnings to those who cause the divisions. 16:17-20.

We must say with Moses Lard: ". . . why he should have introduced the subject of divisions just in this particular conjection is not easily seen." Perhaps after thinking of all the wonderfully good people in the church in Rome he wanted them to know he was aware of the other element also. At whatever purpose this section does stand out separate and apart as a warning to all. We are not here to notice apostates or sectarians, but those who produce parties in the church. There are always some men who want the preeminence and they will have it in one way or another. In the cases here cited, such men draw aside the disciples after them for the purpose of feeding their own stomachs. The method employed by such involves opinionated teaching. Such men could not get a following by teaching the plain truth of the scriptures. An opinion must be taught as God's truth, or such divisions would never occur. In opinions we should have the greatest of liberty, but whenever we enforce our conclusions from the Scriptures with anathemas to all who do not so conclude, we cause stumblings and divisions. We may not do it for the same reason as those of Rome, but we are guilty of the same sin and merit the same censure. One characteristic mark of such division makers is their sanctimonious attitude. The unlearned and weak soon fall victims to such. What are we to do with these people? Mark them first; i.e., take note who they are, then turn away from them, avoid them, separate yourself from them. To do this two things are essential, neither of which we have in any large degree: a knowledge of the Bible and a holy courage to apply it in all cases."

Verse nineteen suggests the thought that such remarks as above (vs. 17-18) do not necessarily apply to the Roman brethren. Verse nineteen is somewhat in the form of an apology. The faith and unity of the Roman saints had been spoken of far and wide. Paul had heard of the reputation of the Romans, and in it he did rejoice. Paul sounds a note of warning in 19b. His earnest desire is to have these brethren very wise in matters of unity and love and very unlearned in matters of parties and sects. This might suggest the seeds of division were ever present in the church at Rome.

Verse twenty contains a wonderful promise and encouragement. "The God of peace" is referred to in contrast to the spirit of faction and war. The promise of the defeat of Satan amounts to a promise of unity. If Satan was crushed in Rome (and we believe he was), then he surely came to life later, for Rome has become well-known today for its scriptural disunity. It is good to read this blessing, "The favor of our Lord Jesus Christ be with you." "If the favor of Christ prevails, Satan will be crushed and division will cease."

d. Salutations of Paul's companions. 16:21-24.

Who is with Paul as the letter is written? Verse twenty-one gives a list of Paul's friends in Corinth who send their greetings. We know of Timothy; Lucius, Jason, and Sosipater are kinsmen of Paul's, probably in the sense that each of them belong to the tribe of Benjamin. Lucius is supposed by some to be the Lucius of Cyrene of Acts 13:1, and Jason the one mentioned in Acts 17:5-7. We do not know if such is true. They do have the same names.

Paul did not himself write the letter, but dictated it to a scribe named Tertius. Evidently Tertius was known to the Christians in Rome, so he sends his personal greetings to them.

The house of Gaius must have been a very spacious one to entertain the whole company with Paul, indeed on one occasion "the whole church." Gaius greets the Romans. How good it is to have men of means to help the cause of Christ.

The influence of the good news in Corinth reached among the leaders of the city. The treasurer of the city was found among the faithful and wished to let it be known to the saints in Rome. We know nothing of Quartus.

Once again Paul wishes the favor of Christ for the holy of Rome. Some ancient manuscripts omit this second benediction.

e. Closing Doxology. 16:25-27.

This is a most beautiful manner in which to close the letter. Such is done in a number of others. cf. Jude 24. Paul states that according to his preaching of Jesus Christ, God is able to establish the saints in Rome so firmly in the faith that no one or no circumstance can move them from it. This good news respecting Jesus Christ was before now a mystery and kept secret. It was a secret until the days of the prophets when it began to be revealed by the command of the everlasting God to these men who wrote by inspiration a prophetic description of the one that was to come. The purpose of the present revelation of Christ through the gospel was to produce faith and obedience among all nations. In other words, "he that believeth and is baptized shall be saved." cf. Mk. 16:15, 16.

416. Who wrote the letter for Paul? From where?
417. The gospel had wide influence in the city of Corinth. How do we know?
418. We can be so firmly established in the faith that no one or no circumstance can move us from it. How?
419. What was the purpose of the gospel?
420. What was involved in "the obedience to the faith"?

Verse twenty-seven concludes the letter in a most appropriate manner. The omniscience of God and the eternal glory coming to him through Jesus Christ are called upon for the benediction. May we be able to say of ourselves and the church where we worship and serve—"Amen."

SPECIAL STUDIES
IN ROMANS

ARE THE HEATHEN SAVED?

A Study in 2:12-16

A SURPASSING RECONCILIATION

A Study in 5:12-16

By WILBUR FIELDS

ARE THE HEATHEN SAVED?

Special Study on 2:12-16

1. *What is the spiritual standing of the "Jews" and "Greeks" under consideration in these verses?*

   Answer: They are sinners, both Jews and Greeks, not having accepted the gospel. We say this for the following reasons:

   a. Since Paul is discussing the universal need of the gospel, it is only logical that he should illustrate this need by those who did not have access to the gospel and those who, having had access to the gospel, had not accepted it. Inasmuch, therefore, as the Jews and Gentiles under consideration had not accepted the gospel, they were sinners, not Christians.

   b. Paul places the basis of judgment for the Jew as "the law." This would NOT be the case if these Jews under discussion had been Christians, for they would then have been under the law of Christ, hence, would be judged according to the gospel as Christians.

   c. The Greeks are spoken of as having "sinned without the law" and thus they would "perish"—be judged "without the law." If they had been Christians they would be judged by the gospel, and it would have been placed as the basis of judgment.

   d. It is self-evident that the Gentiles described in the verses being discussed (1:18-32; 2:14-15) were sinners and could under no consideration be counted as Christians. To suggest otherwise seems absurd.

   Therefore, we must conclude that Paul is discussing those Jews and Gentiles of his day who had not accepted the gospel. Let us not forget that in this discussion he demonstrates their desperate need of the justification found in the gospel. Both the Gentile (chap. 1) and the Jew (chap. 2) when measured by their own law are found guilty.

2. *Why take the gospel to the heathen of today if they can be saved without it?* The answer is threefold.

   a. We should take the gospel to the heathen of today because they are not saved in their present state.

   (1) They are lost, but not because they rejected Christ, for they never had the opportunity to either accept or reject him. If they had had this opportunity through access to the gospel, it would be a different matter; but we are discussing those who never had the opportunity to accept Christ.

(2) The heathen of today are surely, actually and eternally lost because they are not conscientious about keeping their law and because they actually try to withstand God. Notice what Paul has to say upon this point.

    (a) In describing the Gentiles in chapter one, he says, among other things, that they "hinder the truth in unrighteousness"; "they exchanged the truth of God for a lie"; "they refused to have God in their knowledge"; "wherefore God gave them up . . ." (1:18b, 25, 28). Thus using the pronouns (they, their and them) with no qualification whatever, he places the greater part, if not all, of the Gentile world under the wrath of God.

    (b) Again in chapter three in summing up the matter, he writes in verses 9-12: ". . . for we before laid to the charge both of Jews *and Greeks* that they are all under sin; as it is written, There is none righteous, no, not one; There is none that seeketh after God; They have all turned aside, they are together become unprofitable; There is none that doeth good, no, not so much as one."

Here it would seem beyond a shadow of a doubt that the vast majority of Gentiles (and Jews) are lost and consequently under the wrath of God.

(3) "Well," someone says, "what about those spoken of in chapter two, verses 6-7 and 10, who were going to be given eternal life, glory, honor and peace because they were patient in well doing and sought for glory and honor and incorruption, and yet never heard the gospel?"

    (a) Well, where are those persons and who are they? According to Paul the number of such persons is practically nil (0).

    (b) God *will* give to such persons JUST WHAT HE PROMISED and upon EXACTLY the basis he promised it; but on that great day when God begins to judge the secrets of the hearts of men, who will be there to enter into eternal life on this plan?

    (c) The message of these verses (2:6, 7, 10) is the basis of God's judgment; the persons referred to are hypothetical.

    (d) In light of what we have just considered, it would seem to our fallible, human understanding that actually there will be but an infinitesimal portion of the Gentiles who will receive eternal life on the basis stated by Paul in the verses under consideration.

Thus we conclude that since the heathen are not saved in their present state, we should take the gospel to them.

b. We should take the gospel to the heathen because of the great, glorious, and immediate benefits to be found in the reception of the gospel. Think for a moment of some of them.

(1) The present knowledge that our sins are all forgiven.

(2) That we have an advocate with the Father, Jesus Christ the Righteous.

(3) That we are the temple of God, the sanctuary of his Spirit.

(4) That we have God's power through his Spirit and word to help us in defeating Satan.

(5) That the purpose of life and creation is now clear to us.

(6) That we are prepared for the judgment.

All these wonderful possessions and more are given to the heathen who accepts Christ. Are not these sufficient reasons for taking the glad news to them? Have we no sympathy for the man who has no present knowledge that his sins are forgiven; who is driven to make appeasement to a dumb idol? Have we no compassion upon those poor benighted souls who have some knowledge of what is right and wrong (unless they have been misled) and yet who, like us, are human and too weak to overcome the efforts of Satan to lead them in the wrong road? Have we no sorrow for those millions who have no inclination to follow in the path of righteousness? Why take the gospel to the heathen? Let us examine our hearts, brethren, if we can see no reason in the above stated information!

c. We would take the gospel to the heathen because the highest authority in heaven and earth has commanded us to take this message to "every creature." The condition of the souls of men the world around is a great constraining force, but above and beyond that is our obedience to our King. He whom we call "Lord" has intrusted us with this task, and to fail is to fail him, yes more, to disobey him. Why preach the gospel to the heathen?—because Christ asked us to do it.

Conclusion: We should preach the gospel to the heathen because they are lost in their present state, because of the benefits they will receive upon accepting it, and because Christ asked us to do so.

3. *How could the conscientious, but nevertheless sinful, persons be saved who never heard of Christ or his blood?*

Answer: The same way that Abraham, Isaac, Jacob and others were saved. cp. Mt. 8:11. Because of their "patience in well doing" or conscientious (though imperfect) obedience to the law, God mercifully accepted their faith as righteousness and anticipatively extended to them the blood of Christ to justify them from their sins. "Abraham believed God and it was reckoned unto him for righteousness." Rom. 4:3. Thus we see a principle whereby the blood of Christ could be applied to those before Christ who had never heard of him. Though we have shown essentially that there are no heathen who are conscientiously trying to keep God's law, they could by the same principle have Christ's blood applied to their sins also.

4. *What about other scripture references which seem to teach that every last Gentile who has not heard the gospel is lost, regardless of what he does?*

a. We will begin our answer by asking two questions:
   (1) Are the persons involved in the reference those that have done the very best they could to obey the law of nature?
   (2) If so, then are they spoken of as being lost?

b. The writer has found no scriptural reference to any person who could be counted as lost, who never heard the gospel or had opportunity to hear and yet lived up to the law of his conscience according to Romans 2:14-15.

c. Find a reference that speaks of a Gentile who never heard of Christ or had opportunity to hear and yet was lost in spite of his "patience in well doing"—faithful obedience to the law of nature (Rom. 2:7, 14-15)—and we will have a case, but not until then.

5. *Would not this teaching give hope to all those who, in all sincerity, were and are following false doctrines?* In other words, if conscientiousness is a basis for eternal life in one case, why wouldn't it be in all cases?

Before we answer this question, please understand that it is *not* our desire that anyone should be lost. cf. II Pe. 3:9. It is the truth we are interested in, for while we might like to see every conscientious person saved, we realize that our personal feelings will not be the basis of judgment on that great day. Jesus said, "He that rejecteth me, and receiveth not my sayings, hath one that judgeth him: the word that I spake, the same shall judge him in the last day." Jn. 12:48; Rev. 20-12

Is conscientiousness in itself a sufficient basis for receiving eternal life? Answer: No, in the light of revealed facts. Here are the facts:

   a. The law of nature, Biblical history and the plain statements of Scripture seem to prove that conscientiousness alone is insufficient.

      (1) The law of nature definitely teaches this fact.

         (a) Suppose that in all sincerity you take some ant poison, thinking it to be cough syrup—will your conscientiousness save you from sickness or possibly death?

         (b) Remember the time you were traveling when you unknowingly took the wrong road? Did your sincerity make the wrong road the right one?

      (2) Biblical history substantiates this fact.

         (a) Saul of Tarsus was as conscientious as any man could be and yet he was lost. Acts 22:3-4; 23:1; Gal. 1:13; I Tim. 1:15

         (b) The Jews of Paul's day were conscientious and yet lost. Rom. 10:1-3

         (c) The Gentiles who had neither the law of Moses nor the gospel of Christ (Rom. 1-2) were not to be judged on the basis of sincerity alone. Rom. 2:14-15. We will discuss more about this in division b.

      (3) Some plain statements of Scripture which seem to bear out this fact.

         (a) "Can the blind guide the blind? shall they not *both* fall into a pit?" Lu. 6:39

         (b) "For they that lead this people cause them to err; and they that are led of them are destroyed." Isa. 9:16

         (c) "There is a way which seemeth right unto a man; But the end thereof are the ways of death." Prov. 14:12; 16:25

      (4) All known facts seem to prove conclusively that conscientiousness alone is no guarantee against being eternally lost.

   b. Conscientiousness in relation to the truth is what will count in the day of judgment.

      (1) This principle illustrated.

         (a) If you suddenly discover that you are about to take a spoonful of ant poison instead of cough syrup, what will you do?—go ahead and take it, hoping that because you are sincere all will be well?

(b) Suppose on your journey across the country you find out that you are on the wrong road, what will you do?—continue on the wrong way, hoping to arrive at your destination regardless?

(c) When Saul of Tarsus found out that he was persecuting Jesus Christ, he ceased, and as a result became Paul, the apostle.

(d) The Gentile of Romans 1-2 was to be judged not upon conscientiousness alone, but upon his sincere (though imperfect) obedience to the truth revealed in nature. This truth was plain enough for all to see who would see (Rom. 1:18-20). cf. Mt. 13:14-15

(e) Only an honest concern for and obedience to the truth will bring anyone to his desired destination. cf. Jn. 3:36 A.R.V.; Jn. 3:5

(2) Application of this principle and conclusion. (While this principle may be applied to many groups of people, we will deal only with two of them at this time.)

(a) When we apply the above principle to those who profess to believe the Bible and claim salvation in Christ through faith only, apart from baptism (immersion), we base our conclusion upon two facts inherent in the principle.

    i. The truth is that if the Bible says anything at all, it says that faith, repentance, confession and baptism are conditions upon which salvation is conferred.

    ii, In their relationship to the truth, they are overlooking or disregarding it and disobeying it.

(b) Will such people be saved simply because they are conscientious? If so, God has not revealed it to us either through nature or revelation. In the light of all known facts, we can only say to such people: "Why risk your life by taking this uncertain pathway? Be safe and go by the sure highway which God has revealed in his word."

(c) It is not within the scope of this book to discuss the application of this principle to those who have been "baptized into Christ" and yet continue to follow false teaching—unscriptural names and practices and other denominational tendencies.

(d) We are responsible to see that all such people receive the truth. Surely, if they are conscientious and we give them the proper teaching and example, they will turn from false teaching and obey only the truth.

6. *Why do injury to those who never heard by preaching to them and thus making them more responsible and liable to condemnation?*

a. It might be well to refer to what has already been said which gives good and altogether sufficient reasons for taking the message to the heathen.

(1) They are lost in their present state.

(2) There are such great and precious benefits in the acceptance of the gospel that can be found nowhere else.

(3) Christ has commanded us to preach "among all the nations."

b. If we but think for a moment, we can see that to take the gospel to them would be to make them responsible to a law that is far easier to fulfill than the one under which they live. Thus, practically speaking, their responsibility would be lessened rather than increased. This of course is true because of the assistance given by God through Christ to the person who obeys the gospel.

c. Then, too, the persons who are "continuing steadfastly in well doing seeking for glory and honor and incorruption" would be the first ones to accept the gospel message; those, among the others, who do not accept the gospel are all lost anyway.

d. This objection is a shallow one from the logical standpoint.

Questions on the Special Study

1. Does the failure to accept Christ figure into the lost estate of the Gentiles? If not, explain why this is not true.

2. Will the Gentiles be judged by law? What will be the result?

3. How can we know the Gentiles are lost being judged by their own law?

4. How many without the gospel are without hope? What does *the text* say?

5. Do verses 2:6;7:10 give hope to any who have never heard of Christ? (No "yes" or "no" answers.)

6. How many do you think there are among the heathen who will be saved according to the standard Paul sets up here?

7. Name from memory three benefits we obtain in Christ Jesus.

8. Why are these benefits sufficient reason for carrying the gospel to the lost?

9. How does the authority of Christ apply to carrying the gospel?

10. Give from memory the three reasons for taking the gospel to those who have never heard.

11. What is the meaning of the word "anticipatively"? If you do not know, look it up.

12. Honestly now, do *you* know of a scripture reference that states *that heathen are lost regardless of what they do?*

13. What *two* thoughts must be in the reference before it would apply to the case?

14. What is the proper attitude as we approach a discussion of the sincere but lost?

15. What is meant by "the law of nature"?

16. Cite two cases of Biblical history which point out that sincerity alone is not enough.

17. What did Jesus mean by "the blind"?

18. With what must sincerity be linked to be of any value on judgment day?

19. Give an illustration of this principle.

20. Were the Gentiles described in Romans cp.2 judged on sincerity alone? If not, why not?

21. What sad conclusion are we forced to make when we apply this principle to those sincere souls among the "faith only" groups?

22. How do *you* feel this principle would apply to those who are following ANY false doctrine?

23. Would we make the heathen more liable to condemnation by taking the gospel to them? If not, why not?

24. Who among the heathen would be the first to accept the gospel?

25. Show how their responsibility would be lessened.

A SURPASSING RECONCILIATION

By WILBUR FIELDS

Romans 5:12-19

INTRODUCTION: 5:12-14

1. God reconciled the world to himself through Christ.
2. To reconcile us, God had to overcome the effects of Adam's sin.
   a. Sin entered through Adam.
   b. Death entered through his sin.
   c. Death passed to all men, because all sinned.
3. The reconciliation which we have in Christ supersedes every evil effect we suffer in Adam.

PROPOSITION: Some aspects of man's surpassing reconciliation.

I. THE POWER OF ADAM'S SIN IS COMPLETELY OVERCOME IN CHRIST. 5:15
   1. The power of Adam's sin brought the death penalty to all.
   2. Christ has power to reverse the death penalty and to provide escape from our own sins.

II. THE SENTENCE OF ADAM IS ECLIPSED BY THE CONTRASTING GIFT OF CHRIST. 5:16
   1. Adam's sentence came because of one sin, which brought condemnation to all men.
   2. Christ's gift brings justification from many sins.

III. THE REIGN OF DEATH THROUGH ADAM'S SIN IS WONDERFULLY OVERTHROWN IN CHRIST. 5:17
   1. Because of the trespass, death reigned through the one man.
   2. Because of the free gift, they that receive it shall themselves reign in life through Jesus Christ.

IV. THE EFFECTS OF ADAM'S SIN ARE CONTRASTED WITH THOSE OF CHRIST'S GIFT. 5:18-19
   1. Through the trespass, judgment came upon all men to condemnation.
   2. Through the one act of justification, the free gift came to all men, bringing justification and life.
   3. This is explained in the fact of imputed conditions.
      a. The many were made sinners in Adam.
      b. The many were made just in Christ.

CONCLUSION

A SURPASSING RECONCILIATION
Introduction

"Therefore, as through one man sin entered into the world, and death through sin; and so death passed unto all men, for that all sinned:—for until the law sin was in the world; but sin is not imputed when there is no law. Nevertheless death reigned from Adam until Moses, even over them that had not sinned after the likeness of Adam's transgression, who is a figure of him that was to come. But not as the trespass, so also is the free gift. For if by the trespass of the one the many died, much more did the grace of God and the gift by the grace of the one man, Jesus Christ, abound unto the many. And not as through one that sinned, so is the gift; for the judgment came of one unto condemnation, but the free gift came of many trespasses unto justification. For if, by the trespass of the one, death reigned through the one; much more shall they that receive the abundance of grace and of the gift of righteousness reign in life through the one, even Jesus Christ. So then as through one trespass the judgment came unto all men to condemnation; even so through one act of righteousness the free gift came unto all men to justification of life. For as through the one man's disobedience the many were made sinners, even so through the obedience of the one shall the many be made righteous." Romans 5:12-19

1. In Christ Jesus God was reconciling the world unto himself. Mankind had made itself an enemy to God because it had rejected its creator. But God "reconciled us to himself through Christ,"[1] and "we can rejoice in God through our Lord Jesus Christ, through whom we have now received the reconciliation."[2]

2. One of the deepest gulfs that God had to span to reconcile us to himself was the gulf created by the violation of Adam.

a. Through this one man Adam, sin entered into the world. Sin is any violation of God's law, and, of course, it makes a man a criminal in the sight of God. Adam's eating the forbidden fruit brought this terrible fact of sin, and all its penalties, into the world.

b. Death entered through that sin. With Adam's disobedience came its penalty, the death of the body of man. The question will inevitably come up, "Was not the death that came upon Adam (and through sin, upon us) SPIRITUAL death?" Our reply is that while Adam's sin certainly had spiritual effects upon him, the only death spoken of for him in the Scriptures is physical death. He lived 930 years "and he died."[3] And if it be objected that it had to be spiritual

1. II Cor. 5:18.
2. Romans 5:11.
3. Gen. 5:5.

death because God said he would die "in the day that thou eatest thereof."[1] Let us remember that although he may have been dead that day in trespasses and sin, God's grace later allowed that these sins be covered by sacrifices. As for his physical death, the Scriptures plainly tell that he did not die that very day, but that God in his grace allowed him to live to bring into being "the seed of the woman"[2] by which they would all be redeemed from the curse of death, "the seed" of course referring to Christ. Furthermore, Paul's words in verse 14 about "death reigning from Adam to Moses"[3] most certainly refer to physical death. Also, other passages will show us that the death that came into the world through Adam's sin must surely be only physical death.

c. This death passed to all men, because all sinned in Adam. This must be the meaning of the statement, "so death passed to all men, for that all sinned."[4] Adam is our progenitor; he is the head of the human race, and by God's decree we as children of Adam all suffer the effects of his sin with him. That is the reason why we die. Of course, our own sins *would* bring death to us, but Adam's sin is THE cause of physical death to mankind. If this be doubted, that we all die because all sinned in Adam, let us remember the period of time from Adam until Moses. There was sin in the world during that time. The Sodomites all died because of their iniquity. But what about their infants who died? They did not share the penalty of death because of the guilt of their wicked parents. There was no law that would transfer the penalty of parents' guilt to the children.[5] But many of these surely died. The only explanation is that physical death spread to them, as to us, because they all were in Adam. Death had full sway during that period, reigning like a king over small and great. None of these person's sins affected their posterity, as did Adam's, but all died, showing that death spread to all in Adam. If one finds this hard to understand, let him remember that the Scriptures say that the Levitical priesthood paid tithes to Melchizidek, whom they had never seen, because Abraham, their distant ancestor,

1. Gen. 2:17.
2. Gen. 3:15.
3. Rom. 5:14.
4. Rom. 5:12.
5. This I take to be the meaning of "but sin is not imputed where there is no law," and "had not sinned after the likeness of Adam's transgression." Certainly there was law at that time, and with a death penalty attached for certain sins. cf. Gen. 9:6. But there was no law that would transmit such penalty to offspring, as did Adam's. When we come to the time of Moses, there MAY be such a law and penalty. cf. Ex. 34:7; 20:5; Dt. 5:9.

so did. "And so to say, through Abraham, even Levi who receiveth tithes, hath paid tithes; for he was yet in the loins of his father
(Abraham) when Melchizidek met him."[1] In the same way, we participate in the effects of Adam's sin, because we were in him, as surely as the sons of Levi participated in the effects of Abraham's act.

3. God looked down upon us, and saw us doomed to die physically, because all are in Adam whose sin affected those after him, and
all doomed to die spiritually because all will sin. God saw that to save
us he must supply one who would affect those after him, as Adam
affected those after him, but who would affect them for good, not
evil, and who would do it in such a way as to overcome every evil
thing we suffer in Adam. MY PROPOSITION is that the reconciliation which we have in Christ supersedes every evil effect we suffer
because of Adam's sin. I submit Paul's demonstration of this proposition to you:

I. *The Power of Adam's Sin Is Overcome in Christ.*

Paul observed that Adam was a type of Christ because his act had
effects upon those who followed him. But he had scarcely expressed
this thought when the contrasts between the two struck him as being
the more prominent. And so he says immediately, "but not as
the trespass, so also is the free gift."[2] The power of the two is vastly
different, both in their aim and their degree. We notice the power
of the act of each one.

1. Note the power of Adam's trespass upon us. Because of that
one violation, the many died. By "many" Paul evidently means
"everyone," and it is in this sense he uses the term all through his argument of the surpassing reconciliation which we have in Christ. The
power of Adam's sin was to bring death to everyone, beginning with
himself, to his own children, and down to our very selves.

2. Be the power of Adam's sin so great, a comparison with the
gratuitous gift of Christ makes it seem weak. For because of the free
gift of Christ, the Holy Spirit, through Paul, says, "Much more did
the grace of God, and gift by the grace of the one man Jesus Christ
abound unto the many."[3]

God's favor because of Christ's death abounded first of all to redeem us all from the grave. "For as in Adam all die, so also in Christ
shall all be made alive."[4] But what would it profit us to be raised
from the death we suffer in Adam, ready only to face God as crim-
inals sentenced to death for our own sins? This make it necessary

1. Heb. 7:9-10.
2. Romans 5:15.
3. Tim 5:15.
4. I Cor. 15:22.

for the gift of Christ, to be sufficient, to do more than redeem us from the grave.

God not only graciously provides in Christ the reversal of the effect of Adam's sin, but also makes a way in him to wash away our own sins. Thus it becomes MUCH MORE powerful than Adam's sin. To summarize, Adam's sin has power to bring death to all. Christ's gift has power to reverse the death we suffer in Adam, and "much more" to provide the escape from the penalty of our own sins. Truly the power of Adam's sin is much more than overcome in Christ.

II. *The Sentence of Adam Is Eclipsed by the Contrasting Gift of Christ.*

The Scripture says, "And not as through one that sinned so is the gift."[1] This passage makes very little complete sense in itself, without understanding it in the light of its explanation which says, "for the judgment (or sentence) came of one (sin) unto condemnation."[2] Therefore we believe that it is Paul's exact thought to say, "The sentence pronounced upon the one that sinned is not like the (outcome of the) gift." The sentence or the judgment of Adam is eclipsed by the entirely different gift of Christ.

1. The sentence through Adam was pronounced because of one sin unto condemnation. One act condemned all to die. Not that we are guilty with Adam of that sin, but our relationship with him causes us to suffer his fate. A foolish helmsman on a boat may be the cause of the sinking of a ship during a storm. Just as he may perish in the sea for his folly, so will the passengers, though they are innocent. So we, being as it were "in the same boat with Adam," he being the progenitor of the race, suffer the sentence or judgment of death with him.

2. But lo! Take a glance at what happens through the gracious gift of Christ. Whereas Adam's one sin brought condemnation to many, Christ's act takes people, bearing the sentence of Adam's sin, and brings them to justification. In God's sight people who are in Christ are "not guilty." We saw that Christ's gift had power to reverse the death which passed to all in Adam's sin, and furthermore, it had power to do "much more." Now we can see even more plainly than previously what that "much more" is. It is that power to take us, with the sentence of Adam's sin upon us, and many of our own sins, and make us just in God's sight.

1. Rom. 5:16.
2. Rom. 5:16.

Some will probably have noticed that the power of Adam's sin and the sentence that came through him amount to one and the same thing, physical death to the whole human race. But the value of considering these various aspects of the disobedience is found in the fact that each view of it gives new light upon the surpassing qualities in Christ's work of reconciliation.

III. *The Resulting Reign Through Adam's Sin Is Wonderfully Overthrown in Christ.*[1]

A still more striking contrast between the free gift of Christ and the trespass of Adam may be seen in the resulting reigns which came through the two acts.

1. Because of the trespass of the one man, DEATH reigned through that one man. In his action death found a channel through which to exercise its dominion. We have suggested this thought previously, and now it is stated plainly.

2. However, because of the free gift of Christ, they that receive the abundance of grace and the abundance of the gift of justification shall themselves "much more reign in life through the one, Jesus Christ."[2] Notice that through Christ WE shall reign, not death. Death's dominion over us is wonderfully overthrown in Christ. Not that we do not die, but death has no power to hold us, and, if we receive the abundance of the gift of justification, WE shall reign in life, when once we be resurrected, and redeemed once for all from death's kingship. Death is overthrown, and we are no longer of them "who through fear of death were all their lifetime subject to bondage."[3]

IV. *The Effects of Adam's Sin Are Contrasted with Those of Christ's Gift.*

Paul began his comparison of Adam's sin with the reconciliation which we have in Christ in verse twelve. In entering into the discussion of Adam's sin, however, his main thought was interrupted, and not really picked up again till verse eighteen. If we connect verse twelve with the last half of verse eighteen we get the main thought of this entire Scripture. "As through one man sin entered into the world and death through sin," "even so through one act of righteousness the free gift came untol all men to justification to life."[4] Verse

1. Although vs. 17 is introduced as though it were explanation by Paul, I treat it as a third comparison, as do authors MacKnight and Sanday.
2. Rom. 5:17.
3. Heb. 2:15.
4. I translate this "justification to life," rather than "of life" with the common versions.

266

eighteen not only completes the argument, but it sums up all the contrasts that have been presented about the power, the sentence, and the resulting reign through Adam's sin, and tells HOW these came about.

1. Through one trespass, Adam's act of eating the forbidden fruit, "judgment came upon all men to condemnation"[1] of death. This summarizes all that has been said about the power, sentence and reign through Adam.

2. However, just as judgment came upon all men through Adam's act, even so "through one act of justification the free gift (of Christ) came unto all men to justification to life."[2] Incidentally, this verse proves positively that the death which the human race suffers in Adam is ONLY physical death, because it is stated unequivocally that as surely as Adam's sin condemns everyone, so does Christ's act save everyone from that condemnation. Of course, we know that no unbeliever will be saved, and so this passage must be understood to say that Christ justifies everyone to physical life, and not to spiritual or eternal life.

3. But how does it work out that a single act on the part of both Adam and Christ completely affects all men, one for bad and the other for good? It was by God's appointment that it is so. In the case of the former decision, God was eminently just, and in the case of the latter, unbelievably gracious.

a. No man sinned personally in Adam. How could anyone have done so? But the Scriptures say that through the one man's disobedience the many, meaning ALL, as in verse eighteen, were MADE sinners. You cannot MAKE a sinner out of a person when he is one already. So it was that in Adam, we, not having sinned personally, were made or constituted sinners by God's appointment, and were imputed the sentence of his disobedience. THUS we were made sinners, in suffering the effect of his act with him. Any other interpretation makes verse eighteen pronounce universal and unconditional salvation, which the word emphatically denies.

b. But God, the just and the justifier, also imputes a righteousness or justification to us, which will enable every man to stand alive before the presence of God in the last day. For "through the obedience of the one shall the many be made righteous,"[3] that is, justified from the eternal power of Adam's penalty. Then shall those who have received the Lord Jesus find themselves eternally alive; and free from all sin, and not merely raised to suffer eternal punishment, the second death, for their own sins.

1. Rom. 5:18a.
2. Rom. 5:18b.
3. Rom. 5:19.

Conclusion

The power, and the sentence, and the resulting reign because of Adam's act are changed, through Christ, from facts bringing everlasting doom to us. If we receive the abundance of God's grace, and the abundance of Christ's gift of justification we have no need to fear the fleshly state we are in; for as surely as death may have reigned over us, we shall reign in life through Jesus Christ. It is no far away theological vagary. This is life itself. And thanks be to God for the unspeakable gift!

BIBLIOGRAPHY

Alford, Dean. *Greek Testament: Romans.*

Archer, Gleason L., Jr. *The Epistle to the Romans*—a study manual.

Barmby, J. *The Pulpit Commentary: Romans.*

Beet, J. A. *St. Paul's Epistle to the Romans.*

Brown, D. *Handbooks for Bible Classes: Romans.*

Brown, J. *Exposition of the Epistle to the Romans.*

Bruce, A. B. *St. Paul's Conception of Christianity.*

Bullinger, E. W. *The Church Epistles: Romans.*

Chalmers, T. *Lectures on the Romans.*

Darby, J. N. *Synopsis of the Books of the Bible: Romans.*

Denney, James. *Epistle to the Romans*—in Expositor's Greek Testament.

Forbes, J. *Analytical Commentary on the Romans.*

Fort, J. *God's Salvation as set forth in the Epistle to the Romans.*

Gairdner, W. H. T. *Helps to the Study of the Epistle to the Romans, Parts I and II.*

Garvie, A. E. *Century Bible: Romans.*

Gifford, E. H. *The Speaker's Commentary: Romans.*

Godet, F. *Commentary on the Romans, Vols. I and II.*

Gore, Bishop. *St. Paul's Epistle to the Romans, Vols. I and II.*

Grubbs, Isaiah Boone. *An Exegetical and Analytical Commentary on Paul's Epistle to the Romans.*

Haldane, R. *Exposition of the Epistle to the Romans.*

Hamilton, Floyd E. *The Epistle to the Romans.*

Henry, Matthew. *Commentary on the Whole Bible, Vol. 6.*

Hodge, C. *Commentary on the Epistle to the Romans.*

Kelly, W. *Notes on Romans.*

Land, Moses E. *Commentary on Paul's Letter to Romans.*

Lange, J. P. *"Romans"*—in Lange's Commentary on the Holy Scriptures.

Liddon, Canon H. P. *Explanatory Analysis on St. Paul's Epistle to the Romans.*

Lightfoot, Bishop J. B. *Notes on the Epistles of St. Paul; Article on "Romans" in Smith's Dictionary of the Bible.*

Luther, Martin. *Commentary on the Epistle to the Romans.*

McGarvey, J. W. and Philip Y. Pendleton. *The Standard Bible Commentary, Thesselonians, Corinthians, Galatians and Romans.*

Maclaren, A. *Expositions of Holy Scripture: The Epistle to the Romans.*

Meyer, H. A. W. *Commentary on the New Testament: Romans, Vols. I and II.*

Morgan, G. Campbell. *The Analyzed New Testament: The Epistle to the Romans.*

Moule, H. C. G. *Epistle of Paul to the Romans*—in The Expositor's Bible.

Neil, C. *The Expositor's Commentary: Romans.*

Newell, W. R. *Bible Class Lessons on Romans.*

Olshausen, H. *Epistle of Paul to the Romans*—Edinburgh, 1866.

Pendleton, Philip Y. and McGarvey, J. W. *The Standard Bible Commentary, Thesselonians, Corinthians, Galatians, and Romans.*

Rutherford, W. G. *St. Paul's Epistle to the Romans.*

Sanday and Headlam. *The International Critical Commentary: Romans.*

Simpson, A. B. *Christ in the Bible: Romans.*

Stifler, J. M. *The Epistle to the Romans.*

Thomas, W. H. Griffith. *St. Paul's Epistle to the Romans.*

Vaughan, C. J. *St. Paul's Epistle to the Romans.*

Wenham, A. E. *Ruminations on the Epistle of Paul the Apostle to the Romans.*

Whiteside, Robertson L. *A New Commentary On Paul's Letter To The Saints At Rome.*